COMMUNICATION-BASED INTERVENTION FOR PROBLEM BEHAVIOR

This book is printed on recycled paper. ♲

COMMUNICATION-BASED INTERVENTION FOR PROBLEM BEHAVIOR
A User's Guide for Producing Positive Change

by

Edward G. Carr, Ph.D.
Professor
Department of Psychology

Len Levin, M.A.
Gene McConnachie, Ph.D.
Jane I. Carlson, M.A.
Duane C. Kemp, Ph.D.
Christopher E. Smith, M.A.

State University of New York
at Stony Brook
and
Developmental Disabilities Institute

·P A U L·H·
BROOKES
PUBLISHING C⁰

Baltimore·London·Toronto·Sydney

Paul H. Brookes Publishing Co.
P.O. Box 10624
Baltimore, Maryland 21285-0624

Typeset by Maple-Vail Composition Services, Binghamton, New York.
Manufactured in the United States of America by
Vail-Ballou Press, Binghamton, New York.

Situations described in this book come from composite multiple case
studies of the authors and their colleagues. The names of individuals, places,
and organizations are pseudonyms. Any similarity to actual individuals or
circumstances is coincidental and no implications should be inferred.

First printing, June 1994.
Second printing, August 1995.

Library of Congress Cataloging-in-Publication Data

Communication-based intervention for problem behavior : a user's guide
  for producing positive change / by Edward G. Carr . . . [et al.].
    p. cm.
  Includes bibliographical references and index.
  ISBN 1-55766-159-6 :
  1. Developmentally disabled—Rehabilitation. 2. Mentally
handicapped—Behavior modification. I. Carr, Edward G., 1947–
HV1570.C65   1994
362.1′968—dc20   94-11800
                                                              CIP

British Cataloguing-in-Publication data are available from the British Library.

It is not incumbent upon you to complete the work but you are not free from doing all that you possibly can.

—*Talmud*

Contents

The Authors

Edward G. Carr, Ph.D., is Professor of Psychology at the State University of New York at Stony Brook, and a research scientist at the Developmental Disabilities Institute on Long Island, New York. He has worked in the field of developmental disabilities for the past 25 years and has contributed over 100 publications to the professional literature, primarily in the areas of problem behavior and communication. Dr. Carr has lectured extensively and given workshops throughout the U.S., Canada, and Europe. He has served on the editorial boards of 12 journals in the field of developmental disabilities and behavior analysis. Dr. Carr is a Fellow of the American Psychological Association and is listed in *American Men and Women of Science*. In 1981, he received a Certificate of Commendation from the Autism Society of America for his work on problem behavior, and in 1982 he received an award from the International Society for Research on Aggression for his book *In Response to Aggression* (co-authored with A.P. Goldstein, W.S. Davidson, & P. Wehr).

Len Levin, M.A., is an applied behavior specialist at the Developmental Disabilities Institute. He has been working with children with developmental disabilities for more than 10 years. Mr. Levin has provided technical assistance to service agencies throughout the New York metropolitan area. He was on-site director for the clinical outcome project that provided the empirical evidence supporting many of the ideas and procedures described in this book.

Gene McConnachie, Ph.D., served as the director for several clinical research projects for the Research and Training Center on Positive Behavioral Support, and as a research associate at the Developmental Disabilities Institute. His interests include the development of intervention for aggression in children and youth, applications of behavior analysis to pediatric populations, and the processes that affect the maintenance of intervention effectiveness.

Jane I. Carlson, M.A., has been a special education teacher in both public and private school programs for people with disabilities. She is presently a Research Associate at the State University of New York at Stony Brook and directs several projects addressing intervention for severe problem behaviors and issues of community integration. Ms. Carlson has presented research and given workshops on these topics throughout the U.S. and Europe.

Duane C. Kemp, Ph.D., is Clinical Director of Adult Residential Services at the Developmental Disabilities Institute and is responsible for program planning in psychology, communication, vocational services, and staff training.

He has worked in the field of developmental disabilities for over 16 years and has provided inservice training and workshops throughout the U.S. and Europe.

Christopher E. Smith, M.A., is a research project coordinator at the State University of New York at Stony Brook. He has conducted numerous staff trainings and workshops as a consultant to schools and agencies across the U.S. He is presently working on research that explores the relationships between biological setting events and problem behavior.

Foreword

Understanding problem behaviors and their management (often referred to as discipline) may be the most pervasive concern among educators and parents in America. Support for this contention is easy to gather: One needs only to browse the shelves of any library or bookstore to discover the multitude of volumes that have been written on this controversial topic. I once read that the amount of space dedicated to a content area is inversely proportional to our understanding of that area; I believe this to be true of problem behaviors. Discipline and behavior management appear to be among the most enduring topics for continuing education requested by teachers in our schools. This enduring interest necessarily is linked to the failure of past efforts. Failure can occur for many reasons: Procedures may be ineffective; procedures may be effective but they are too costly in terms of time and resources to implement; procedures may be effective but they have not been described and disseminated sufficiently for others to implement with fidelity; procedures may be effective in some situations but not in others, and no one has yet determined the conditions under which they are and are not effective; procedures may be effective for a short time, but the changes produced are not durable. This list, which is by no means exhaustive, may illuminate some of the barriers to finding an approach that is at once effective, practical, and enduring. The approach espoused in *Communication-Based Intervention for Problem Behavior: A User's Guide for Producing Positive Change* is uniquely responsive to these many problems.

In the past, our goal for problem behaviors has been to eliminate them. Problem behaviors have been assigned labels such as "undesired," "inappropriate," "maladaptive," "excessive," and "challenging" to name just a few. With elimination as a goal, two common strategies have been employed: 1) explain to the person exhibiting the behavior why his or her behavior is a problem, or 2) punish the person exhibiting the behavior. In neither case were efforts made to understand why the behavior occurred in the first place. We never considered that behavior, regardless of the label assigned, may have a function—that is, it may serve some purpose for that individual. In fact, if it is a behavior of long standing, it may be not only possible but economical to consider it functional and somehow adaptive. If behavior occurs with some frequency and it occurs in a predictable fashion (i.e., under some conditions but not others), then such behavior cannot be identified as random; rather, it would appear to serve a purpose.

This new perspective, that problem behavior has a function for the individual who engages in it, took root in 1977 when Dr. Ted Carr, one of the authors of this book, published an article entitled "The Motivation for Self-Injurious Behavior: A Review of Some Hypotheses." In addition to this position paper, he published research that began in the middle 1970s and continues to this day, which has formed much of the empirical bases for this new perspective. Especially compelling is the evidence for a communication hy-pothesis, which states that problem behavior may be a means of communica-tion for those with severely limited language capabilities. Learners with se-vere intellectual disabilities who have little or no language are much more likely to engage in problem behavior than those individuals who have ac-quired language. Current thinking is that those who lack language are greatly restricted in their means of influencing people and events in their environ-ment. To achieve the same goals in life to which we all strive—to obtain things we want such as attention, affection, and materials and to avoid things we don't want such as pain, discomfort, boredom, and failure—these individ-uals have learned to behave in ways that we label problematic. An important distinction to draw from this communication perspective is separating the *form* of a behavior from its *function*. The function or purpose of the behavior is to obtain some universally human goal. All of us behave to secure these same goals, but what differs is the form of the behavior used to achieve them. We have unwittingly taught those referred to as having disabilities (in fact, the label may in large part be determined by problem behavior) to behave in socially maladaptive ways to secure their entirely human wants and needs.

If this perspective is correct, then our goal must change from the elimina-tion of problem behaviors to understanding their function so that we can craft an intervention designed to teach a new form of behavior that is at least as successful in achieving the identified function as the old, more coercive form. The implications of this change in perspective and approach are revolution-ary. Blame ought not be leveled at the learner because the problem behavior develops in a social context that actually taught the learner to behave in this way. That is, if someone aggresses toward us (with the purpose of maintaining personal distance) and, as a consequence, we remain at a distance, we have taught this individual to aggress to achieve his or her end. Ideally, we would assess the situations in which aggression occurs and the consequences of the aggression in order to understand its function and then we would teach an acceptable alternative, such as, "Give me some space!" By sharing responsibil-ity for the aggression, those of us who interact with the learner have an oppor-tunity to change the form of the learner's behavior. Just as the problem behav-ior was learned in transactions with social partners, it can be unlearned and new, more adaptable replacement behaviors can be acquired.

Communication-Based Intervention for Problem Behavior contains so many unique features that a complete listing is beyond the scope of this fore-word; however, a sampling of these features will highlight for readers what they can anticipate. First, the book is unusually consumable, written in a user-friendly format rich with description and examples of sophisticated pro-cedures. For years, perhaps decades, a common complaint of practitioners has been that research does not inform practice: The content and the findings of research have little relevance for the issues facing practitioners. In collabora-tion with five colleagues, Dr. Carr, who is among the premier researchers in studying problem behavior of individuals with disabilities, has crafted a book that bridges the gap between research and practice. Because of his expertise and extraordinary grasp of the content, the information provided is techni-cally accurate and appropriately qualified (even humble on occasion). What is most remarkable, however, is the authors' facility with introducing very sophisticated procedures in a form that can be understood by those charged with implementing such procedures (i.e., parents, teachers, teachers' aides, group home staff).

In the context of this user-friendly format, the authors have skillfully in-fused many of the most innovative concepts that have been empirically tested only recently. Among these are *setting events*, which are events that are temporally distant (i.e., occur earlier in time) from problem behaviors but have a pervasive influence on their probability of occurrence; *interpersonal effects*, which encompasses a recognition of the reciprocity of influence between learner and teacher and defines how individuals manipulate, often unintentionally, the behavior of others; and *response efficiency*, which becomes a consideration only after a functionally equivalent response has been identified. If the new desired response is less successful at achieving the goal than the problem behavior, it will not compete successfully, and therefore interventionists need to consider the amount of effort required to make the response, as well as how quickly and how consistently the response produces the desired outcome. Other concepts include *embedding*, which involves strategies for enhancing the positive climate of the context so that when a request or demand is embedded, the probability of compliance is increased; providing more opportunities for *making choices* enables individuals with disabilities to exercise more control over events in their lives; and *rapport-building*, which is an innovative strategy for enhancing the quality of relationships between learners and those who interact with them. Rapport-building functions as a necessary prerequisite for other strategies, such as *building tolerance* for delays in reinforcement or in gratification, which is implemented following communication intervention because as learners first discover they can obtain desired outcomes and avoid undesired ones by using their newly acquired responses, they use them often and are at risk of overwhelming (i.e., nagging) their social partners.

Among the unique features of the book is its emphasis on assessment and evaluation. The entire first half of the book is devoted to functional assessment (i.e., determining the function or purpose of the behavior for the individual). Without this information, there is no way for an interventionist to develop a program that is logical and rational, and that "fits" the problem behavior and the context in which it occurs. Throughout the book, assessment and evaluation are emphasized as continuing processes. Although an intervention may produce impressive results, conditions change and new people enter the lives of the learners with whom we work; familiar people leave; schedules change; and physical growth, maturation, and changing peer groups modify an individual's needs and preferences for activities and people. Interventionists need to continually assess in order to be responsive to ongoing change.

A feature that distinguishes this book from others on the same subject is its emphasis on problem-solving and decision-making rather than on providing a "cookbook" of recipes for intervention. The authors acknowledge the complexity of the phenomenon they are studying and the depths of what still remains to be known and understood. Every individual is different and unique and the same set of strategies that is effective in one circumstance for one individual will not be so for another. Carr et al. provide guidelines to be considered when selecting strategies, and all of these guidelines are based on careful, thorough, and continual assessment.

Inherent in this problem-solving format are potential pitfalls that can be anticipated when implementing particular strategies. The authors' recognition of these pitfalls and their suggestions for remediation were made possible from the extensive field testing that is the foundation of all of their recommendations. This means that when a failure of intervention occurs, possible explanations for the failure are provided that allow formulation of another logical strategy. Again, no certain recipes are offered, but considerations are delineated that enable informed decisions. Rather than avoiding one of the most frequent criticisms of this approach—what to do when the problem behavior occurs during the teaching of communicative alternatives—the authors address this concern directly by describing strategies for crisis management. They warn that these strategies ought to be short term and are not to be considered ends in themselves but rather means to the end of teaching functionally equivalent, alternative ways of meeting goals. For example, when embedding fails to produce the intended effect, the authors suggest that rapport-building be assessed because without rapport, embedding will not yield its optimal effect. Rapport-building is a necessary condition that empowers the embedding strategy. Explication of conditions under which a strategy will and will not work is rare in a book such as this (or anywhere for that matter). Such consideration reflects a recognition of the complexity of human behavior with which we grapple.

Also unique is the humanistic perspective that infuses this book. For example, a common theme is enhancing the control that individuals with disabilities have over their environments. Teaching and facilitating an enhanced communicative repertoire permits an individual to have more active and interactive participation with people and events. Providing choice may be the most obvious example of sharing control with the individuals with whom we work. The authors argue convincingly that our past attitude about people with disabilities was discriminatory; we forced decisions upon them with little recognition of their preferences and decision-making capacities. One final example is especially compelling: If an individual with problem behavior begins to get upset, we are quick to intervene because of his or her reputation. We do not always consider the context in which the behavior developed. All of us become upset at times. It is important to consider the situation and to ask if there is general consensus that any reasonable person might become agitated in such a situation. If the answer is yes, then we need to allow people with disabilities the same freedom to be upset that the rest of us take for granted.

The outcomes sought in this volume and the measures of success go well beyond elimination of problem behaviors. Lifestyle changes, the authors' explicit goal, encompass active participation by individuals with disabilities in their neighborhoods, schools, communities, and work settings as well as in fulfilling and meaningful social relationships with family, peers, and members of the community. These broad-based and socially valid outcomes contrast sharply with traditional goals of problem behavior reduction or elimination. Lifestyle change is a lofty and challenging goal that is not easily achieved, but this book provides many of the necessary conditions and considerations that make such a goal feasible and possible.

James W. Halle, Ph.D.
Department of Special Education
University of Illinois, Champaign
Editor
Journal of The Association for Persons with Severe Handicaps

REFERENCE

Carr, E.G. (1977). The motivation for self-injurious behavior: A review of some hypotheses. *Psychological Bulletin, 84*, 800–816.

Foreword

I still remember attending an American Psychological Association convention sometime in the mid- to late 1970s and listening to a presentation by Ted Carr. I still remember this event even though it occurred during my graduate student days because I was stunned by his presentation. He was making the case that some forms of aberrant behavior (my term, not his) might actually serve an operant function. And because the behavior served environmental functions, we could possibly treat it by replacing it with more acceptable behavior. It wasn't until much later that I discovered his seminal article on this topic in the *Psychological Bulletin* (Carr, 1977). It was even later, when I became familiar with Iwata et al.'s (Iwata, Dorsey, Slifer, Bauman, & Richman, 1982) functional analysis methodology, that I began to appreciate more fully the implications of Carr's (1977) analysis. I mention his presentation and article because I think it is fair to say that Carr has devoted over 15 years to the preparation of this book. He and his colleagues have published extensively on virtually every component described in this book, and the book is, indeed, comprehensive. If anyone is qualified to write this book, it is Ted Carr.

I spend much of my time working in hospital-based outpatient clinics where I evaluate children and young adults with problem behaviors. I have frequent contact with many agencies and parents who sincerely want to help their clients or children to stop engaging in problem behavior. My first reaction to this book, which occurred while reading the second section, "The Core Intervention," was that I should give this book to those individuals. This is the highest compliment I can pay to the authors. I am convinced that the book will be an extremely positive and thought-provoking resource to care providers, especially those who have already been exposed to functional assessment practices and functional communication training and who are struggling to blend these approaches into the everyday activities in their particular settings.

I am pleased that Carr and his associates waited 15 years to write this book: It shows. The 15 years of field-tested experience show in the book's comprehensive approach, in its careful specification of necessary conditions, and in the numerous "gems" described in the book. I believe that the field is ready for this book, and I doubt that many consumers will be disappointed.

If I were to summarize this book in a schematic way, using the most simplistic terms possible, it would be as follows:

Functional Communication Training
↓
Choice-Making
↓
Social Communication

Functional communication, if taught in a correct manner, may lead to choice-making, which may in turn lead to positive, reciprocal interactions between the client and others in the environment. I say "may" because, as the authors note, not everyone will respond positively to this approach. But those who do may benefit in sustained, generalized ways that make the overall environment more positive. There are few downsides to the recommended procedures.

There are three main sections to this book, each organized in the following manner. In each section, the authors make some well-grounded assertions, followed by believable case examples, followed by commentary. Subsections conclude with a checklist. By using this format, the authors are able to avoid writing a "cookbook" but are still able to provide bottom-line information in a practical format. Readers can choose to simply follow the checklist or, instead, read the narrative and develop their own checklists.

In the first section, the authors provide an excellent explanation of why they have written the book in this manner, offering some cautionary statements, and reviewing some of the literature supporting their assertions. Especially appreciated is their brief discussion of crisis management, which could be used as the basis for a helpful handout for care providers. This first section is an appropriate establishing condition for the remainder of the book. Read it carefully, consider the conservative approach, and keep this information in mind as you read the remainder of the book. If, for example, you react negatively to certain terms (in my case, to decidedly nonbehavioral terms), remember that you were warned. If you react to certain procedures (in my case, to panel discussions), remember that the authors are being pragmatic.

The heart of the book is the second section on core intervention. It is in this section where the authors' experience and expertise clearly contribute. In essence, this section is a masterful piece of writing because so many difficult concepts are presented in such a well-organized, clear manner. Also, the majority of assertions are based directly on previous experimental studies or conceptual analyses that give the assertions both credibility and substance. The notion of "functional equivalence," for example, was well described by Carr (1988) and has been discussed in the literature by numerous authors (e.g., Mace & Roberts, 1993). The description of reciprocal effects was nicely demonstrated by Carr, Taylor, and Robinson (1991). Their suggestions, therefore, are based on a literature that they and others have systematically developed.

In this section, the authors provide numerous hints or gems that I think most readers will find to be credible. These are especially appealing because these suggestions are almost never based solely on conventional wisdom; they have been studied in the literature. The authors have simply made it possible for parents and practitioners not to have to spend countless hours reviewing the literature (although I should note that the reference lists are valuable to researchers as well).

Ensuring that the alternative communicative behavior is functionally equivalent to the problem behavior (and emphasizing the need for verification through experimentation) and focusing on the discriminability and efficiency of the communicative response are key points of this approach. Also of great importance and interest are those sections that describe the reciprocal interactions that occur with functional communication training. The authors provide a clear, concise description of the needed context (e.g., motivated staff) and the need to "enjoy" the client. I find these types of topics to be frequently avoided or presented in an overly harsh manner. The authors, fortunately, are both experienced and sensitive.

The final major section on generalization and maintenance is excellent. The need to program explicitly for generalization cannot be overstated, and I appreciated the authors' suggestions for accomplishing this type of programming. One gem in this section is the discussion about how a maintenance problem can often be a stimulus generalization problem. I am betting that many care providers will read this and be able to understand their own experiences of past difficulties.

This book is for individuals who know something about communication training, or who are learning about it, and now want to incorporate it more fully into daily practice. As I read the book, I was reminded, once again, of how fortunate I have been. As I entered the field, Ted Carr and Brian Iwata were already making it possible for me, as an applied behavioral researcher and clinician, to be more successful in my work. I suspect that numerous care providers will feel equally fortunate to have read this book prior to implementing the procedures. It really is that good.

David P. Wacker, Ph.D.
Division of Development Disabilities
Department of Pediatrics
University Hospital School
The University of Iowa, Iowa City

REFERENCES

Carr, E. (1988). Functional equivalence as a mechanism of response generalization. In R. Horner, R. Koegel, & G. Dunlap (Eds.), *Generalization and maintenance: Life-style changes in applied settings* (pp. 221–241). Baltimore: Paul H. Brookes Publishing Co.

Carr, E.G. (1977). The motivation of self-injurious behavior: A review of some hypotheses. *Psychological Bulletin, 64*, 600–616.

Carr, E., Taylor, J., & Robinson, S. (1991). The effects of severe behavior problems in children on the teaching behavior of adults. *Journal of Applied Behavior Analysis, 24*, 523–535.

Iwata, B.A., Dorsey, M.F., Slifer, K.J., Bauman, K.E., & Richman, G.S. (1982). Toward a functional analysis of self-injury. *Analysis and Intervention in Developmental Disabilities, 2*, 3–20.

Mace, F.C., & Roberts, M. (1993). Factors affecting selection of behavioral interventions. In J. Reichle & D. Wacker (Eds.), *Communication and language intervention series: Vol. 3. Communicative alternatives to challenging behavior: Integrating functional assessment and intervention strategies* (pp. 113–133). Baltimore: Paul H. Brookes Publishing Co.

Preface

From time to time, students have asked me, "Why did you pursue psychology as a career?" My answer has been the same for the past 25 years: "I became a psychologist because I'm interested in why people do things." My guiding light has been the concept that people do things for a reason. Human behavior, even the most severe problem behavior shown by people with developmental disabilities, is not the result of some accidental process. Behavior occurs because it typically serves a purpose for the individual displaying it; that is why problem behavior occurs so frequently, why it lasts so long, and why it is often so difficult to deal with. The concept that problem behavior has a purpose is the central theme of this book, a theme that permeates every assessment and intervention strategy described in this book.

The major challenge in writing a book about problem behavior involves sensitivity to professionals on the one hand and consumers on the other. Many professionals, particularly those who have a behaviorist orientation, are uncomfortable with mentalistic language involving ideas such as "purpose." Many consumers, as well as professionals who do not have a behaviorist orientation, dislike and are often confused by the strict, technical terminology associated with behavioral intervention. We have tried to address the concerns of behaviorists by providing an extensive list of references and resources that document the rationale and scientific support for the various strategies that we use. We have tried to address the concerns of consumers and nonbehavioral professionals by minimizing the use of jargon when describing strategies, choosing instead nontechnical language such as "purpose," "motivation," and "goals." We adopted this approach because we want to disseminate information to as wide an audience as possible, to those with little background in behaviorism as well as to those who are experts.

In Chapter 1, we present a synopsis of the major ideas on which our approach is based:

1. Problem behavior is purposeful;
2. Assessments must be done to identify what purpose problem behavior serves;
3. Intervention for problem behavior must focus on education, not simply behavior reduction;
4. Problem behavior typically serves many purposes and therefore requires many interventions;
5. Intervention involves altering the way in which individuals with and without disabilities interact and, therefore, intervention involves changing social systems; and
6. Lifestyle change rather than the elimination of problem behavior per se is the ultimate goal of intervention.

We end the chapter by noting that our intervention approach, while generally applicable, is not meant to address all problem behavior, particularly that having a biological basis.

Chapter 2 focuses on crisis management, which involves dealing with aggressive and self-injurious behaviors at the moment they are occurring. This topic is of immediate concern to parents, teachers, and others because unmanaged crises pose threats to the safety of everyone involved in a social interaction. Furthermore, our experience has shown that there is little practitioner interest in long-term solutions to problem behavior unless practitioners know and can use specific strategies for defusing dangerous situations. To respond to this concern, we discuss five crisis management strategies in this chapter.

Chapter 3 is of special interest to professionals and researchers who want to understand the scientific basis for the approach that we take. We discuss at length the research demonstrating that problem behavior serves many purposes, and we explore the notion, central to our book, that problem behavior may function as a primitive form of communication, influencing people in ways that are adaptive for the individual displaying it. This communication concept is developed with reference to the research literature in child psychology as well as to the extensive literature in developmental disabilities.

Over the years, many service providers have told us that the most difficult task related to intervention planning is the assessment. For this reason, Chapters 4, 5, and 6 are devoted to the detailed explanation and illustration of assessment procedures that can be used to determine what purposes particular instances of problem behavior serve. We describe individuals with whom we have worked so that the reader has a clear sense of how interviews and direct observation can contribute to identifying purpose. We illustrate how the information gathered can be reduced to a manageable number of categories that facilitate intervention planning. We discuss how practitioners can verify if the identified purposes are indeed the reasons why the individual is engaging in problem behavior. Finally, we highlight the important role that social, physical, and physiological contexts can play in determining whether problem behaviors will occur and how to address the impact of context in planning intervention.

In Chapter 7, we take up the issue of building rapport. This chapter reflects a central theme of our book, that intervention is not simply the application of procedures for altering the behavior of people with disabilities. Rather, intervention involves changing relationships, that is, the ways in which people with and without disabilities interact with one another. The essence of rapport-building is to make yourself likeable to the person with disabilities and, just as important, to help the person with disabilities become likeable to you. When two people have established good rapport, they are more motivated to communicate with one another. Thus, by establishing positive relationships, a basis is provided on which to build communication skills that replace problem behavior.

The educational nature of our intervention approach is the primary focus of Chapter 8. The goal of intervention is not simply to reduce the level of problem behavior but rather to broaden the individual's social repertoire so that he or she acquires new skills that replace problem behavior. Communication skills are critical to this approach. We show how individuals can learn to use communication to achieve the same goals that they achieved through their problem behavior. For example, simple conversational skills may be taught that replace aggression as a way of obtaining attention from other people. Since there are many communication systems available (including speech, sign language, and gesture), we also discuss issues involved in selecting communication systems as well as the forms within a system that should be taught first. Given the large number of purposes that problem behavior can serve for an individual, this chapter also makes clear that replacing problem behavior requires that an individual learn many different forms of communication in order to cover the full range of goals formerly achieved through the problem behavior.

Even the best intervention strategies fail if they are implemented in an unsupportive context. Chapter 9 demonstrates the necessity of changing social systems in order to produce good outcomes. An appropriate context for communication requires that a number of cooperative and motivated people are involved in the intervention. These people also need to agree that intervention should, whenever possible, be carried out in the community where its members live, work, and recreate, in contrast to the sterile and restrictive environments that have historically served people with disabilities. Finally, functional education, that is, education that promotes a rich variety of opportunities for communication as well as living and enjoying life as independently as possible, must be a priority. All of these system changes just noted help ensure that meaningful and beneficial long-term outcomes can occur.

We have noted already that because problem behavior serves so many purposes, intervention almost invariably requires the use of many procedures over and above communication training per se. Chapters 10, 11, and 12 amplify this point by discussing three additional forms of intervention: building tolerance for delay of reinforcement, embedding, and providing choices, respectively. All of us have to accept the fact that our needs cannot always be gratified immediately. People with disabilities must also learn this. In Chapter 10, we describe strategies to help people with disabilities learn to tolerate the inevitable delays in having our needs met that all of us experience daily. In Chapter 11, we present an additional strategy that can be used with escape-motivated problem behavior such as aggression and self-injury, which serve the purpose of extricating the person with disabilities from unpleasant situations, for example, academic tasks or work demands. This approach involves embedding demands in a positive context that evokes a good mood. Because the situation then becomes less aversive, there is no longer need for escape-motivated aggression or self-injury. Our final presented procedure, providing choices (Chapter 12), highlights again the need to alter social systems in order to produce good outcomes. Traditionally, people with disabilities have not been given many choices. They have been told what tasks they must perform, with whom they may interact, where they must be, when they may do certain activities, and what rewards they may have. In short, they are encouraged to be passive and helpless. We argue, as have others before us, that the time has come to encourage people with disabilities to make their own choices. Not only does encouraging choice-making represent a radical change in the typical social system for people with disabilities, but it also results in a marked reduction in problem behavior.

Chapter 13 takes up the issue of generalization, which is ensuring that gains made in one situation transfer to other situations. We discuss strategies for producing generalized intervention effects. Most important, this chapter highlights a dominant theme in our book, which is that lifestyle change, rather than the elimination of problem behavior per se, is the ultimate goal of intervention. Thus, through the use of many detailed examples, we demonstrate how to bring about generalization across a wide variety of tasks, people, and settings. The result is that the individual is free of problem behavior and, at the same time, able to function in diverse community situations from which he or she was previously excluded. We end Chapter 13 with a discussion of how occasional failures of generalization can be used to redesign and update interventions, keeping them effective.

We close our book with a discussion of maintenance. Maintenance refers to the extent to which intervention effects last over time. Again, we return to the idea that successful intervention involves changing social systems, not just the person with disabilities. For example, people with disabilities are sometimes held to a stricter standard of what constitutes inappropriate behavior than the rest of us. Thus, if following intervention, a person with disabilities begins to show minor or even justifiable problem behavior, others declare that intervention effects did not maintain, ignoring the fact that all of us, from time to time, display problem behavior. Here, the solution is to educate the community about the unfair double standard, thereby altering one aspect of the social system in which the person with disabilities lives. Another aspect of this issue concerns maintenance failures that are the result of inadequate support for the people—parents, teachers, and others—who themselves support people with disabilities. For example, if a mother fails to respond to the appropriate communication of her son because she is physically exhausted or overwhelmed with other obligations, should we conclude that subsequent problem behaviors represent a failure of maintenance? We do not think so. We believe that the failure here is of the social support network and that the solution is to alter the social system, in this case, by providing occasional respite for the mother. Intervention does not occur in a vacuum but within the context of a social system and when that system is deficient, it must be altered in order to give intervention efforts a chance to produce long-term maintenance.

Professionals and consumers alike often ask us whether there are sources they can refer to that provide additional information on the various topics that we discuss in this book. In response to this request, we provide an extensive resource list of books and journal articles that the reader can consult to obtain more information about each topic covered, as well as detailed analyses of the rationale for each of the procedures described.

Finally, in the Appendix, we provide the results of field tests on the assessment and intervention procedures described in this book. Our results are based on tests involving almost 200 people with disabilities as well as several hundred interventionists—group home staff, parents, and teachers—who used the procedures we present here. Outcomes were positive. Interventionists were able to carry out the assessment and intervention procedures and generally chose to use them because the procedures worked and produced a variety of desirable and educationally sound changes in people with disabilities. Problem behavior decreased markedly and, most important, broad, meaningful changes in lifestyle occurred.

If you interact with a person with disabilities who shows serious problem behavior, you have good reason to believe that you can change this behavior. By viewing the person's behavior as purposeful and by focusing your efforts on education (rather than simply on behavior reduction), you have an excellent opportunity to deal successfully with the problem behavior and help make the life of the person with disabilities richer and happier, and that is the best reward of all.

Acknowledgments

We would like to thank the many people who contributed to this book. Joe Pancari, Denise Berotti, Karen Pierce, Julie Soriano, Tracey Vaiano, Sandi Diamond, Lisa Storey, and the Innes family helped carry out the interventions and collect data. Theresa Giacobbe and Becky MacDonald oversaw the field testing. We especially thank Rob Horner for continuous, ongoing, detailed feedback and enthusiastic support.

The Developmental Disabilities Institute cooperated through all phases of the research leading up to this book and we are grateful to its Executive Director, Dr. Martin Hamburg. We thank Sharon Krass for her patience in typing the endless revisions of the manuscript, and Carol Hollander and Molicca Behm of Brookes Publishing Co. for editorial support. Finally, we acknowledge the National Institute on Disability and Rehabilitation Research (Grants #G0087C0284, #H133G2f0098, and #H133B20004) for providing the funding that made this entire project possible.

One of us (Ted Carr) would like to dedicate this book to the memory of his Uncle Manny and Aunt Ida, who, like so many people labeled as retarded, were forgotten in life but here, at least, they are remembered in death.

COMMUNICATION-BASED INTERVENTION FOR PROBLEM BEHAVIOR

PART I

BACKGROUND, CRISIS MANAGEMENT, AND FUNCTIONAL ASSESSMENT

Chapter 1

Preliminary Considerations

The purpose of this book is to describe a communication-based intervention for severe problem behavior in persons with developmental disabilities. We need to be clear about what each of the terms used in the preceding sentence means. "Communication-based intervention" refers to an approach that reduces or eliminates problem behavior by teaching an individual specific forms of communication. Because the communicative forms that are taught are more effective ways of influencing others than the problem behavior, they eventually replace the problem behavior itself. Although the intervention of "communication training" is central to the approach, other interventions are also involved and that is why we use the term communication-"based" rather than simply "communication." By communication training, we mean that individuals are taught specific language forms including, for example, speech, signing, and gestures that can be used to influence other people in order to achieve important goals. Severe problem behavior includes intense forms of aggression (punching, scratching, biting, and kicking others), self-injury (head-banging, self-biting, and self-slapping), property destruction, and tantrums (prolonged screaming and crying, often accompanied by one or more of the other forms of problem behavior just described). "People with developmental disabilities," in this book, typically refers to those people with mental retardation or autism, although we have also used the intervention approach with people with aphasia, neurological impairments, brain damage, developmental delays, and schizophrenia.

MAJOR THEMES

Six major themes recur throughout this book, which we now introduce.

Problem Behavior Usually Serves
a Purpose for the Person Displaying It

You are probably used to hearing problem behavior described as "aberrant," "random," "psychotic," or "maladaptive." We think that these terms are misleading. To the contrary, problem behavior can be adaptive and that is why it is displayed so often. If a young girl learns that the only way to get her father's undivided attention is by banging her head against the table, then head-banging becomes a useful and adaptive response because it guarantees that the girl will receive continued contact with and influence over a very important person in her life.

Functional Assessment Is Used to
Identify the Purpose of Problem Behavior

Because problem behavior is typically purposeful, you cannot change it successfully in the long run without trying to discover what the purpose of the behavior is. This process is referred to in the scientific literature as "functional analysis" or "functional assessment." To continue with our example, you may be able to suppress the young girl's head-banging temporarily by shouting at her to stop, but such punishment does not take into consideration why the girl is head-banging in the first place. Sooner or later, she will crave her father's attention again and she will resume head-banging. Therefore, if you want to help her in the long run, you must discover the reason for her head-banging, in this example, attention-seeking. Then you will be in a position to help her by teaching her new ways of getting her father's attention, for example, by talking to him.

The Goal of Intervention Is Education,
Not Simply Behavior Reduction

The most important implication of functional assessment is that intervention for problem behavior involves education. Because problem behavior often serves a purpose for the individual displaying it, the main goal of intervention is to teach the individual new ways of influencing other people so that problem behaviors are no longer necessary. This educational approach contrasts sharply with more traditional approaches that have focused on eliminating or reducing problem behavior without considering what types of skills must be learned to bring about the *permanent* replacement of problem behavior.

Problem Behavior Typically Serves Many
Purposes and Therefore Requires Many Interventions

Problem behavior does not occur in a vacuum. It occurs in a social context. In the social context of the community, problem behavior tends to serve many purposes. For example, the young girl described earlier may bang her head to get her father's attention when she is at home, bite her classmate to get her teacher to stop asking her to do schoolwork, and throw a tantrum to get her mother to buy her a chocolate bar in the supermarket. The three contexts (home, school, supermarket) evoke problem behaviors that serve different purposes (attention-seeking, escape from work, and obtaining desired foods, respectively). Because problem behavior can serve many different purposes, it is almost a certainty that multicomponent interventions will be needed. In other words, it is usually wrong to think that you can affect all of an individual's severe problem behavior in the community by using a single intervention procedure.

Intervention Involves Changing Social Systems, Not Individuals

Because social context is so important, intervention is not something that you do *to* a person who has disabilities; rather, it is something that you do *with* a person who has disabilities. This is especially true when operating within a communication-based model of intervention. For communication to be successful, both people must be motivated to interact with one another. After all, given a choice, we all prefer to interact with people whose company we prefer and with whom we have a good relationship. Therefore, interpersonal factors such as rapport and shared interests become important considerations. In this context, intervention does not mean applying specific procedures to change the behavior of the person with disabilities. Instead, it implies the process of mutual give and take and of reciprocal influence, which lead to desirable behavior change on the part of everyone involved. *In short, intervention involves altering social systems, not individuals.*

Lifestyle Change Is the Ultimate Goal of Intervention

The broader goal of intervention is to produce change that positively affects how people live their lives. Reducing problem behavior is not enough, particularly if the only result is to produce a quiet, docile individual who does not bother parents, teachers, or others. Problem behavior, more often than not, emerges from a background of exclusion, segregation, lack of personal control, and impoverished lifestyles. Therefore, interventions for problem behavior need to improve the life of the person with disabilities so that he or she is no longer excluded, segregated, and controlled by others. Successful interventions allow a person with disabilities to influence others without having to resort to problem behavior. Most important, successful interventions permit an individual to participate directly in the community, and have more social, vocational, and leisure opportunities than ever before. These opportunities do not occur in "special settings" exclusive to disability but, rather, in the wider world of people who do not have disabilities. *Lifestyle change is the ultimate goal of intervention.*

ABOUT THIS BOOK

Intended Audience

We have field tested the various components that make up this book and have found the material to be useful for teachers, parent trainers, behavior specialists, speech-language pathologists, residential and vocational administrators, and psychologists. Parents, residential staff, and job coaches have also found the material helpful, but, unless they had some prior background in behavior modification and methods of functional assessment, they required support and consultation from the professionals listed above. This book is also intended for use in behavior management courses in special education, human development, and child clinical psychology.

HOW TO USE THIS BOOK

For the most part, we have used a format in which the *background and rationale* of a particular component of our approach are first introduced, followed by *examples* of how the component may be put into practice, then *commentary* on important considerations to bear in mind when implementing the component, and finally a *checklist* of the critical elements that go into the successful use of the component.

We have avoided the use of a "cookbook" approach to intervention with severe problem behavior. In fact, intervention does not generally occur in a set order, proceeding from component to component. Instead, the various procedures in our model should be viewed not as a recipe but as an array of options, only some of which may be relevant in a specific situation for a specific individual. For example, some individuals may show few escape-motivated problem behaviors. For them, the embedding procedures described later will play little, if any, role in intervention. In contrast, procedures such as rapport-building, and generalization and maintenance tactics are important for all individuals. The decision of which components to use with an individual is typically the result of consensus established by discussion among parents, teachers, and other concerned individuals. Important, too, as discussed in the later section on choice-making, the individuals with disabilities themselves influence the decision process through the choices they make and the impact that they have on other people in their social system (family, school, neighborhood).

In sum, our position is that intervention is a gradual process that unfolds over time. It is not a good idea to establish an intervention protocol at the beginning and remain rigidly committed to it. Instead, as the individual's life expands and becomes more varied and more community-based, it will be necessary to confront new issues that were not present at the start. Thus, additional assessments will have to be made and new interventions designed. We have purposely written this book to reflect the evolving nature of assessment and intervention in real life.

Although our approach to intervention is undoubtedly behavioral, we have chosen to minimize the use of jargon. Repeatedly, parents as well as many professionals have told us in field tests that the use of technical language is distracting and annoying. Therefore, although we introduce behavioral concepts in various places throughout the book, we have generally tried to express ideas in general terms. This tactic sometimes leads to the use of mentalistic language (talking about the "purpose" of problem behavior rather than reinforcers, functions, and maintaining variables). We hope our behavioral colleagues will support our use of nontechnical language. Our aim, simply stated, is to create a user-friendly product to help professionals of diverse orientations and training to communicate with one another as well as with the parents and others with whom they consult.

APPROPRIATE USE OF COMMUNICATION-BASED INTERVENTION

The approach that we describe is likely to be effective in intervening with many instances of problem behavior. However, it will not be effective in all instances. Too much is still unknown about problem behavior to expect that any approach will be universally effective. Generally, a communication-based approach is relevant to instances of problem behavior that are influenced by attention from others, escape from unpleasant situations, and attainment of tangible items such as foods and toys, as well as preferred activities. There are, however, other variables that have been identified or proposed in the scientific literature as also being important. You should be aware of some of these variables so that you do not misapply the procedures described in this book. To that end, a brief discussion is in order, followed by a short reference list that will direct you to additional information.

There are at least three important variables other than those listed above that have been identified as controlling severe problem behavior and for which our intervention model is not relevant.

These are sensory, homeostatic, and organic factors. By "sensory," we mean that self-injury, for example, may be maintained by the sensory stimulation that it produces (Favell, McGimsey, & Schell, 1982). For instance, a child may repeatedly poke him- or herself in the eye because this produces interesting patterns of visual effects called phosphenes. (You can demonstrate this effect for yourself by closing your eyes and pressing your eyeballs with your fingers for a few seconds.) By "homeostatic," we mean that sometimes self-injury is a response to too little or too much stimulation from the environment (Guess & Carr, 1991). If the environment offers very little stimulation, then the child may generate his or her own stimulation by head-banging or face-slapping, for example. Alternatively, if the environment is overstimulating (with too much noise or too many people), then the child may attempt to block out the extra stimulation by engaging in various forms of self-injury. Finally, by "organic," we mean that self-injury may sometimes be the result of certain biological factors (Carr, 1977; Cataldo & Harris, 1982; Lowry & Sovner, 1992; Schroeder, Rojahn, Mulick, & Schroeder, 1990). For example, some scientists have suggested that certain instances of self-injury may represent a type of addictive behavior. The idea is that each time the individual bangs his or her head, for example, opiate-like substances are released into the bloodstream, producing a natural "high." Therefore, the individual becomes addicted to his or her own behavior because of the pleasant effects that result from it. In this example, the use of opiate blockers, such as the drug naltrexone, may be a fruitful intervention (Barrett, Feinstein, & Hole, 1989; Herman et al., 1987; Sandman, Barron, & Colman, 1990). Assessment of and intervention planning for problem behavior controlled by sensory, homeostatic, or organic factors are complicated and require professional consultation.

It is worth repeating that the types of problem behavior discussed in this book are not controlled by sensory, homeostatic, or organic factors. However, the problems that we do discuss are very common and, fortunately, responsive to communication-based intervention.

There is one other point worth emphasizing about the appropriate use of communication-based intervention. Specifically, the model that we describe is not meant to replace a general language curriculum, although it can certainly be an important part of such a curriculum. A comprehensive curriculum must address a large number of issues involving expressive and receptive language skills applied across many different social contexts. These issues have been dealt with expertly by others (Goetz, Schuler, & Sailor, 1981; Hart & Risley, 1978; Mirenda, Iacono, & Williams, 1990; Musselwhite & St. Louis, 1988). The model that we discuss has more modest goals, namely, teaching functional communication skills to replace serious problem behaviors.

THE PEOPLE THIS BOOK IS ABOUT

The intervention model that we describe is based on observations of over 100 individuals who participated in our research on communication-based intervention for severe behavior problems over 10 years. More recently, we have conducted field tests in the community that involved well over 100 additional individuals. (See the appendix at the end of this book for results.) For purposes of illustration, we frequently refer to three individuals who represent the focus of a 5-year longitudinal study, and we will describe these participants briefly. At the beginning of intervention, Val was 15 years old, Gary was 18, and Juan was 39. Val and Gary each lived at home with their respective parents, and Juan lived in a group home. Val had been diagnosed with mental retardation and cerebral palsy. Gary and Juan had both been diagnosed as having autism with mental retardation. Val was able to speak in full sentences and had some conversational skills. Gary spoke in short sentences and single words. Juan was nonverbal but would on occasion indicate his needs through gestures. During the day, Val attended school where part of her curriculum was devoted to helping her make the transition to living in a community residential program. Gary also attended school for part of the day. The rest of the day, Gary was involved in a supported employment program in a greenhouse. All three participants displayed severe problem behaviors that included some combination of self-injury, tantrums, aggression, and property destruction. In short, we were dealing with people who posed serious threats to themselves and others and who were frequently involved in crises in the home, school, and community. Because a crisis requires an immediate response from others, we need to focus on this topic next before considering longer-term intervention issues.

REFERENCES

Barrett, R.P., Feinstein, C., & Hole, W.T. (1989). Effects of naloxone and naltrexone on self-injury: A double-blind, placebo-controlled analysis. *American Journal on Mental Retardation, 93*, 644–651.

Carr, E.G. (1977). The motivation of self-injurious behavior: A review of some hypotheses. *Psychological Bulletin, 84*, 800–816.

Cataldo, M.F., & Harris, J. (1982). The biological basis for self-injury in the mentally retarded. *Analysis and Intervention in Developmental Disabilities, 2*, 21–39.

Favell, J.E., McGimsey, J.F., & Schell, R.M. (1982). Treatment of self-injury by providing alternate sensory activities. *Analysis and Intervention in Developmental Disabilities, 2*, 83–104.

Goetz, L., Schuler, A.L., & Sailor, W.S. (1981). Functional competence as a factor in communication instruction. *Exceptional Education Quarterly, 2*, 51–60.

Guess, D., & Carr, E. (1991). Emergence and maintenance of stereotypy and self-injury. *American Journal on Mental Retardation, 96*, 299–319.

Hart, B., & Risley, T.R. (1978). Promoting productive language through incidental teaching. *Education and Urban Society, 10*, 407–429.

Herman, B.H., Hammock, M.K., Arthur-Smith, A., Egan, J., Chatoor, I., Werner, A., & Zelnick, N. (1987). Naltrexone decreases self-injurious behavior. *Annals of Neurology, 22*, 550–552.

Lowry, M.A., & Sovner, R. (1992). Severe behavior problems associated with rapid cycling bipolar disorder in two adults with profound mental retardation. *Journal of Intellectual Disability Research, 36*, 269–281.

Mirenda, P., Iacono, T., & Williams, R. (1990). Communication options for persons with severe and profound disabilities: State of the art and future directions. *Journal of The Association for Persons with Severe Handicaps, 15*, 3–21.

Musselwhite, C., & St. Louis, K. (1988). *Communication programming for persons with severe handicaps: Vocal and augmentative strategies* (2nd ed.). Boston: College-Hill Press.

Sandman, C.A., Barron, J.L., & Colman, H. (1990). An orally administered opiate blocker, naltrexone, attenuates self-injurious behavior. *American Journal on Mental Retardation, 95*, 93–102.

Schroeder, S.R., Rojahn, J., Mulick, J.A., & Schroeder, C.S. (1990). Self-injurious behavior: An analysis of behavior management techniques. In J.L. Matson & J.R. McCartney (Eds.), *Handbook of behavior modification with the mentally retarded* (2nd ed., pp. 141–180). New York: Plenum Press.

Chapter 2

Crisis Management

The most common question that we are asked by parents and teachers is what to do at the moment that a crisis is occurring. That is, what can be done when a person with disabilities is banging his or her head against a wall to the point of drawing blood, or severely biting people, or throwing heavy objects at windows and trashing a room? It is situations such as the ones just described that cause many people, out of fear or desperation, to become willing to use extreme or even bizarre procedures to end the crisis. We ought not to fault them for doing so. It is not easy to watch another person mutilate himself or herself nor is it possible to stand by and do nothing while others are injured. The situations described call for some form of crisis management and no approach to managing severe problem behavior is ever likely to be taken seriously unless the issue of crisis management is addressed.

PROCEDURES FOR MANAGING CRISES

Over time, people, ourselves included, have learned to deal with crises on a case-by-case basis using procedures that are almost common sense in nature. We have found five categories of procedures to be useful in managing crises: 1) when feasible, *ignore* the behavior problem; 2) *protect* the individual or others from the physical consequences of the problem behavior; 3) *momentarily restrain* the individual during episodes of problem behavior; 4) *remove* anyone who is in danger from the behavior problem from the vicinity where the crisis is occurring; and 5) *introduce cues* (technically known as "discriminative stimuli") that evoke nonproblem behavior.

CRISIS MANAGEMENT PROCEDURES
ARE NOT A FORM OF INTERVENTION

The purpose of crisis management procedures is very modest, namely, to interrupt or control an otherwise dangerous or unmanageable situation. Unfortunately, many people find these procedures so helpful and are so relieved when the crisis ends that they forget to develop an intervention. "Intervention," as the term is used in this book, refers to a long-term educational approach that focuses on teaching individuals new skills that make problem behavior unnecessary. Since crisis management procedures do not teach new skills, they really cannot be viewed as an intervention given our definition. In fact, if you focus on crisis management alone, what you typically find is that the problem behaviors occur again at some future time, thereby making more crisis management necessary. You can become trapped in a scenario that has no end, except frustration and despair. We do not know yet whether the crisis strategies that we describe work in all cases of severe problem behavior. The field of education and clinical practice has not systematically explored the issue of crisis management per se. What we do know, from our own efforts with several hundred individuals as well as from talking with large numbers of practitioners on the "front lines," is that the procedures are generally adequate for the *temporary* control of problem behavior. The procedures provide a window of opportunity for parents, teachers, and others to undertake the more serious and beneficial long-term task of educating the individual in such a way as to undermine the necessity for engaging in problem behavior in the future. This book is largely a description of what to do when that window of opportunity is opened. First, however, we describe some situations that illustrate the use of crisis management strategies. We do so because our experiences have shown us that until the window of opportunity has been opened, caregivers and support personnel are too anxious, demoralized, and distracted to consider anything else except how to end the crisis at hand.

CRISIS MANAGEMENT IN ACTION

Examples: Val, Gary, and Juan

For Val, Gary, and Juan, the crisis management options for the most severe instances of problem behavior centered on *protect*, *restrain*, or *remove*. Thus, when Juan slapped or kicked a group home staffperson, the staffperson would use his or her hands to deflect Juan's blows (protect). Likewise, if Juan threw a chair or radio at a staffperson, that person would use a chair or some other large object to deflect the oncoming projectile (protect). When Gary punched his mother, she would back off beyond the reach of his fist (remove) to avoid further punches but if he tried to bite himself on the hand, she blocked his hand before he could put it in his mouth (protect).

If Val hit a classmate, her teacher immediately put herself between Val and the victim (protect) and then, while attending to the victim, removed him or her from the vicinity of Val (remove). If Val grabbed another's hair and began to pull vigorously, the teacher unclenched Val's fingers to release her grip (protect) and continued to hold Val's arm (restrain) until the teacher's aide got the classmate who was in danger out of the area (remove).

Restraint proved to be the least desirable tactic for Val because she appeared to like the contact and individual attention she received during the procedure. Her teacher worried that restraint might therefore become something that Val sought out. Thus, for Val, momentary restraint was sometimes associated with temporary increases in the level of aggression (struggling). Yet, in spite of this clear disadvantage, Val's teacher sometimes used restraint in order to obtain a few extra seconds of time to implement remove and protect strategies that benefitted the victims of Val's aggression.

Sometimes, ignoring was used as a crisis management strategy. The crisis strategy of ignoring a behavior problem is not the same as the intervention strategy of extinction. Extinction involves the systematic and consistent removal of those events (reinforcers) that maintain a behavior problem. Ignoring, in contrast, is an occasional strategy used for instances of the problem behavior that are not dangerous but which have the potential to become dangerous if they are treated inappropriately. For example, Val would sometimes get angry and throw her cosmetics at the wall. When her teacher pleaded with her to stop, Val appeared to behave worse, often screaming loudly and hitting others. Clearly, pleading was not an effective strategy. When the teacher switched strategies and began to ignore Val when cosmetics were thrown about, Val typically stopped misbehaving. Similarly, Juan's group home staff and Gary's mother found that by ignoring minor instances of problem behavior (Juan's loud grunting and Gary's light hand-biting directed at himself), they could prevent these problems from escalating into more serious ones. Ignoring, then, was a good way of defusing a potentially serious problem situation.

There were some situations in which it was possible to manage a crisis by introducing a cue for nonproblem behavior. For example, even while Gary was biting his hand severely and attempting to punch others, it was often possible for his mother to interrupt the crisis by asking him a question such as, "What do you want?". Through use, this question became a powerful cue for Gary to stop his problem behavior. He would often respond to the question by asking for a break from doing a task or he might request some music or the opportunity to make a sandwich. Of course, this strategy only worked after some communication training. Nonetheless, it was a useful strategy because Gary and other individuals invariably showed brief relapses from time to time even after extensive communication skills training. Therefore, it was good to have a back-up crisis management strategy when things got out of hand.

Val's teacher had learned that introducing a cue could work for Val even before Val had learned specific communication skills to replace her problem behavior. Specifically, the teacher noticed that Val rarely showed problem behavior when either of two aides from another classroom (Tim and Fred) were present. When either Tim or Fred were around, Val would try to engage them in conversation. She might act silly but she would not become aggressive. In other words, Tim and Fred were powerful cues (discriminative stimuli) for nonproblem behavior. Val's teacher decided to make use of this fact. When an especially serious crisis arose, it was often possible for the teacher to get Tim or Fred to come into the classroom. Val almost always responded to their presence by breaking off her aggressive attacks, calming down, and eventually beginning a conversation with them. Of course, Val's teacher could not always rely on Tim or Fred to be around to help, but, when they were available, their presence was used as part of a helpful approach to crisis management.

Comment: After the Crisis

The five crisis management procedures that we have described are not clever, not long-lasting in their effects, and, most important of all, not interventions given our definition that intervention must involve teaching new skills that replace problem behavior over time. What *is* good about the procedures is that they often stop people with disabilities from harming themselves, others, and you. Also, the procedures work quickly. Whether they always have these effects, no one knows because crisis management has not received the scientific scrutiny that it deserves and that practitioners desire.

Crises typically occur before intervention has begun or early in intervention. However, as noted, it is a mistake to think that once an intervention is well underway, you no longer need to worry about serious outbursts and the necessity for crisis management. Many people with disabilities have long histories of intense problem behavior and do not give up their old ways so easily. Therefore, even after you have successfully implemented the intervention procedures that we describe later in this book, you can expect occasional relapses. Such relapses do not mean that the intervention is a failure nor does it mean that people with disabilities are fundamentally different from the rest of us. All of us, from time to time in our lives, experience crises and some of us without disabilities respond with extreme behavior to those crises. The issue is not whether a person has disabilities but rather what to do when a person, including someone with a disability, exhibits dangerous behavior. The procedures that we have described are one way of addressing this situation.

Unfortunately, once the crisis has passed, many caregivers or other involved individuals feel that they have done enough and walk away from the situation. We cannot blame them for doing so. After all, dealing with a crisis is emotionally draining and physically exhausting. However, if the only thing you do is disengage yourself once the crisis is over, you will find that there will be many more crises to face in the future and that life with the person who has the disability will resemble the proverbial walking on eggshells. It is *essential* for caregivers to take advantage of the quiet period between crises in order to build skills that make problem behavior unnecessary and, therefore, new crises rare. Ironically, the best time to implement an intervention for problem behavior is when no problem behavior is occurring.

✔ CHECKLIST OF THINGS TO DO

1. Implement crisis management strategies when problem behavior is likely to increase to a serious level if not stopped or when it has reached a level that poses a danger to the person with disabilities or to others around him or her.
2. Use the ignore strategy to handle minor problem behavior that has a history of leading to more serious problem behaviors if not stopped. Use the momentary restraint strategy for problem behavior that is so dangerous that it must be stopped immediately to prevent further injury to the person with disabilities or to others around him or her.
3. When the crisis is over, begin to or continue to implement the intervention procedures described in the remainder of this book.
4. Monitor for success. Success means that the problem behavior stops quickly and for a long enough period of time for you to begin implementing long-term communication-based intervention strategies.

Chapter 3

The Purposeful Nature of Problem Behavior: Conceptual and Empirical Background

The purposeful nature of problem behavior is best illustrated by the many research studies that document the roles of attention, escape, and tangible items in motivating problem behavior. Consider, first, instances of problem behavior that serve to get attention from others. All too often, people with developmental disabilities are ignored unless they display some dramatic form of behavior. Under such circumstances, people soon learn that problem behavior is an effective way, sometimes the only way, of getting others to interact with them. This notion was directly confirmed in a study by Taylor and Carr (1992a). In this study, the behavior of teachers was measured directly to see how the aggression, tantrums, and self-injurious behavior of children influenced the social behavior of the adults. We found that teachers responded to the severe problem behavior of the attention-seeking children by increasing the amount of attention given to them, providing higher levels of physical contact with them, and presenting activities that required continuous adult–child interaction. In other words, the problem behavior was a very effective way of getting more social contact from adults. There are many demonstrations in the scientific literature of the attention-seeking function of a wide variety of serious problem behaviors (e.g., Carr & McDowell, 1980; Durand, Crimmins, Caulfield, & Taylor, 1989; Lovaas, Freitag, Gold, & Kassorla, 1965; Lovaas & Simmons, 1969; Martin & Foxx, 1973; Taylor & Carr, 1992b).

Consider next those instances of problem behavior that serve to help individuals escape from unpleasant situations. In one study (Carr, Newsom, & Binkoff, 1980), teachers worked with two children, both with a diagnosis of mental retardation. When these children were asked to carry out simple academic tasks, they responded by biting, scratching, and kicking the teacher. When the tasks were withheld, the children displayed almost no aggression. This pattern of behavior suggested that the children may have learned that by being aggressive they could cause the teachers to stop making demands on them. In other words, aggression paid off by helping the child escape from having to do work. This notion was directly confirmed in a study by Carr, Taylor, and Robinson (1991). In this study, the behavior of the teachers was measured directly to see how aggression influenced their presentation of work tasks. We found that teachers were unlikely to present tasks that set off a lot of aggression but were likely to present tasks that seldom set off aggression. Apparently, the children used their aggression to control teacher behavior, specifically, to get teachers to stop presenting tasks that were unpleasant or otherwise unacceptable to them. There are many other studies in the literature demonstrating the escape function of some instances of problem behavior (e.g., Carr & Newsom, 1985; Carr, Newsom, & Binkoff, 1976; Churchill, 1971; Durand, 1982; Durand et al., 1989; Plummer, Baer, & LeBlanc, 1977; Repp, Felce, & Barton, 1988; Romanczyk, Colletti, & Plotkin, 1980; Sailor, Guess, Rutherford, & Baer, 1968; Steege, Wacker, Berg, Cigrand, & Cooper, 1989; Weeks & Gaylord-Ross, 1981; Wolf, Birnbrauer, Williams, & Lawler, 1965).

Finally, consider those instances of problem behavior that serve to help individuals gain access to tangible items such as preferred activities, toys, and food. In one study (Edelson, Taubman, & Lovaas, 1983), a variety of self-injurious behaviors increased when individuals were asked to give up a desired object, specifically, the individual was asked to let go of a toy, or when a desired object such as a toy was taken away, or when the individual was physically prevented from participating in a desired activity, for example, a locked door prevented access to the play area. Such individuals may in the past have learned that the tangible item would be reinstated following an outburst of self-injury; for instance, an anxious parent may try to soothe a child by giving back the toy whose earlier withdrawal resulted in head-banging (Lovaas et al., 1965). There is a body of literature suggesting that problem behavior is sometimes exhibited because it helps the individual to gain or regain access to preferred or desired tangible items (e.g., Billingsley & Neel, 1985; Day, Rea, Schussler, Larsen, & Johnson, 1988; Durand & Crimmins, 1988; Horner & Budd, 1985; Wiesler, Hanson, Chamberlain, & Thompson, 1985).

Although we have been discussing the distinctly different purposes that problem behavior can serve, it is very important to emphasize that, in real-life settings, a given individual is likely to use the same problem behavior to achieve many different goals (Goldiamond, 1974). The same individual may use aggression to get attention from others in one setting, to escape from an unpleasant event in another setting, and to gain access to tangible items in still another setting. For example, in one study (Carr & Durand, 1985a), a 5-year-old girl with brain damage engaged in self-biting, hitting others, and screaming in order to escape a vocabulary development task; however, she used the same problem behaviors to gain her teacher's attention whenever the teacher failed to pay sufficient attention to her. There is a growing body of scientific evidence demonstrating that an individual with disabilities may learn, over time, to use his or her problem behavior to achieve many different goals depending on specific circumstances (Carr & Carlson, 1993; Durand, 1982; Durand & Carr, 1991; Guess & Carr, 1991; Heidorn & Jensen, 1984; Iwata, Dorsey, Slifer, Bauman, & Richman, 1982; Maisto, Baumeister, & Maisto, 1978; Smith, Iwata, Vollmer, & Zarcone, 1993).

PROBLEM BEHAVIOR IN NORMAL CHILD DEVELOPMENT

It is important to note that studies of normal child development show that a variety of disruptive behaviors in young children without disabilities appears to occur for the same reasons and serve the same purpose as the more severe problem behaviors that we have been discussing. For example, Bayley (1932) observed that infants would cry for a variety of reasons, including escape from unpleasant testing situations, seeking the attention of the mother, and to obtain certain tangible items. The same patterns were observed later in a detailed study of infant crying carried out by Wolff (1969). Apparently, children with disabilities are not very different from those without disabilities in the ways that they use their problem behavior to influence others.

Perhaps the single most important concept to emerge from the study of crying in normal child development is that *crying may be viewed as a primitive form of communication.* In fact, this concept has been around for thousands of years. For example, the ancient Greek philosopher Plato, writing in about 348 B.C., observed:

> New born beings have from the very first a way of screaming. . . .
> So when the nurse would discover its desires she guesses from these
> indications what to offer it; if the child is quiet when something is
> offered it, she thinks she has found the right thing, but the wrong if it
> cries and screams. (c. 348 B.C./1960, p. 174)

In other words, according to Plato, the nurse does not view the child's screaming merely as a problem behavior that needs to be eliminated. Rather, she views it as a behavior that serves a purpose for the child (in this case, obtaining a tangible item). Furthermore, she treats the behavior as a primitive form of communication, that is, as if the child was saying, "I want this." By trying to determine the purpose of the behavior and treating it as if it were an act of communication, the nurse is adopting a strategy very much like the one we advocate in this book. Indeed, most parents with young children will recognize that they too routinely respond to screaming and crying by trying to determine what purpose the behavior serves for the child. Parents try to calm the child down by treating the behavior as if it is a form of communication that requires an appropriate response and not simply suppression. The link between disturbing behaviors such as crying on the one hand and communication on the other is spelled out even more directly in the writings of the 18th-century French philosopher Rousseau, who observed, "When children begin to speak, they cry less. This is a natural progression. One language is substituted for another. As soon as they can say with words . . . why would they say it with cries?" (1762/1979, p. 77)

More recently, child psychologists and psycholinguists have demonstrated that children communicate long before they can speak (Bates, 1976; Bates, Benigni, Bretherton, Camaioni, & Volterra, 1977; Bates, Camaioni, & Volterra, 1975; Prizant & Wetherby, 1987). Thus, Bruner, like Rousseau, concluded that, "There is a progressive development of these primitive procedures for communicating, and typically they are replaced by less primitive ones until eventually they are replaced by standard linguistic procedures" (1979, p. 268). Bell and Ainsworth (1972) studied the evolution of these "primitive procedures" into more sophisticated communication by observing a group of infants during their first year of life. As did other investigators, they found that crying had a powerful influence on adults, particularly in getting adults to come closer to the infants, to pick them up and hold them, to talk to them, to feed them, and to offer them toys. However, the most important finding of all was that the infants who were the first to develop more advanced forms of communication such as facial expressions, gestures, and noncrying vocalizations were also the first to give up crying as a primary way of influencing adults. In other words, the "primitive procedure" of crying was replaced by "standard linguistic procedures" such as gesture and, eventually, speech.

The Bell and Ainsworth study supports the idea that disturbing behavior such as crying can be viewed as the precursor of communication or perhaps as a primitive form of communication itself.

Crying is not the only nonverbal behavior that has been suggested to be a primitive form of communication. Aggression has also been viewed in this way. Specifically, Brownlee and Bakeman (1981) explored aggression in toddlers. They found that certain aggressive acts influenced other children in reliable ways. For example, when one child hit another with an open hand, the other child quickly stopped interacting with the aggressor. Brownlee and Bakeman suggested that aggression in this circumstance was a communicative act that was equivalent to saying, "Leave me alone." In contrast, hitting that involved objects, for example, a light hit with a stuffed teddy bear, promoted pleasant social interaction, especially play. The investigators suggested that aggression in this circumstance functioned communicatively to express the notion, "Hey, wanna play?" All of these observations were true for 2-year-olds but not for 3-year-olds. The older children appeared to rely more on speech than aggression to influence their peers. Again, a sophisticated mode of communication (speech) replaced a primitive mode of communication (aggression). In sum, the literature on normal child development suggests that problem behavior serves a purpose for the individual displaying it. Most important, it seems that as individuals acquire new ways of achieving their goals (through the use of speech), they tend to give up their old ways (crying, screaming, and aggression) of reaching those goals.

PROBLEM BEHAVIOR IN CHILDREN AND ADULTS WITH DISABILITIES

The main message from the literature on child development is that children tend to "outgrow" problem behavior such as screaming, crying, and aggression as they become more proficient at communicating through speech and gesture. Nevertheless, there are children with various disabilities who do not become communicatively competent over time. What happens to them? In one study, Stevenson and Richman (1978) assessed a group of 3-year-old children who showed expressive language delay and compared them with a similar age group whose expressive language was not delayed. They found a marked association between problem behavior and expressive language delay. Children whose communication skills lagged behind those of others their age were much more likely to show a wide variety of problem behaviors. In fact, a number of studies have demonstrated that children whose communicative development is impaired are more likely to be described as aggressive, noncompliant, or hostile (Aram, Ekelman, & Nation, 1984; Baker & Cantwell, 1982; Cantwell, Baker, & Mattison, 1980; Caulfield, Fischel, DeBaryshe, & Whitehurst, 1989).

Similar findings have also been reported in the research literature concerning people with developmental disabilities. For example, Talkington, Hall, and Altman (1971) studied a number of individuals with mental retardation, some of whom had relatively poor
communication skills and others whose communication skills were
considerably better. The individuals with poor communication
skills were rated as showing higher levels of aggressive behavior.
Again, communicative impairment appeared to be strongly associated with serious problem behavior, an observation that Talkington
and Hall (1969) made with respect to a group of individuals who
had been diagnosed as having hearing impairments as well as retardation. Similar findings have been obtained with respect to self-
injury from a study of children with autism (Shodell & Reiter,
1968). These researchers found that self-injury was much more
common in children who had poor communication skills. The various investigators whose work we have just discussed all reached
similar conclusions based on their data. Specifically, they suggested
that aggression and self-injury are used as primitive forms of communication by individuals who lack more sophisticated ways of
communicating such as speech and sign language. Furthermore,
these investigators implied that if these individuals could learn
more sophisticated and effective ways of communicating, then they
would have no further need to engage in self-injury or aggression
and these behaviors would become less frequent or disappear altogether.

THE COMMUNICATION HYPOTHESIS OF PROBLEM BEHAVIOR

The scientific studies that we have just reviewed led several investigators to propose what has been referred to as the "communication hypothesis" of problem behavior. This hypothesis is that problem behavior often functions as a primitive form of communication
for those individuals who do not yet possess or use more sophisticated forms of communication that would enable them to influence
others to obtain a variety of desirable outcomes, termed "reinforcers" in the literature (Carr, 1985; Carr & Durand, 1985b; Donnellan, Mirenda, Mesaros, & Fassbender, 1984; Doss & Reichle, 1989;
Neel & Billingsley, 1989; Reichle & Yoder, 1979). There are two
very important points that need to be stressed in order to fully understand the communication hypothesis. First, the hypothesis does
not state that only people who cannot talk will use problem behavior to influence others. Frequently, people who have quite a lot of
speech will nevertheless use problem behavior when, for example,
they want to escape from an unpleasant situation. For whatever reason, they have not yet learned that they can use their speech skills

(rather than aggression or self-injury) to extricate themselves from situations that they do not like. Second, the communication hypothesis does *not* state that individuals systematically and intentionally use their problem behavior to influence others. There is no evidence that a person with disabilities is actually thinking to him- or herself, "I don't like the vocabulary task that the teacher is presenting to me. Therefore, I will frighten her by biting myself on the arm and then pulling her hair." The communication hypothesis is, in reality, a metaphor that suggests that problem behavior often functions *as if* it was a form of communication. As we will see next, this hypothesis is useful not because it tells us what people with disabilities are thinking but rather because it suggests a constructive and educational way of addressing problem behavior.

DECREASING PROBLEM BEHAVIOR BY TEACHING COMMUNICATION SKILLS

As noted, the major implication of the communication hypothesis in terms of intervention is that by strengthening relevant communication skills, it may be possible to replace problem behavior so that such behavior becomes much less frequent or is eliminated altogether. Carr and Durand (1985a) carried out a study that systematically analyzed this possibility. The four individuals involved in this study had a variety of disabilities, including autism, brain damage, and developmental delay. Their problem behaviors consisted of several forms of aggression, self-injury, and tantrums. In the first part of the study, which took place in a classroom, an assessment was made to determine what purpose the problem behavior served. In the case of two of the individuals, problems worsened when the individuals were asked to participate in a difficult vocabulary development exercise. Thus, the purpose of the problem behavior appeared to be escape from the frustrating vocabulary task. In the case of one of the individuals, problems worsened when the teacher reduced the amount of attention to the individual in order to work with another child. Thus, the purpose of this individual's problem behavior seemed to be attention-seeking. The fourth individual showed problem behavior that seemed to be both escape-motivated and attention-seeking, depending on the situation. Once the purpose of the problem behavior had been identified, specific forms of communication were taught to the individuals that directly addressed the relevant factors. For example, if attention-seeking were the important factor, the individual was taught to solicit the teacher's attention by using an appropriate communicative initiation such as holding up completed work and saying, "Am I doing good work?" or, "Look what I've done!" If escape were the important factor, the individual learned to make the work situation less frustrating by seeking assistance with the communicative phrase, "I don't understand" or, "Help me." When the individuals were taught these relevant communicative phrases, their self-injury, aggression, and tantrums fell to very low levels. A large and growing number of studies have demonstrated positive intervention effects, that is, decreased problem behavior, following communication-based interventions (Billingsley & Neel, 1985; Bird, Dores, Moniz, & Robinson, 1989; Casey, 1978; Day et al. 1988; Duker, Jol, & Palmen, 1991; Durand & Kishi, 1987; Ellsworth, 1975; Horner & Budd, 1985; Horner & Day, 1991; Horner, Sprague, O'Brien, & Heathfield, 1990; Hunt, Alwell, & Goetz, 1988; Hunt, Alwell, Goetz, & Sailor, 1990; Northup et al., 1991; Rowe & Rapp, 1980; Smith & Coleman, 1986; Steege et al., 1990; Wacker, Northup, & Kelly, in press; Wacker & Steege, 1993; Wacker et al., 1990).

GENERALIZATION AND MAINTENANCE FOLLOWING COMMUNICATION TRAINING

Although initial positive intervention effects are a welcome outcome of any intervention, generalization and maintenance of these effects must also occur if the intervention is to be truly meaningful. "Generalization" means that positive intervention effects are also seen in new situations that go beyond the original situation in which the intervention first occurred. Durand and Carr (1992) found that following communication training involving one teacher, individuals were able to use their newly acquired communication skills when they encountered new teachers and, further, the individuals showed virtually no problem behavior in the presence of the new teachers. Similarly, Bird et al. (1989) found that individuals who had received communication training in one situation showed improvements in communication skills and reductions in problem behavior when they encountered new settings, new staff, and new tasks. Also, Hunt et al. (1990) reported improvements in the presence of new peers. Apparently, communication-based intervention can, if appropriately applied, generalize to a variety of situations beyond the one originally used in teaching.

"Maintenance" means that initial intervention effects are durable. In a study by Durand and Carr (1991), three students in a classroom situation were taught communication skills and followed up for 18–24 months. These students continued to display their communication skills, and problem behaviors greatly decreased over this long time period. In a recently completed 5-year study of communication training involving three individuals with developmental disabilities, Carr et al. (1992) observed that communication skills maintained for at least 2–2½ years across a wide variety of home, school, and neighborhood settings. Also during this time period, problem behaviors remained negligible.

In sum, the scientific literature supports the idea that a communication-based intervention designed to address the many purposes that problem behavior can serve not only produces good initial intervention effects but is also associated with generalization and maintenance of those effects. Since the first step in using a communication-based approach is to identify the purpose of problem behavior, we turn to this issue next.

REFERENCES

Aram, D.M., Ekelman, B.L., & Nation, J.E. (1984). Preschoolers with language disorders: 10 years later. *Journal of Speech and Hearing Research, 27*, 232–244.

Baker, L., & Cantwell, D.P. (1982). Developmental, social, and behavioral characteristics of speech and language disordered children. *Child Psychiatry and Human Development, 12*, 195–206.

Bates, E. (1976). *Language and context: The acquisition of pragmatics.* New York: Academic Press.

Bates, E., Benigni, L., Bretherton, I., Camaioni, L., & Volterra, V. (1977). From gesture to the first word: On cognitive and social prerequisites. In M. Lewis & L. Rosenbaum (Eds.), *Conversation and the development of language* (pp. 247–307). New York: John Wiley & Sons.

Bates, E., Camaioni, L., & Volterra, V. (1975). The acquisition of performatives prior to speech. *Merrill-Palmer Quarterly, 21*, 205–226.

Bayley, N. (1932). A study of the crying of infants during mental and physical tests. *Journal of Genetic Psychology, 40*, 306–329.

Bell, S.M., & Ainsworth, M.D.S. (1972). Infant crying and maternal responsiveness. *Child Development, 43*, 1171–1190.

Billingsley, F.F., & Neel, R.S. (1985). Competing behaviors and their effects on skill generalization and maintenance. *Analysis and Intervention in Developmental Disabilities, 5*, 357–372.

Bird, F., Dores, P.A., Moniz, D., & Robinson, J. (1989). Reducing severe aggressive and self-injurious behaviors with functional communication training. *American Journal on Mental Retardation, 94*, 37–48.

Brownlee, J.R., & Bakeman, R. (1981). Hitting in toddler–peer interaction. *Child Development, 52*, 1076–1079.

Bruner, J. (1979). Learning how to do things with words. In D. Aaronson & R.W. Rieber (Eds.), *Psycholinguistic research* (pp. 265–284). Hillsdale, NJ: Lawrence Erlbaum Associates.

Cantwell, D.P., Baker, L., & Mattison, R.E. (1980). Psychiatric disorders in children with speech and language retardation. *Archives of General Psychiatry, 37*, 423–426.

Carr, E.G. (1985). Behavioral approaches to language and communication. In E. Schopler & G. Mesibov (Eds.), *Current issues in autism: Volume 3. Communication problems in autism* (pp. 37–57). New York: Plenum Press.

Carr, E.G., & Carlson, J.I. (1993). Reduction of severe behavior problems in the community using a multicomponent treatment approach. *Journal of Applied Behavior Analysis, 26*, 157–172.

Carr, E.G., & Durand, V.M. (1985a). Reducing behavior problems through functional communication training. *Journal of Applied Behavior Analysis, 18,* 111–126.

Carr, E.G., & Durand, V.M. (1985b). The social-communicative basis of severe behavior problems in children. In S. Reiss & R. Bootzin (Eds.) *Theoretical issues in behavior therapy* (pp. 219–254). New York: Academic Press.

Carr, E.G., Levin, L., McConnachie, G., Carlson, J.I., Smith, C.E., & Kemp, D.C. (1992). *A long-term multicomponent communication-based intervention for severe problem behavior.* Unpublished manuscript, State University of New York at Stony Brook, Department of Psychology, Stony Brook, NY.

Carr, E.G., & McDowell, J.J. (1980). Social control of self-injurious behavior of organic etiology. *Behavior Therapy, 11,* 402–409.

Carr, E.G., & Newsom, C.D. (1985). Demand-related tantrums: Conceptualization and treatment. *Behavior Modification, 9,* 403–426.

Carr, E.G., Newsom, C.D., & Binkoff, J.A. (1976). Stimulus control of self-destructive behavior in a psychotic child. *Journal of Abnormal Child Psychology, 4,* 139–153.

Carr, E.G., Newsom, C.D., & Binkoff, J.A. (1980). Escape as a factor in the aggressive behavior of two retarded children. *Journal of Applied Behavior Analysis, 13,* 101–117.

Carr, E.G., Taylor, J.C., & Robinson, S. (1991). The effects of severe behavior problems in children on the teaching behavior of adults. *Journal of Applied Behavior Analysis, 24,* 523–535.

Casey, L.O. (1978). Development of communicative behavior in autistic children: A parent program using manual signs. *Journal of Autism and Childhood Schizophrenia, 8,* 45–59.

Caulfield, M.B., Fischel, J., DeBaryshe, B.D., & Whitehurst, G.J. (1989). Behavioral correlates of developmental expressive language disorder. *Journal of Abnormal Child Psychology, 17,* 187–201.

Churchill, D.W. (1971). Effects of success and failure in psychotic children. *Archives of General Psychiatry, 25,* 208–214.

Day, R.M., Rea, J.A., Schussler, N.G., Larsen, S.E., & Johnson, W.L. (1988). A functionally based approach to the treatment of self-injurious behavior. *Behavior Modification, 12,* 565–589.

Donnellan, A.M., Mirenda, P.L., Mesaros, R.A., & Fassbender, L.L. (1984). Analyzing the communicative functions of aberrant behavior. *Journal of The Association for Persons with Severe Handicaps, 9,* 201–212.

Doss, S., & Reichle, J. (1989). Establishing communicative alternatives to the emission of socially motivated excess behavior: A review. *Journal of The Association for Persons with Severe Handicaps, 14,* 101–112.

Duker, P.C., Jol, K., & Palmen, A. (1991). The collateral decrease of self-injurious behavior with teaching communicative gestures to individuals who are mentally retarded. *Behavioral Residential Treatment, 6,* 183–196.

Durand, V.M. (1982). Analysis and intervention of self-injurious behavior. *Journal of The Association for Persons with Severe Handicaps, 7,* 44–53.

Durand, V.M., & Carr, E.G. (1991). Functional communication training to reduce challenging behavior: Maintenance and application in new settings. *Journal of Applied Behavior Analysis, 24,* 251–264.

Durand, V.M., & Carr, E.G. (1992). An analysis of maintenance following functional communication training. *Journal of Applied Behavior Analysis, 25,* 777–794.

Durand, V.M., & Crimmins, D.B. (1988). Identifying the variables maintaining self-injurious behavior. *Journal of Autism and Developmental Disorders, 18,* 99–117.

Durand, V.M., Crimmins, D.B., Caulfield, M., & Taylor, J. (1989). Reinforcer assessment I: Using problem behavior to select reinforcers. *Journal of The Association for Persons with Severe Handicaps, 14,* 113–126.

Durand, V.M., & Kishi, G. (1987). Reducing severe behavior problems among persons with dual sensory impairments: An evaluation of a technical assistance model. *Journal of The Association for Persons with Severe Handicaps, 12,* 2–10.

Edelson, S.M., Taubman, M.T., & Lovaas, O.I. (1983). Some social contexts of self-destructive behavior. *Journal of Abnormal Child Psychology, 11,* 299–312.

Ellsworth, S. (1975). If only Jimmy could speak. *Hearing and Speech Action, 43*(6), 6–10.

Goldiamond, I. (1974). Towards a constructional approach to social problems. *Behaviorism, 2,* 1–84.

Guess, D., & Carr, E. (1991). Emergence and maintenance of stereotypy and self-injury. *American Journal on Mental Retardation, 96,* 299–319.

Heidorn, S.D., & Jensen, C.C. (1984). Generalization and maintenance of the reduction of self-injurious behavior maintained by two types of reinforcement. *Behaviour Research and Therapy, 22,* 581–586.

Horner, R.H., & Budd, C.M. (1985). Acquisition of manual sign use: Collateral reduction of maladaptive behavior, and factors limiting generalization. *Education and Training of the Mentally Retarded, 20,* 39–47.

Horner, R.H., & Day, H.M. (1991). The effects of response efficiency on functionally equivalent competing behavior. *Journal of Applied Behavior Analysis, 24,* 719–732.

Horner, R.H., Sprague, J.R., O'Brien, M., & Heathfield, L.T. (1990). The role of response efficiency in the reduction of problem behaviors through functional equivalence training: A case study. *Journal of The Association for Persons with Severe Handicaps, 15,* 91–97.

Hunt, P., Alwell, M., & Goetz, L. (1988). Acquisition of conversation skills and the reduction of inappropriate social interaction behaviors. *Journal of The Association for Persons with Severe Handicaps, 13,* 20–27.

Hunt, P., Alwell, M., Goetz, L., & Sailor, W. (1990). Generalized effects of conversation skill training. *Journal of The Association for Persons with Severe Handicaps, 15,* 250–260.

Iwata, B.A., Dorsey, M.F., Slifer, K.J., Bauman, K.E., & Richman, G.S. (1982). Toward a functional analysis of self-injury. *Analysis and Intervention in Developmental Disabilities, 2,* 3–20.

Lovaas, O.I., Freitag, G., Gold, V.J., & Kassorla, I.C. (1965). Experimental studies in childhood schizophrenia: Analysis of self-destructive behavior. *Journal of Experimental Child Psychology, 2,* 67–84.

Lovaas, O.I., & Simmons, J.Q. (1969). Manipulation of self-destruction in three retarded children. *Journal of Applied Behavior Analysis, 2,* 143–157.

Maisto, C.R., Baumeister, A.A., & Maisto, A.A. (1978). An analysis of variables related to self-injurious behavior among institutionalized retarded persons. *Journal of Mental Deficiency Research, 22,* 27–36.

Martin, P.L. & Foxx, R.M. (1973). Victim control of the aggression of an institutionalized retardate. *Journal of Behavior Therapy and Experimental Psychiatry, 4,* 161–165.

Neel, R.S., & Billingsley, F.F. (1989). *Impact: A functional curriculum* handbook for students with moderate to severe disabilities. Baltimore: Paul H. Brookes Publishing Co.

Northup, J., Wacker, D., Sasso, G., Steege, M., Cigrand, K., Cook, J., & DeRaad, A. (1991). A brief functional analysis of aggressive and alternative behavior in an outclinic setting. *Journal of Applied Behavior Analysis, 24,* 509–522.

Plato. (1960). *The laws* (A.E. Taylor, Trans.). London: J.M. Dent.

Plummer, S., Baer, D.M., & LeBlanc, J.M. (1977). Functional considerations in the use of procedural timeout and an effective alternative. *Journal of Applied Behavior Analysis, 10,* 689–706.

Prizant, B.M., & Wetherby, A.M. (1987). Communicative intent: A framework for understanding social-communicative behavior in autism. *Journal of the American Academy of Child and Adolescent Psychiatry, 26,* 472–479.

Reichle, J.E., & Yoder, D.E. (1979). Assessment and early stimulation of communication in the severely and profoundly mentally retarded. In R.L. York & E. Edgar (Eds.), *Teaching the severely handicapped* (Volume 4, pp. 180–218). Seattle: American Association for the Education of the Severely/Profoundly Handicapped.

Repp, A.C., Felce, D., & Barton, L.E. (1988). Basing the treatment of stereotypic and self-injurious behaviors on hypotheses of their causes. *Journal of Applied Behavior Analysis, 21,* 281–289.

Romanczyk, R.G., Colletti, G., & Plotkin, R. (1980). Punishment of self-injurious behavior: Issues of behavior analysis, generalization, and the right to treatment. *Child Behavior Therapy, 2,* 37–54.

Rousseau, J.J. (1979). *Emile* (A. Bloom, Trans.). New York: Basic Books.

Rowe, J.A., & Rapp, D.L. (1980). Tantrums: Remediation through communication. *Child Care, Health, and Development, 6,* 197–208.

Sailor, W., Guess, D., Rutherford, G., & Baer, D.M. (1968). Control of tantrum behavior by operant techniques during experimental verbal training. *Journal of Applied Behavior Analysis, 1,* 237–243.

Shodell, M.J., & Reiter, H.H. (1968). Self-mutilative behavior in verbal and nonverbal schizophrenic children. *Archives of General Psychiatry, 19,* 453–455.

Smith, M.D., & Coleman, D. (1986). Managing the behavior of adults with autism in the job setting. *Journal of Autism and Developmental Disorders, 16,* 145–154.

Smith, R.G., Iwata, B.A., Vollmer, T.R., & Zarcone, J.R. (1993). Experimental analysis and treatment of multiply controlled self-injury. *Journal of Applied Behavior Analysis, 26,* 183–196.

Steege, M.W., Wacker, D.P., Berg, W.K., Cigrand, K.C., & Cooper, L.J. (1989). The use of behavioral assessment to prescribe and evaluate treatments for severely handicapped children. *Journal of Applied Behavior Analysis, 22,* 23–33.

Steege, M.W., Wacker, D.P., Cigrand, K.C., Berg, W.K., Novak, C.G., Reimers, T.M., Sasso, G.M., & DeRaad, A. (1990). Use of negative reinforcement in the treatment of self-injurious behavior. *Journal of Applied Behavior Analysis, 23,* 459–467.

Stevenson, J., & Richman, N. (1978). Behavior, language, and development in three-year-old children. *Journal of Autism and Childhood Schizophrenia, 8,* 299–313.

Talkington, L.W., & Hall, S.M. (1969). Hearing impairment and aggressiveness in the mentally retarded. *Perceptual and Motor Skills, 28,* 303–306.

Talkington, L.W., Hall, S., & Altman, R. (1971). Communication deficits and aggression in the mentally retarded. *American Journal of Mental Deficiency, 76*, 235–237.

Taylor, J.C., & Carr, E.G. (1992a). Severe problem behavior related to social interaction. II: A systems analysis. *Behavior Modification, 16*, 336–371.

Taylor, J.C., & Carr, E.G. (1992b). Severe problem behaviors related to social interaction. I: Attention seeking and social avoidance. *Behavior Modification, 16*, 305–335.

Wacker, D.P., Northup, J., & Kelly, L. (in press). Proactive treatment of self-injurious behavior based on functional analysis. In E. Cipani & N. Singh (Eds.), *Treatment of severe behavior problems: A handbook for practitioners*. New York: Springer-Verlag.

Wacker, D.P., & Steege, M.W. (1993). Providing outclinic services: Evaluating treatment and social validity. In S. Axelrod & R. Van Houten (Eds.), *Effective behavioral treatment: Issues and implementation* (pp. 297–319). New York: Plenum Press.

Wacker, D.P., Steege, M.W., Northup, J., Sasso, G., Berg, W., Reimers, T., Cooper, L., Cigrand, K., & Donn, L. (1990). A component analysis of functional communication training across three topographies of severe behavior problems. *Journal of Applied Behavior Analysis, 23*, 417–429.

Weeks, M., & Gaylord-Ross, R. (1981). Task difficulty and aberrant behavior in severely handicapped students. *Journal of Applied Behavior Analysis, 14*, 449–463.

Wiesler, N.A., Hanson, R.H., Chamberlain, T.P., & Thompson, T. (1985). Functional taxonomy of stereotypic and self-injurious behavior. *Mental Retardation, 23*, 230–234.

Wolf, M.M., Birnbrauer, J.S. Williams, T., & Lawler, J. (1965). A note on apparent extinction of the vomiting behavior of a retarded child. In L. Ullman & L. Krasner (Eds.), *Case studies in behavior modification* (pp. 364–366). New York: Holt, Rinehart & Winston.

Wolff, P.H. (1969). The natural history of crying and other vocalizations in early infancy. In B.M. Foss (Ed.), *Determinants of infant behavior* (Volume 4, pp. 81–109). London: Methuen.

Chapter 4

Functional Assessment: Describe

We have already discussed that individuals engage in problem behavior for many different reasons. Problem behavior is purposeful. Now, we discuss *assessment*, which aims to discover the reasons why a particular individual engages in severe problem behavior. When you understand what purpose the behavior serves, you are better able to design interventions that provide individuals with meaningful alternatives to their problem behaviors.

Some people mistakenly assume that they can begin an intervention without doing any assessment. Over the years, we have heard people say, "Let's not waste time trying to figure out why Jamal is head-banging. The important thing is to stop this problem now." Consider this point before rejecting the need for assessment. When your own son or daughter cries, or your spouse is angry, do you just jump in and try to change their behavior or do you try to find out the reasons why they are behaving the way they are? If you try to answer the "why" question, then you are doing an assessment. If you feel that the behavior of people without disabilities deserves some form of assessment whereas the behavior of people with disabilities does not, then you are not taking people with disabilities very seriously and you ought to examine your conscience and possibly your prejudices.

Traditionally, functional assessment involves trying to discover the functions that problem behavior serves, that is, the reasons that problem behavior occurs. The three components of functional assessment are interview, direct observation, and experiment. (If you read some of the scientific literature cited at the end of this book, you will see that "experiment" is sometimes referred to as "functional analysis.") What do each of these three terms—interview, direct observation, and experiment—mean? Consider, first, the interview. An interview consists of the person doing the assessment asking classroom staff, group home staff, or parents, for example, to describe the nature of the behavior in specific detail, the circumstances in which the problem is most likely to occur, and the reaction that it evokes from others when it does occur. Direct observation means that the person doing the assessment may follow the individual around for a number of weeks. During this time, the individual is carefully and directly observed in a variety of ordinary daily situations, including those that were identified in the interview process as being associated with problem behavior. Finally, in the experiment component, the person doing the assessment may purposely and systematically arrange certain situations in order to determine if problem behavior occurs consistently in those situations.

PRACTICAL STRATEGIES

The assessment method that we use involves elements of the three procedures that we just discussed. However, we are not asking you to carry out these procedures in the precise and often laborious way described in scientific journals. In extensive field tests, we have found that when parents, teachers, and residential staff, for example, were asked to take a lot of data in complicated natural environments, they often became overwhelmed by the task and were reluctant to continue. Therefore, we have adopted a middle ground that has proven to be practical as well as effective. Specifically, when possible, we avoid asking overworked direct service providers (particularly in the early stages of intervention) to carry out detailed data collection procedures. We choose instead to have a number of professionals and supervisory staff bear the brunt of data gathering. Our assessment strategy can be summarized in terms of three stages: *describe, categorize, verify.* These stages are described fully in this and the following chapters.

Describe, the initial step, involves both interview and direct observation in order to get a clear picture of the social context for the problem behavior, the specific nature of the problem behavior, and the reaction that the problem behavior evokes from others. (If you read some of the resource materials listed at the end of this book, you will see that many scientific papers refer to description as an "ABC" analysis, meaning antecedents, behaviors, consequences. Knowing this terminology will help you to integrate what we are talking about with how other people refer to this topic.) *Categorize,* the second step, involves grouping all the information gathered from the description by specific situations according to the different purposes that the problem behaviors appear to serve. Finally, *verifiy*, the last step, involves systematically changing the social reaction to problem behavior, as well as the social and physical context, in order to be more certain if a specific instance of problem behavior does indeed serve a specific purpose (function). Now we discuss in detail how to carry out the describe, categorize, and verify procedures.

DESCRIBE: INTERVIEW AND DIRECT OBSERVATION

There are two components to this stage of the assessment, interview and direct observation. There are three possible connections between direct observation and interview that we have seen time and again: 1) direct observation confirms the description obtained from the interview process, 2) direct observation fails to confirm the description obtained from the interview process, 3) direct observation identifies a new problem that was not described during the interview process.

DIRECT OBSERVATION CONFIRMS INTERVIEW

Example: Val

Joan was Val's classroom teacher. During the first few months of the school year, Joan had noticed that Val behaved very poorly many times each day and things seemed to be getting worse. Therefore, Joan invited the school psychologist, Jacki, into her classroom to assess the problem. This is the interview that followed:

Jacki: *What is it that Val does that upsets you?*

Joan: *She's very disruptive and mean to the other students. Actually, she's a sweet kid, but sometimes I think she's being spiteful or jealous.*

Jacki: *There are lots of ways of being disruptive and mean. Could you give me some specific examples?*

Joan: *Sure, Val will scream or spit at me. She'll grab another student by the hair or throw all her schoolwork off her desk.*

Jacki: *You mentioned before that Val was sometimes spiteful or jealous. When does she act this way? All the time?*

Joan: *No, no, not all the time. If I'm working with her or talking with her, she's fine. But if I start talking to another student or get busy with some paperwork that I need to do, all hell will break loose.*

Jacki: *So in other words, if she's got your attention, she's pretty*

> *well behaved, but if you can't socialize with her, she gets angry.*

Joan: *That's the truth.*

Jacki: *I'm just curious. When she does get angry and grabs another student or spits at you, how do you react?*

Joan: *I'll tell you: I don't tolerate it. I lay down the law and let her know that that is not how a young lady acts in my classroom!*

Jacki: *When you say "lay down the law," do you mean that you tell her "No" or is there more to it?*

Joan: *Oh, much more. I tell her that we do not allow that kind of behavior here. I ask her how she would feel if I spit at her or grabbed her hair. And I tell her that I know she is capable of much better behavior and that I expect her to act more grown up from now on.*

Jacki: *How long do you talk to her like this?*

Joan: *Oh, not long, maybe 3 or 4 minutes.*

Jacki: *What is Val's reaction to all this?*

Joan: *Well, that's the thing that bothers me the most. Very often, she simply becomes silly and starts laughing or making funny faces at me and then I have to lay down the law again.*

Jacki: *So, in fact, once Val gets off on the wrong track, you might be talking to her for much longer than 3 or 4 minutes. That must be tiring after a while.*

Joan: *Yes, that's why I invited you here.*

Jacki: *OK, this was helpful. I have a better idea now of what's going on. Since you mentioned that there are quite a few other times when Val goes off, I'd like to talk to you about those times as well. When we're done, though, I'd like to hang out in your classroom at various times during the next 2 weeks so that I can observe things more directly. That will give me a much better idea of what you and Val are going through and it will also help me to get a sense of the day-to-day routine here.*

During the next 2 weeks, Jacki made good on her promise to visit Joan's classroom and did so for about 1 hour every day in order to make a series of direct observations. She scattered her visits across various times of the day so that she could sample as many different aspects of the classroom routine as possible. The interview had provided Jacki with many tips about where she could best focus her observation efforts. Recall that Joan had told her that Val's problem behavior was especially bad when she was unable to attend to Val because she needed to work with another student or to complete some paperwork. During each visit, Jacki recorded each incident of problem behavior on an index card, using the format that we developed over many years of observing individuals with problem behavior. Figure 1 shows three examples of the format that related directly to the information that Joan had provided.

Figure 1a. illustrates the types of information recorded. In addition to listing the *name of the person being observed* (Val), the *name of the person making the observation* (Jacki), the *date of the observation* (11/12/87), and the *time of the observation* (10:00 A.M.), each episode is described in terms of the *general context*, which refers to the overall activity taking place at the time the observation was made (group instruction). Jacki did not record any of these items of information until there was an episode of problem behavior. At that time, she recorded the information just described and, most important of all, she noted the specific *interpersonal context*. She wrote down which people were around at the time the problem occurred and what interaction these people were having. This information is central because, as noted earlier, the communication-based approach is only appropriate when you suspect that problem behavior is influenced by the social interactions that occur between people. As can be seen from Figure 1a., the situation in which the problem behavior occurred was distinctly social in nature, with Joan speaking to a student while Val and the others listened. Jacki also wrote down the specific nature of the *problem behavior* so that she could compare it later with the description given to her by Joan during the interview. The yelling and aggressive behavior that Jacki observed were consistent with Joan's earlier description. Finally, and of greatest importance, Jacki noted the *social reaction* that Val's problem behavior evoked from significant others, in this case, Joan. It was very clear that Joan responded vigorously and at length to Val's inappropriate behavior. In other words, problem behavior was followed by long periods of attention from Joan, a fact that had also come out during the interview process.

Figure 1b. describes a different general context and interpersonal context in which yelling and aggression took place. Here, too, Jacki observed that when Joan could not attend to Val (in this case Joan was talking to another teacher), Val showed problem behavior. As in Figure 1a., Val received a great deal of individual attention from Joan following the outburst. Val also received much attention from the male teacher to whom Joan was talking. Figure 1c. depicts a third context associated with multiple forms of aggression. This time, Joan could not attend to Val because Joan was busy preparing

NAME: Val	OBSERVER: Jacki	DATE: 11/12/87

GENERAL CONTEXT: Group instruction	TIME: 10:00 A.M.

INTERPERSONAL CONTEXT: Joan was asking each student in turn to identify some pictures from a magazine and to tell a story about each one.

BEHAVIOR PROBLEM: Val knocked the magazine out of Joan's hand and yelled, "You're stupid," to the student who had been speaking.

SOCIAL REACTION: Joan angrily told Val to pick up the magazine and tried to make her apologize to the other student. When Val refused, Joan persisted for approximately 7 minutes in her efforts to get an apology.

a.

NAME: Val	OBSERVER: Jacki	DATE: 11/18/87

GENERAL CONTEXT: Recess	TIME: 1:45 P.M.

INTERPERSONAL CONTEXT: The students were sitting on the grass near the playing field or walking around the courtyard. Joan was standing at the doorway talking to a male teacher.

BEHAVIOR PROBLEM: Val ran up to the male teacher and yelled, "Hey, nubbie!" in his face. When Joan tried to intercede, Val grabbed Joan's shirt sleeve and ripped it in the struggle that followed.

SOCIAL REACTION: Joan severely berated Val for about 5 minutes, telling her that she should not interrupt when people were talking to one another and that she should apologize for tearing her shirt. The male teacher repeated many of Joan's comments to Val.

b.

NAME: Val	OBSERVER: Jacki	DATE: 11/19/87

GENERAL CONTEXT: Lunch	TIME: 12:00 P.M.

INTERPERSONAL CONTEXT: Val was seated at the lunch table with the other students. Joan was busy putting the finishing touches on some birthday cupcakes in honor of one of the students.

BEHAVIOR PROBLEM: Val suddenly yelled, "I'm not hungry." When Joan turned around and made eye contact, Val pulled the hair of the birthday student while staring at Joan. As Joan approached Val to protect the other student, Val spit at Joan, cursed repeatedly, and tried to scratch Joan several times.

SOCIAL REACTION: Joan pried Val's fingers off the other student and told Val she had better start acting more grown-up or nobody would want to be her friend. This theme continued for about 8 minutes.

c.

Figure 1. Index cards used in the functional assessment of Val's problem behavior. The three cards are examples of situations in which direct observation confirmed the description obtained in the interview.

food. Again, Val's problem behavior resulted in a great deal of social interaction with Joan.

Example: Gary

Cal was Gary's job coach. Gary had gotten a part-time job working in a greenhouse where, in addition to other responsibilities, he planted bulbs in pots, which were then sold. Gary ran into trouble almost immediately. His frequent and accelerating bouts of aggression, although defused by the job coach, were beginning to annoy his fellow workers and his job was in jeopardy. Cal asked Rob, the supervisor of the supported employment program, to come to the greenhouse to assess the problem. The interview went as follows:

Rob: *You're having some difficulties.*

Cal: *We sure are. Gary's going to kill someone in here if things keep going this way unless, of course, he gets fired first.*

Rob: *What do you mean by "kill"?*

Cal: *I mean that he's a terror and everybody's afraid to come near him. He's a wild man at times.*

Rob: *Exactly what does he do when he's a "wild man" and a "terror"?*

Cal: *I'll give you an example of what just happened this morning. I asked him to bring over a big bag of potting soil that we needed for a job, but instead of bringing it over, he let out a yell and punched me right in the face. I don't think he's a big fan of physical labor.*

Rob: *I noticed you said that you asked for a big bag of soil. What happens if it had been a little bag?*

Cal: *Actually, nothing would have happened. He probably would have been OK.*

Rob: *That seems to fit in with your statement that he doesn't like physical labor. Am I right?*

Cal: *Come to think of it, Gary is mostly aggressive when he gets tired from working a lot and the task just becomes too much for him.*

Rob: *What do you do when Gary starts swinging?*

Cal: *Do you want to know the truth?*

Rob: *Yes.*

Cal: *We get the hell out of here. He's big and when he lands a good punch, it hurts. My life insurance policy is not big enough.*

Rob: *So, in other words, when he becomes aggressive, you don't
        make him complete his work before giving him a break?*

Cal: *Let me put it this way, Rob: One punch and we go to lunch.*

Rob: *I think I get the message. There are a number of other prob-
        lem situations that I want to talk to you about. Once I get
        some more information from you, I'd like to come by pretty
        much every day for the next 2 weeks to see Gary in action.
        That'll give me a clearer picture of what's happening and
        what we need to do about it.*

During the next 2 weeks, Rob made a series of direct observations in the greenhouse in much the same way that Jacki did in the
classroom. Rob used the information he obtained in the interview
to check closely Gary's behavior. In all three situations depicted in
Figure 2, Rob's direct observations seemed to confirm what Cal had
told him in the interview: Gary displayed various forms of aggression when he was asked to initiate or continue to carry out a physically demanding task. In each situation shown in Figure 2, Cal responded to Gary's aggression by pulling back and not asking Gary
to complete the task. Gary's aggression got him out of the work situation.

Example: Juan

Bill was the service coordinator for Juan in his group home. Juan
had moved to the community home from a state psychiatric hospital where he had lived for 30 years. Although he showed a remarkable ability to adjust to life in the community, the fact that he could
not speak often made things difficult for him. Bill felt that Juan
became frustrated and aggressive because he lacked the requisite
skills to make himself understood. Bill was eager to begin teaching
Juan specific communication skills to reduce the frustration. However, Bill was confused about exactly what it was that set Juan off
and, thus, what skills to teach. Because Bill felt that he was too
close to the problem, he asked the supervisor of the group home,
Glen, to come by and help assess the problem. Glen's interview was
as follows:

Glen: *Tell me what's happening with Juan.*

Bill: *He has these random outbursts where he suddenly loses it.
        He'll be doing great in the home, seeming to enjoy himself,
        and then he'll let us have it.*

Glen: *What do you mean exactly when you say, "He'll let us
        have it?"*

Bill: *He just gets very angry.*

NAME: Gary	OBSERVER: Rob	DATE: 3/10/87

GENERAL CONTEXT: Gathering work materials   **TIME:** 9:30 A.M.

INTERPERSONAL CONTEXT: Cal asked Gary to bring over a wheelbarrow full of potting soil to the workbench.

BEHAVIOR PROBLEM: Gary punched Cal in the chest and tried to punch him a second time in the face but Cal ducked.

SOCIAL REACTION: Cal told Gary to "keep cool" and moved away from him. After a few minutes, Cal got the wheelbarrow himself.

a.

NAME: Gary	OBSERVER: Rob	DATE: 3/23/87

GENERAL CONTEXT: Potting bulbs   **TIME:** 1:00 P.M.

INTERPERSONAL CONTEXT: Gary potted about 10 bulbs then stopped working. After 2 minutes, Cal said to Gary, "Come on, Gary, let's get on with the job."

BEHAVIOR PROBLEM: Gary threw a pot at Cal and bit himself severely on the hand while jumping up and down on the floor.

SOCIAL REACTION: Cal said to Gary, "Calm down. Calm down. Everything's OK." After 5 minutes, Cal got out a soda and offered some to Gary.

b.

NAME: Gary	OBSERVER: Rob	DATE: 3/24/87

GENERAL CONTEXT: Planting flower beds   **TIME:** 2:45 P.M.

INTERPERSONAL CONTEXT: After 5 minutes of work, Gary slowed down his output to the point where he was putting in about one plant every 2 minutes. Cal said to Gary, "We have to pick up the pace a bit," and demonstrated the technique.

BEHAVIOR PROBLEM: Gary grabbed a plant out of Cal's hand and tore it to pieces. Then, Gary grabbed Cal's shirt and ripped several buttons off it in the struggle that followed.

SOCIAL REACTION: Cal disengaged himself from Gary and backed off about 10 feet. After 5 minutes, Gary calmed down. At that point, Cal finished the planting by himself.

c.

Figure 2. Index cards used in the functional assessment of Gary's problem behavior. The three cards are examples of situations in which direct observation confirmed the description obtained in the interview.

Glen: *I see. He's angry. What does he do when he's angry?*

Bill: *Oh, he'll kick you or slap you or scream a lot.*

Glen: *Earlier, you told me that Juan had a lot of random out-bursts. Do you mean that you have no idea at all when Juan will kick or slap?*

Bill: *No, no. We can see it coming. It's when he gets frustrated.*

Glen: *What would be a good example of a situation that frus-trates him?*

Bill: *Well, most of the time, it's when he's trying to get a point across and nobody understands him. Then, he'll really let you have it.*

Glen: *What kind of point does he try to get across?*

Bill: *Oh, he'll want to watch some TV program but he won't be able to because someone else has the TV on another chan-nel. Then, he'll race up to us screaming and yelling and we have to guess what he wants. Sometimes, I guess right but when I don't, I have to get ready for some heavy duty wres-tling.*

Glen: *How do you wrestle with him? How do you react?*

Bill: *I was just kidding. What we do is to try to keep guessing for as long as he'll let us. Sometimes we luck out, guess right, and there's no more problem. Once he starts attacking, however, we give him a wide path and hope he'll go for the thing he wants. If he finds it, he becomes calm again.*

Glen: *So, in other words, when he's aggressive, he usually wants something and you try to get it for him or hope he'll get it for himself?*

Bill: *Yeah, that's it.*

Glen: *OK, I think I'll hang out here over the next couple of weeks. I need to talk to you also about some of the other problem situations that you reported to me. But I would like a chance to observe Juan directly for about 2 weeks so I can see what it's like and what we can do about it.*

Glen followed up his interview with a period of direct observa-tion spread out over 2 weeks. He, like Jacki and Rob, used the infor-mation he had gathered from the interview to guide his observa-tions of Juan. In Figures 3a., b., and c., we see that Glen's direct observations seemed to confirm what Bill had told him. Specifi-cally, Juan was most likely to become aggressive when he lost ac-cess to a preferred activity, such as watching TV, or when his at-tempts to request an item he desired, such as popcorn or a

NAME: Juan   OBSERVER: Glen   DATE: 5/15/88

GENERAL CONTEXT: Sitting in backyard   TIME: 6:30 P.M.

INTERPERSONAL CONTEXT: Several residents are relaxing on lounge
chairs eating snacks. Juan starts saying, "orn, orn," over and over again
excitedly. Sam, a new staff member, asks Juan, "What do you want?
What are you saying?"

BEHAVIOR PROBLEM: Juan runs at Sam and slaps him several times
on the hands and arms. Then, Juan starts kicking Sam.

SOCIAL REACTION: Sam backs away and says, "It's OK, It's OK" to
Juan. As Sam moves about 5 feet away from Juan, Juan suddenly runs
by Sam and goes into the kitchen. He comes back with a bag of popcorn.
Sam helps Juan open the bag and Juan becomes calm.

a.

NAME: Juan   OBSERVER: Glen   DATE: 5/16/88

GENERAL CONTEXT: Standing in the hallway   TIME: 7:00 P.M.

INTERPERSONAL CONTEXT: Juan, Bill, and Sam are gathered together
in the hallway. Juan is pointing upstairs repeatedly. Bill and Sam ask,
"What's wrong?"

BEHAVIOR PROBLEM: Juan grabs Bill by the arm roughly and pulls him
toward the stairs. When Bill resists, Juan hits Bill on the side of the
head and screams several times.

SOCIAL REACTION: Bill and Sam move away from Juan. Juan rushes
past them and goes up the stairs to his bedroom. He returns calmly
holding his favorite videotape.

b.

NAME: Juan   OBSERVER: Glen   DATE: 5/18/88

GENERAL CONTEXT: Watching television   TIME: 9:30 P.M.

INTERPERSONAL CONTEXT: Juan is watching a TV program that he
likes. Another resident enters the room and turns the TV to another station. Juan turns it back. The other resident turns the TV off.

BEHAVIOR PROBLEM: Juan runs into the kitchen and pulls one of the
staff members into the TV room while screaming. Juan slaps and kicks
the staff member.

SOCIAL REACTION: The staff member says, "You'll be all right, Juan.
Calm down." Juan contines slapping. The staff member then turns on
the TV and says, "Look, Juan, your favorite program. Now, will you calm
down?" Juan stops slapping after about 5 seconds and watches TV.

c.

Figure 3. Index cards used in the functional assessment of Juan's problem behavior.
The three cards are examples of situations in which direct observation confirmed the
description obtained in the interview.

particular videotape, were not heeded or understood by the staff. It is important to note that aggressive behavior was typically followed by Juan's attainment of the desired object or activity. Juan's problem behavior was strongly associated with obtaining tangible items.

Comment: Who Should Do the Assessment?

Each example that we have just discussed demonstrates that the information gathered during the interview was accurate since it was subsequently confirmed through direct observation.

One important question concerns who should gather the information; that is, who should do the assessment? Because accurate assessment requires specific technical training and experience, the assessor is typically an education specialist, psychologist, parent trainer, group home manager, or vocational supervisor. Of course, there are other people who are qualified and competent to carry out assessments, including those with direct service responsibilities. For example, in principle, many classroom teachers could carry out the assessment. The problem is that if a person is directly involved in providing services, it is often difficult for that person to find the time to carry out detailed assessments on a given individual, particularly when the person is also responsible for providing services to many other individuals as well. Also, direct service providers are sometimes too close to the problem behavior, which can interfere with thorough and accurate assessment. For example, if a teacher becomes involved in almost daily battles with a student, then he or she may be too busy managing aggressive and self-injurious behavior to notice all of the relevant and sometimes subtle social cues that form part of the context of the behavior problem. Finally, and unfortunately, repeated episodes of problem behavior may destroy the relationship between the direct service staff and the person with the disability. Thus, a teacher who comes to fear or even actively dislike the individual exhibiting problem behavior is less apt to be an accurate observer for purposes of assessment. For all these reasons, we have found that the people who are most directly involved with the person displaying the problem behavior function better, at least initially, in the role of informant than assessor. In this respect, good informants may include teachers (classroom, art, music, and gym, to name a few), speech-language pathologists, physical and occupational therapists, residential staff, job coaches, and, especially, parents. Over time, however, we have found that once the initial assessment has been completed and interventions formulated, many informants are able to continue the assessment and intervention process with only modest support from the original assessors. Later in the book we emphasize this through the examples in which the parent, residential staff, or classroom teachers, for instance, actively formulate and carry out various aspects of intervention in a sophisticated and knowledge-able manner.

In the examples of Val, Gary, and Juan just described, the infor-mants provided rather vague descriptions of the problem behavior at first. Thus, Val's teacher used words such as "spiteful" and "jeal-ous;" Gary's job coach used the words "wild man" and "terror"; and Juan's service coordinator used the phrases "random out-bursts" and "loses it." However, these descriptions are very subjec-tive and can mean different things to different people. When Jacki pressed Val's teacher to be more specific, the teacher defined Val's screaming and spitting as "spiteful" and "jealous." Most people would not think of screaming and spitting as definitions of spiteful and jealous. More likely, jealousy, for instance, would be implied by a sarcastic comment or perhaps ridicule. Because of this possible confusion, Jacki was right in asking Val's teacher to give very spe-cific examples of what she meant by spiteful and jealous. In this way, everybody interacting with Val could be clear about what her specific problem behavior was.

In addition to getting informants to define the problem behav-ior precisely and concretely, assessors must use the interview pro-cess to get information on the social context of and social reaction to the problem behavior. This information is later used to formulate hypotheses as to *why* individuals are engaging in aggression and self-injury. As we later describe, these hypotheses then form the basis for intervention selection and planning. Thus, Rob not only asked Cal what the nature of Gary's problem behavior was but also what the specific social context for the problem behavior was. In the example of working in the greenhouse, the situation was com-plicated and involved many different tasks, people, and settings. Therefore, Rob was careful to narrow down all the possibilities in order to discover the specific situation that appeared to cause Gary to aggress. The interview revealed that it was not work in general or even getting potting soil in general that set Gary off. Rather, it was heavy labor, such as carrying big bags of soil over a period of time, that caused the problem behavior to occur.

Once the social context is clear, the assessor continues the in-terview to pin down the nature of the social reaction. That is, the assessor tries to determine how other people respond to aggressive and self-injurious behavior. Information on the social reaction often provides the best clue for understanding the purpose of the prob-lem behavior. Therefore, Glen (the assessor) was right to press Bill (the informant) to be very precise in describing how Bill and others responded to Juan in the social context of people sitting around watching television. Glen was able to learn from the interview that

Bill and others responded to Juan's screaming and slapping by trying to guess what TV program Juan wanted. Correct guessing resulted in Juan's calming down whereas incorrect guessing resulted
in Juan's escalating his aggressive behavior. It would appear, therefore, that in this social context, the purpose of Juan's aggression
was to gain access to specific television programs. As we will
shortly see, this type of information is very helpful in intervention
planning.

FOLLOW-UP

It is essential to follow up the interview with at least 2 weeks of
direct observation in order to confirm the accuracy of the interview
information. You may ask, "Why bother with the interview at all if
you are going to do direct observation?" The answer is that the
interview helps the assessor to know where to look. Although Glen
eventually watched Juan in many situations, he knew to keep an
especially sharp eye on the television-watching situation because it
had been identified in the interview as particularly likely to set off
problem behavior. Thus, given limited time, Glen made sure to
make a top priority of observing Juan directly in the television-
watching situation.

As we have noted already, the interview typically results in
many leads for further observation and it is necessary to conduct
observations in a variety of different settings to ensure that all the
problem situations are adequately sampled. It is also necessary to
scatter observations across enough different settings to address the
possibility that the informant may have missed or forgotten to re-
port certain problems that occur on a regular basis.

Assessment Difficulties

Even if you follow all of the recommendations that we have made,
the assessment will be incomplete if either of two difficulties arise.
First, a 2-week observation period may not be long enough if the
problem behavior occurs very infrequently. You can overcome this
difficulty by extending the period of direct observation by several
weeks. This option is reasonable if the problem behavior is not too
severe. Usually, however, it is more practical to keep the 2-week
observation period but schedule periodic, brief follow-up observations after intervention has begun. For example, problem behavior
may occur only when a particular substitute teacher takes over the
classroom. If the substitute teacher is present once on the average
of every 3 months, you should certainly not extend the period of
direct observation to 3 months, but rather you should visit the
classroom when you know that the substitute teacher is there, even
if intervention is already ongoing at that point. There is an im-

portant message here: *Direct observation, in particular, and functional assessment, in general, are not things that occur at the beginning of an intervention program and are then dropped. Rather, functional assessment is an ongoing process that must be continued periodically throughout the entire course of intervention, especially when there is reason to believe that new information may be gained from additional assessment.*

A second assessment difficulty arises, after intervention has begun, when significant changes occur in work schedules, curricula, and staffing schedules. In these situations, new problem behavior may emerge due to factors that are different from those already assessed. Again, the solution is to carry out additional interviews and direct observations. It is clear that functional assessment needs to be an ongoing process and not simply an activity that is conducted once at the beginning of intervention planning and then discontinued.

As noted, we have recommended that the information gathered during direct observation be transferred onto index cards. Although there are many other ways of coding information, service providers have told us that the index card format is practical and easy to use. In all likelihood, people find this system workable because this format resembles teacher notes or parent diaries, and is a familiar system of coding information.

To make the discussion easy to follow, we provided example index cards in which each individual displayed problem behavior that was governed by a single purpose. Specifically, Val's problem behavior was a function of attention-seeking, Gary's was a function of escape from unpleasant situations, and Juan's was a function of obtaining tangible objects (e.g., food) or activities such as watching TV. In reality, as we shall see later, problem behavior for a given individual typically serves more than one purpose depending on the context. You can be sure that for most individuals you will generate a number of index cards that reflect a wide variety of purposes. A single individual may use aggression to escape from classroom work, to get attention during a play period, and to gain access to favorite foods during dinner. Therefore, there can be no *single* intervention for aggression. Instead, each situation calls for a specific intervention that addresses the relevant purpose of the problem behavior.

✔ CHECKLIST OF THINGS TO DO

1. Decide who will be the assessor.
2. Decide who will be the informant(s).

(continued)

3. In the interview, the assessor must ensure that the informant describes the nature of the problem behavior in specific, concrete terms.

4. In the interview, the assessor must make sure to get information regarding the social context for and the social reaction to the problem behavior.

5. After the interview has been completed, the assessor should conduct at least 2 weeks of direct observation in a variety of settings and at different times.

6. If the problem behavior occurs infrequently, it may be necessary to use a longer period of direct observation. More likely, it will be necessary to carry out additional assessments at specific times associated with situations known to evoke problem behavior. In practice, this strategy means that assessments need to be carried out on an ongoing basis even when intervention has begun. Ongoing assessment is the rule rather than the exception.

7. New assessments will be needed after intervention has begun if there have been significant changes in the life situations of the individual who is being observed. Since change is typical for most people, assessment is clearly an ongoing process.

8. Summarize all direct observation information using the index card format.

9. Monitor for success. Success means that the information derived from the interview process is corroborated by later direct observation.

DIRECT OBSERVATION FAILS TO CONFIRM INTERVIEW

Example: Val

After Val had been involved in intervention for several months for her attention-seeking aggressive behavior (described later), Joan noticed that although Val's behavior was much improved there were still times when problem behavior occurred. Val's remaining problems seemed more related to the curriculum and so Joan consulted Wayne, the education specialist at her school.

Wayne: *I understand that Val has improved quite a bit but she still has outbursts. What does she do during her outbursts?*

Joan: *Oh, pretty much the same old stuff that we have been working on for the past 6 months. She'll grab another student by the hair or throw all of her work off her desk.*

Wayne: I thought that you and Jacki had pinned this pattern down to attention-seeking? Does the behavior still occur in social situations? What I mean is, does the behavior occur, for instance, more if you start talking to another student or get busy with paperwork so that you can't attend to Val?

Joan: No, I think we've addressed that issue. The problem is much more likely to occur when I try to get Val to do certain tasks.

Wayne: For instance?

Joan: Well, if I ask her to clean up after lunch or put away the books and magazines at the end of the day, she'll tear up the magazines or spit at me or grab another student by the hair.

Wayne: Is she less disruptive if you pay more attention to her when you ask her to do these tasks?

Joan: No, that's the point. It doesn't matter if I pay attention to her and give her positive encouragement to complete the task or whether I leave her on her own to do the task independently. She'll become aggressive either way.

Wayne: How do you react to her aggression?

Joan: Oh, I'll prompt her through the task and make sure that she completes it.

Wayne: So, you don't let her use her aggression to allow her to get out of doing work?

Joan: Absolutely not.

Wayne: Okay. I think I have enough to begin with. Let me look in on your classroom during the next 2 weeks. Since you mentioned that you don't ask Val to clean up every day, tell me which days and times you ask her to do the task we're interested in and I'll schedule my visits then.

When Wayne visited Joan's class, he confirmed some of what Joan had described, but there were also some very important differences. Figure 4 summarizes what happened during a visit when Wayne observed one situation, cleaning up magazines and books. Direct observation confirmed part of what was learned from the interview: that Val misbehaved when asked to clean up at the end of the day. However, direct observation failed to confirm the most important aspect of the interview, which was Joan's insistence that she reacted to Val's problem behavior by making Val complete the task and not allowing her to escape it by becoming aggressive. Di-

NAME: Val	OBSERVER: Wayne	DATE: 3/13/87

GENERAL CONTEXT: Final clean-up   TIME: 2:45 P.M.

INTERPERSONAL CONTEXT: Joan asked Val to pick up all of the books and magazines around the class and place them back on the class-room shelves.

BEHAVIOR PROBLEM: Val screamed and tore up several magazines. She then spit at Joan.

SOCIAL REACTION: Joan repeated her request. When Val failed to com-ply, Joan physically prompted Val to pick things up. Val ignored the prompts, stared at the mirror, and made silly faces. Joan continued to clean things up without Val but now and then urged Val to help. Val ignored these requests.

Figure 4. Index card used in the functional assessment of Val's problem behavior. The figure is an example of a situation in which direct observation failed to confirm part of the description obtained in the interview.

rect observation showed instead that Val ignored her teacher's prompts to get the job done. The actual consequence of aggression in this case was that Joan completed the clean-up instead of Val. Aggression, therefore, was an effective way for Val to escape from what was for her an unpleasant task.

Example: Gary

Gary's mother, Mrs. Ibsen, had been following the assessment of her son at work in the greenhouse. She was anxious to have Gary's behavior improve in other community settings as well, for example, in the supermarket where she and Gary sometimes shopped to-gether. Mrs. Ibsen contacted Bob, the parent trainer at the agency that coordinated services for her son. Together, Bob and Mrs. Ibsen determined that Gary's aggressive behavior in the supermarket was related to his trying to obtain tangible items. Gary typically became aggressive when he wanted something, for example, a soda, but could not have it immediately. Bob and Mrs. Ibsen designed an intervention program that was very successful. However, 4 months into the intervention program, Gary's aggressive behavior began to increase. This development upset Mrs. Ibsen very much and she contacted Bob once more.

Bob: *I understand that Gary has started to become aggres-sive again in the supermarket.*

Mrs. Ibsen: *Yes, he has and I don't understand why. The inter-vention that we had developed was working fine. It really seemed that all of Gary's aggression was just his way of trying to get food items that he wanted.*

Bob: *Does he still ask for items that he wants and do you honor his requests?*

Mrs. Ibsen: *Yes, he knows to ask for things while we are going up and down the aisle and I am almost always able to give him what he wants.*

Bob: *Then there must be some new situation that sets off his aggression.*

Mrs. Ibsen: *Yes, I think there is. He's fine until we have to line up at the cashier to pay.*

Bob: *What happens then?*

Mrs. Ibsen: *Well, he's OK for the first few minutes, then he becomes fidgety, and then he starts yelling and ripping open items that we haven't yet paid for.*

Bob: *Then what happens?*

Mrs. Ibsen: *I tell him that he can't open things until we've paid for them but he continues to be agitated.*

Bob: *So, it looks like his aggression in this new situation is still linked to getting his favorite items.*

Mrs. Ibsen: *Yes, but when you and I first began the intervention, Gary was fine in line.*

Bob: *That's true. I remember. Just one question, though, you said that Gary is okay for the first few minutes but as he has to wait longer, he becomes aggressive. As I recall, when we began intervention, you never had to wait in line for more than a few minutes. Has the supermarket gotten more crowded?*

Mrs. Ibsen: *No, I forgot to mention that since Gary has been doing so well I've been buying a lot more groceries so it takes the cashier longer to ring them up.*

Bob: *When we first began, you used to get only a few items and then leave. Now you're saying that the shopping list is much longer.*

Mrs. Ibsen: *Oh, yes, it's much longer.*

Bob: *Well, that could be important. Let me go to the supermarket with you and Gary the next few times so that I can see what's happening more clearly.*

When Bob visited the supermarket, he confirmed some of what Mrs. Ibsen had described, but there were also some significant differences. Figure 5 illustrates what happened when Bob observed

```
NAME:  Gary              OBSERVER:  Bob              DATE:  4/14/88

GENERAL CONTEXT:  Supermarket                        TIME:  7:30 P.M.

INTERPERSONAL CONTEXT:  Gary and Mrs. Ibsen were waiting at the
   checkout stand for about 5 minutes while the cashier rang up various
   items.
BEHAVIOR PROBLEM:  Gary suddenly screamed and started tearing up
   several of the grocery items and throwing them about the checkout area.
   He then ran toward the exit.
SOCIAL REACTION:  Mrs. Ibsen appeared very embarrassed and she
   said, "Gary, don't do that, people are looking." She escorted Gary out of
   the store into the car where he was allowed to wait. Gary calmed down
   almost immediately and sat quietly in the car. Mrs. Ibsen returned to the
   checkout area to wait while the cashier bagged various items.
```

Figure 5. Index card used in the functional assessment of Gary's problem behavior. The figure is an example of a situation in which direct observation failed to confirm part of the description obtained in the interview.

one of the supermarket expeditions. Direct observation confirmed that Gary became agitated when he had to wait in line, but, direct observation did not confirm an important part of the interview, Mrs. Ibsen's assertion that Gary's aggressive behavior continued to be motivated by his trying to get certain favorite foods. Gary tore up the food boxes but made no attempt to eat the food. Many of the items he tore up were nonfoods such as detergent and toilet paper. Also, Mrs. Ibsen did not tell Gary that he could have his favorite items later. Instead, she took Gary from the store and had him wait in the car. Gary became calm once he was out of the store. Apparently, food had little to do with Gary's aggression in this situation. The purpose of his behavior appeared to be related to his desire to avoid having to wait in line while the cashier rang up all of the items and bagged them.

Example: Juan

Juan's behavior had improved greatly in the group home. Although his aggression had decreased, to negligible levels, he would occasionally slap the side of his face very lightly with his open hand. This behavior worried staff in the group home because many years before while living in an institution Juan had engaged in high intensity self-injury, including face-slapping, the result of which was that he had permanently deformed ears. Staff were eager to avoid any recurrence of such extreme behavior. Because the behavior seemed to occur more at night, Bill contacted Rick, the night supervisor, for a consultation.

Rick: So, Juan's aggression is way down but you still see some self-injury.

Bill: We do and we're worried that if we don't do something, it may replace aggression and become more and more severe.

Rick: Does the behavior occur in the same situations as the aggression used to occur?

Bill: I believe it does and that's what bothers us. You'd think that the successful intervention that we developed for aggression would have controlled the self-injury too.

Rick: Yes, I agree. You're saying that, for example, if Juan is watching TV late at night and someone switches off his favorite program, then he'll start to slap himself?

Bill: Exactly.

Rick: And if you turn the TV back on to the channel he was watching, he'll stop slapping?

Bill: It seems that way to us. It seems that the slapping is just another way he has of getting what he wants.

Rick: Let me drop by over the next few days and watch Juan in the various situations that worry you.

When Rick visited Juan at the group home, he paid special attention to the television-watching situation. As Figure 6a. shows, when the television was switched off during Juan's favorite program, he did indeed hit himself once or twice very lightly. This observation seemed to confirm what Rick was told during the interview. However, when the television was turned back on, Juan also hit himself a few times. Because Rick failed to see any pattern to the hitting, he continued to observe Juan over a number of days in several other situations. Rick failed to see any pattern emerge. Thus, Juan was observed to hit himself a few times when he could not obtain his favorite foods. Yet he also hit himself a few times while he was eating popcorn. The other times that Juan's hitting seemed to occur were when he was alone in his room at night (Figure 6b.), or sitting alone outside in the back yard, or otherwise unoccupied. In short, Juan's hitting did not seem to be related to obtaining tangible items or preferred activities as the staff had suggested. Most likely, Juan's self-injury was nonsocial in nature. Perhaps it was a way of generating stimulation in otherwise unstimulating situations such as being alone with nothing to do.

Comment: Reason for Discrepancies Between Direct Observation and Interview

The three examples that we just described illustrate that functional assessment is not something that takes place only at the beginning

NAME: Juan   OBSERVER: Rick   DATE: 11/20/88

GENERAL CONTEXT: Watching television   TIME: 9:30 P.M.

INTERPERSONAL CONTEXT: Juan was first prevented from watching one of his favorite TV programs. Juan was then allowed to watch the program.

BEHAVIOR PROBLEM: Juan hit himself lightly, several times, in each of the TV situations.

SOCIAL REACTIONS: Staff did not respond to the hitting.

a.

NAME: Juan   OBSERVER: Rick   DATE: 11/20/88

GENERAL CONTEXT: In bedroom   TIME: 11:00 P.M.

INTERPERSONAL CONTEXT: Bill wished Juan a good night's sleep and left Juan alone in his bedroom.

BEHAVIOR PROBLEM: For about an hour, audible face slaps could be heard in the hallway outside Juan's bedroom. About 25 slaps occurred.

SOCIAL REACTION: As was the rule, staff respected Juan's privacy and made no effort to enter his room or admonish him.

b.

Figure 6. Index cards used in the functional assessment of Juan's problem behavior. The figures are an example of situations in which direct observation failed to confirm part of the description obtained in the interview.

of an intervention and is then dropped. In each case, Val, Gary, and Juan had been participating successfully in ongoing intervention, but problem behavior was still evident. This outcome prompted additional functional assessment, as it always should. All three observation sessions represent instances in which direct observation failed to confirm part of what was reported in the interview.

Inaccurate Description of Social Reaction: Val Val's situation is quite typical. Her teacher (Joan) was accurate in describing the problem behavior in its interpersonal context. However, Joan was not accurate in describing her social reaction to Val's aggression. She said that she did not allow Val to get out of completing a task just by being aggressive. In fact, she did allow Val to escape. In general, we find that when informants provide inaccurate information in an interview, it is the description of the social reaction that is most often in error. Because intervention is based on what purpose the problem behavior is thought to serve, it is crucial to verify whether the informant's description of the social reaction is accurate. If Joan really had not permitted Val to stop working following aggressive behavior, then it would be unlikely that the purpose of Val's aggression was to help her escape from an unpleasant situation. However, because direct observation revealed that Joan *did* allow Val to stop working following aggressive behavior, it seems that the purpose of the aggression was indeed related to escape. The fact that descriptions obtained from interviews can be inaccurate is a powerful reason always to check interview accuracy by means of direct observation.

Changes in Motivation: Gary Gary provides a second reason why direct observation sometimes fails to confirm what is reported in interviews. When Gary's mother first consulted with Bob, Bob carried out a new functional assessment. This tactic was wise because, as we have already noted, additional assessments are almost always needed when a situation is different from that already assessed. The work situation in which Gary had been successful was certainly different from the new supermarket situation to which Mrs. Ibsen had introduced Gary. Just as important, Bob realized in the interview that the supermarket situation that he and Mrs. Ibsen had examined and dealt with successfully months before had changed in certain important respects. That is why Bob carried out the functional assessment process once again. Bob suspected that Gary's aggression while in line was no longer due to his wanting to eat foods, although Mrs. Ibsen's self-described social reaction implied that obtaining food remained the real reason behind Gary's problem behavior. Bob's suspicion was based on Mrs. Ibsen's statement that she had greatly expanded the shopping list and this change, in turn, greatly increased the amount of time that Gary now had to wait in line. Direct observation failed to confirm Mrs. Ibsen's belief that tangible-seeking (obtaining food) was the root cause of Gary's deteriorating behavior. Bob observed that Gary became very calm when he was allowed to leave the checkout line and wait in the car. Apparently, over time, Gary's aggression in one situation (the checkout line) developed as that situation changed and he had to wait longer because of the larger number of items now purchased. In fact, the motivation or purpose of Gary's aggression had changed, at least in this situation, from tangible-seeking to escape. Changes in motivations due to changes in situations are a common reason why problem behavior reappears over time, and this under-lines the necessity for carrying out additional functional assess-ments when changes are suspected or known.

Assumed Purpose of Problem Behavior Is Incorrect: Juan

Juan represents a third reason why direct observation some-times fails to confirm what is reported in the interview process. As was true for Val and Gary, the starting point involved concern by significant others (for Juan, the group home staff) about residual problem behavior or possible worsening of problem behavior. Bill could not understand why Juan's face-slapping did not go away during the television-watching given that the interventions devel-oped for dealing with aggression in that situation were successful. Bill told Rick that the staff were reasonably sure that Juan's self-injury served the purpose of regaining access to favorite television programs that had been intentionally or inadvertently switched off by others. Yet, direct observation seemed to contradict Bill's de-scription of the staff's social reaction to the self-injury. Specifically, self-hitting appeared to occur at low but constant rates regardless of whether Juan did or did not have access to his favorite television programs. Furthermore, staff did not respond to the self-injury. In short, there did not seem to be any social influence on the self-injury. Therefore, Rick wisely decided to look at a few other sit-uations to see if he could discern whether Juan's self-injury was related to the social influences of significant others. In the pop-corn situation, Rick saw the same lack of a pattern as he did in the television-watching situation. Specifically, face-slapping occurred at a low, steady rate regardless of whether other people provided Juan with the popcorn that he desired. The fact that two different situations failed to show that self-injury was systematically related to the social reaction of others made Rick suspect that this particu-lar problem behavior was controlled by factors other than social interaction variables. Therefore, Rick purposely observed Juan in nonsocial situations (when he was alone in his bedroom or alone outside in the back yard). Rick noticed that self-injury increased somewhat in these nonsocial situations. Because Rick was familiar with the research literature (described earlier), he concluded that it was likely that Juan's self-injury was nonsocial. Therefore, Rick did not attempt the social-communicative procedures that we describe later. Instead, he focused on enhancing environmental stimulation for Juan. As this example shows, direct observation fails to confirm descriptions obtained from interviews when the informant assumes that the problem behavior is related to socially based variables such as escape, attention, and tangible items provided by others but, in fact, the purpose of the problem behavior is nonsocial in nature. In Juan's situation, the problem behavior was the result of an under-stimulating environment.

> ✔ **CHECKLIST OF THINGS TO DO**
>
> 1. Carry out additional functional assessments if any of these events occur: 1) significant changes occur in the person's life (work or educational activities, staff, living situations, or social relationships) and these changes are associated with new instances of problem behavior; 2) there is residual problem behavior after an otherwise successful intervention; 3) problem behavior that was once under control has begun to reappear.
> 2. Carefully compare the descriptions generated through interview with the descriptions generated through direct observation. Pay particular attention to discrepancies in the descriptions of the social reaction to the problem behavior.
> 3. Monitor for success. Success means that you are now able to identify the nature of the discrepancy, thereby allowing you to continue the intervention process using the new information. The discrepancy (failure to confirm interview information with direct observation) typically takes one of three forms: 1) the social reaction specified in the interview is different from that seen in direct observation, 2) the motivation (purpose) of the problem behavior specified in the interview is not the same as the one inferred through direct observation because there have been significant changes in the person's living situation, 3) the purpose of the problem behavior specified in the interview is identified as social but the purpose inferred from direct observation is nonsocial.

DIRECT OBSERVATION IDENTIFIES A NEW PROBLEM NOT DESCRIBED IN THE INITIAL INTERVIEW

Example: Val

As noted earlier, Wayne told Joan that he would visit her classroom many times in order to directly observe Val. One day, Joan was out sick and a substitute teacher, Cheryl, took her place. Wayne observed Val carry out a task that he had never seen Joan ask her to do before, specifically, washing laundry. As can be seen in Figure 7, when Cheryl asked Val to sort the clothes into "darks" and "lights," Val screamed, spit, cursed, and hit Cheryl. Cheryl appeared shocked and backed away from Val. Within a minute, Val calmed down and appeared quite cheerful. One-half hour later, Cheryl tried to reintroduce the laundry task with the same result.

```
┌─────────────────────────────────────────────────────────────────┐
│  NAME:  Val           OBSERVER:  Wayne          DATE:  4/14/88    │
├─────────────────────────────────────────────────────────────────┤
│  GENERAL CONTEXT:  Doing laundry                TIME:  4:15 P.M.  │
├─────────────────────────────────────────────────────────────────┤
│  INTERPERSONAL CONTEXT:  Cheryl, a substitute teacher, asked Val  │
│    to sort the laundry into dark and light colors.                │
│  BEHAVIOR PROBLEM:  Val screamed, spit, cursed, and hit Cheryl.   │
│  SOCIAL REACTION:  Cheryl moved away from Val and did not try to  │
│    get Val to complete the task.                                  │
│                                                                   │
│                                                                   │
│                                                                   │
│                                                                   │
│                                                                   │
└─────────────────────────────────────────────────────────────────┘
```

Figure 7. Index card used in the functional assessment of Val's problem behavior when direct observation uncovered a new problem not identified in the initial interview.

Because Wayne did not remember Joan's talking about this situation during his initial interview with her, he decided to interview her again.

Wayne: *The other day, when you were out sick, Cheryl asked Val to do the laundry. Val immediately became very aggressive and destructive. Do you have the same problem with Val?*

Joan: *Oh, I haven't asked her to do the laundry for the past 6 months.*

Wayne: *Why not?*

Joan: *Because we had so many other problems that we didn't want to set her off unnecessarily.*

Wayne: *Does that mean that she also behaved poorly when you asked her to do the laundry?*

Joan: *Oh, definitely.*

Wayne: *Since Val has improved in so many areas now, would you be willing to reintroduce the laundry task?*

Joan: *Yes, I would. It would help her adjust to living in the community.*

Wayne was wise to follow up on his initial interview with Joan by carrying out many direct observations. Joan had stopped doing the laundry with Val many months before Wayne interviewed her. Therefore, it never occurred to Joan to tell Wayne about Val's aggression during the laundry task. Instead, she focused on those situations that were currently a problem. If Wayne had not done multiple direct observations, he would not have known about the laundry problem. From long experience, Wayne knew that it was often the case that new people, tasks, or settings can be associated with problem behavior. If Wayne had not taken the time to observe Val in a wide variety of situations (not just those described by Joan), he would have missed an important opportunity to help Val adjust to a common task that is familiar to most people in the community. Furthermore, by interviewing Joan a second time, he was able to confirm that she too had once experienced the same difficulties that Cheryl had. The laundry task was confirmed as a situation that reliably produced problem behavior and therefore required a plan for intervention.

Example: Gary

Bob knew that it was always a good idea to make direct observations in a variety of settings over time. Therefore, in addition to working with Mrs. Ibsen in the supermarket, he made several assessment visits to the home. In Figure 8, Bob recorded a situation that he had not seen before. Specifically, Mrs. Ibsen asked Gary to clean up after lunch. Gary responded aggressively and Mrs. Ibsen did not make him clean up. Because Mrs. Ibsen had not mentioned this situation during Bob's initial interview with her, he decided to interview her again.

NAME: Gary	OBSERVER: Bob	DATE: 6/25/88
GENERAL CONTEXT: Lunch		TIME: 12:30 P.M.

INTERPERSONAL CONTEXT: Gary had just finished eating his lunch. Mrs. Ibsen was very busy trying to get a number of things done so that she and Gary could make a doctor's appointment. Because she was so busy, she asked Gary to clean the table and put away the dishes. She had to make several requests to get Gary moving.

BEHAVIOR PROBLEM: Gary responded by biting his hand, spitting, and trying to slap his mother.

SOCIAL REACTION: Mrs. Ibsen backed away. When Gary had calmed down, she quickly cleaned up the table and put the dishes in the sink.

Figure 8. Index card format used in the functional assessment of Gary's problem behavior. The card shows a situation in which direct observation uncovered a new problem not identified in the initial interview.

Bob: *Yesterday when I was here, I noticed that Gary be-
                came very aggressive and upset when you asked him
                to clean up after lunch. Does this happen often?*

Mrs. Ibsen: *It used to happen all the time but I got fed up and
                just decided not to ask Gary to clean up anymore.*

Bob: *Why did you ask him yesterday then?*

Mrs. Ibsen: *Well, I was desperate because we had to make a doc-
                tor's appointment and we were running late. It was
                the first time I had asked in over a year. I got pun-
                ished again.*

Bob: *Yes, it was rough. Since Gary is doing so well in so
                many other settings now, would you like to work on
                clean-up time?*

Mrs. Ibsen: *Definitely. It would make life easier.*

We see again that it is not possible to expect to get all the information needed for a thorough assessment of problem behavior
from one interview. Because Mrs. Ibsen had not asked Gary to
clean up after lunch for more than 1 year, she did not mention
the situation to Bob at first. It was only after Bob had made a number of home observations that he saw, quite by accident, that lunch
was a problem situation for Gary. By interviewing Mrs. Ibsen a
second time, Bob was able to confirm that lunch time was associated with problem behaviors and that Mrs. Ibsen had intentionally avoided certain situations (cleanup) because she had been attacked by Gary in the past whenever she allowed those situations
to occur.

Example: Juan

Glen had been making periodic follow-up visits to the group home
to observe Juan for many months. During one 2-week period when
Bill, Juan's service coordinator, was on vacation, a new service coordinator, Al, took Bill's place. Al had an interest in physical fit-
ness and was worried that Juan's sedentary lifestyle was unhealthy,
and Al tried to motivate Juan to exercise more. Glen happened to
be visiting the home during one of the first exercise sessions, and
Juan responded very poorly to the demands of the exercise regimen
(Figure 9). For example, almost every time that Al asked Juan to
increase the level of his exercising, Juan began to scream and kick.
This outburst caused Al to back off and stop advocating that Juan
exercise. Because Glen had not seen this pattern before, and because Bill had not mentioned in the initial interview that exercise
was a problem, Glen waited until Bill returned from vacation and
interviewed him again.

NAME: Juan	OBSERVER: Glen	DATE: 7/10/88
GENERAL CONTEXT: Exercise		TIME: 4:30 P.M.

INTERPERSONAL CONTEXT: Al asked Juan to increase the level of exercising from 5 to 10 sit-ups, or from 3 to 6 toe touches.

BEHAVIOR PROBLEM: Juan began to scream and then kick Al.

SOCIAL REACTION: Al moved away from Juan and did not try to make Juan complete his exercise.

Figure 9. Index card used in the functional assessment of Juan's problem behavior. Direct observation uncovered a new problem not identified in the initial interview.

Glen: When you were away on vacation, I visited the group home and watched Al and Juan. When Al asked Juan to increase his exercise, Juan became very aggressive. Have you ever seen this pattern before?

Bill: Actually, I haven't because we've never asked Juan to exercise.

Glen: You weren't aware that exercise sets Juan off?

Bill: No, although now that you mention it, I remember one of the former staff who left here when I first came 2 years ago told me that Juan did not like to work out physically and that it was best not to push him too hard. I must have taken that advice to heart because we've never discussed exercise as a program goal for Juan.

Glen: Now that you are aware of the problem, would you be willing to set up a program to help motivate Juan to exercise more?

Bill: Definitely. We're all worried that Juan spends too much time in front of the TV and is not active enough. We'd like to have a positive relationship with Juan in which exercise routines become an enjoyable part of Juan's life.

Once again we see the limitations of interviewing only one informant and observing only a few situations. Because Glen observed Juan over a long period of time in many different situations, he was able to identify problems that even Bill was unaware of.

Also, we see the necessity for carrying out functional assessment not just once at the beginning of intervention but many times, even after intervention has been ongoing for some time. Apparently, other staff had tried to get Juan to exercise in the past with poor results. These staff then discouraged others from trying exercise programs with the result that this problem activity was simply eliminated from Juan's daily list of activities. Only when Al, a substitute staff member who was unaware of past difficulties arrived, was an exercise program reintroduced.

Comment: Interpersonal Effects and Functional Assessment

In all the examples, new problem situations that were not described in the initial interview were identified when additional direct observations were made. Once again, the extreme importance of conducting functional assessment periodically even after intervention had begun is clear. It is necessary to sample a wide variety of situations, not just the ones specified by the informant in the first interview. Furthermore, because situations keep changing, it is necessary to continue functional assessment over a period of many months, even years. Of course, these assessments need not be conducted often, but they do need to be made when new problems are reported to occur or changes take place in an individual's social situations and pattern of activities.

At the time the first interviews were made, certain situations were not in effect. Thus, Val was not being asked to do the laundry; Gary was not being asked to clean up after lunch; and Juan was not being asked to exercise. Because these situations were not occurring, none of the informants mentioned them during the interview. Therefore, the interview did not provide a full picture of each individual's problem behavior. A full picture was obtained only after additional direct observations were made. The observers followed up with a second interview in order to determine why these problem situations were not mentioned in the first interview. In each case, it was clear that the problem situation in question had been a part of the individual's routine a long time ago but had been dropped because it generated too much aggression or disruption. In other words, the parent, teacher, or group home staff person had been punished (physically attacked) for trying to get the individual to participate in a particular activity. The parent, teacher, and group home staff person responded to this punishment by dropping the activity altogether. Technically, what we have just described is referred to in the scientific literature as "child effects." Child effects simply means that children can affect adults by misbehaving. Thus, it is wrong to think that adults can affect children but children cannot affect adults. Of course, we have been describing individuals who are themselves adults and, perhaps, a more appropriate term for what we have been describing would be "interpersonal effects." It is entirely accurate to say that people with developmental disabilities can affect us just as we can affect them. Social interaction is, after all, a two-way street. Interpersonal effects are very common. Many situations that were once problematic will have been discontinued by the time the informant is interviewed. This fact further justifies the necessity for periodic, long-term observation because it is typical for the problem situation to be reintroduced at a later time. If the observer is present at that time, he or she will discover important new information about the individual concerned.

The interpersonal effects that we have been describing are all related to escape behavior, which means that the individual displayed problem behavior in order to escape having to perform a requested activity. Thus, by being aggressive, Juan got out of having to exercise. We have focused on examples of escape behavior because we have found them to be extremely common. Interpersonal effects, however, are not limited to escape-motivated problem behavior. Direct observation, for example, sometimes reveals that a teacher spends a tremendous amount of time with a student on one-to-one tasks that involve much individual attention rather than in group activities that involve very little individual attention. The reason for this pattern becomes clear when one day a substitute teacher focuses on group activities only to find that the particular student becomes aggressive. Follow-up interviews with the original teacher reveal that he or she had many negative experiences with group instruction and few with one-to-one instruction. In a sense, the student punished the teacher for focusing on group activities and rewarded the teacher for focusing on one-to-one activities. It is likely, in this case, that the student's problem behavior is attention-seeking rather than escape-motivated. Thus, as long as the teacher emphasizes one-to-one activities, few problem behaviors will occur and the student will appear to have less difficulty than he or she really does. Furthermore, the teacher will be less likely to mention the eliminated problem situation as a source of difficulty.

Interpersonal effects may also be a factor in problems related to obtaining tangible items. Thus, direct observation may reveal, for example, a routine in which a particular individual (Juan) is always served first at dinner. One day, a new staff member who is not familiar with the routine serves another (Paul) first only to find that Juan grabs Paul's plate and a struggle breaks out. Follow-up interviews with veteran staff reveal that there was a long history of aggression if Juan was not served first. In other words, they were punished for not serving Juan first and rewarded when they did serve

him first. Therefore, they eliminated all situations in which Juan
was not served first. In all likelihood, Juan's problem behavior was
based on obtaining tangibles. Just as important, the interpersonal
effects process made Juan look better than he really was, as was
apparent when the new staff member inadvertently altered the normal dinner routine. The key point, however, is that veteran staff
would be unlikely to mention the eliminated failure-to-serve-Juan-
first situation as a source of difficulty.

   In summary, the existence of interpersonal effects can result in
interviews that fail to give a full picture of the extent of an individual's problem behavior, a difficulty that can be resolved only when
functional assessment is an ongoing, long-term process.

✔ CHECKLIST OF THINGS TO DO

1. Conduct periodic functional assessments over time and in many
   different situations, not just in those situations specified by the
   original informant. Assessments should continue to be carried out
   even after intervention has begun and especially when new problems are reported or when changes have occurred in an individual's
   social situations and pattern of activities.
2. If a new problem is identified, interview the original informant
   again to determine why he or she did not mention the situation in
   the earlier interview. Try especially to discuss whether the original
   informant discontinued the newly discovered situation because he
   or she was punished in the past for permitting the situation to occur. If the situation is totally new, try to observe it again to make
   sure that the problem behavior is predictable and reasonably frequent.
3. Monitor for success. Success means that the new problem situation
   has been confirmed through repeated observation and/or validated
   through interview of the original informant. Success also means
   that sufficient information has been gathered about the social reaction to the problem behavior that it is possible to hypothesize what
   the purpose of the problem behavior is and proceed with an intervention plan based on the hypothesized purpose.

Chapter 5

Functional Assessment: Categorize

The describe component that we have outlined typically generates a large number of index cards. For the three individuals we have been discussing, we generated more than 100 cards per individual. Clearly, some way must be found to organize all of these descriptions efficiently so that we can proceed with intervention planning. The categorization process that we have found successful can be broken down into several steps.

STEP 1: FORMULATE HYPOTHESES ABOUT PURPOSE

Earlier, we reviewed the scientific literature concerning the variables that influence problem behavior. These variables include socially mediated outcomes (reinforcers) such as attention, escape, and tangible items, as well as nonsocial factors that are sensory, homeostatic, or organic in nature. These variables represent many of the purposes that problem behavior can serve. A useful first step in categorization is to use this knowledge of purposes to formulate hypotheses as to why an individual is showing problem behavior in a specific situation.

To begin, we create a panel of three people to meet and examine each index card. This panel consists of any two people who have been involved in carrying out the assessment, and a third person who is a direct service provider such as a parent, teacher, job coach, or a group home staff member. This third person needs to have learned about the empirical research pertaining to variables that can control problem behavior. Otherwise, this person may come up with hypotheses for which there is no scientific support, such as, "I think it's due to phases of the moon," "His mother didn't love him enough," or "He hates himself," which are not useful in intervention planning.

After the panel has been established, each member looks at each index card independently and is asked to answer the following question: "What did the individual want to happen as a consequence of engaging in the problem behavior?"

Example: Val

In Figure 10, the panel consisted of two of the original assessors (Jacki and Wayne) and Val's teacher, Joan. Each of the three observers read the index card independently and each decided that the purpose of Val's aggression at recess was to gain attention from the male teacher by yelling in his face and to gain attention from the female teacher by tearing her clothing, thus precipitating a lecture from that teacher. Since the three members of the panel agreed with one another, a new information category, *Hypothesis*, was created on the index card. Following *Hypothesis* was the entry: "Val aggresses during the recess situation in order to get the attention of teachers who are not attending to her at the moment." (ATTENTION) The word "ATTENTION" following in parentheses summarizes the purpose of the problem behavior. For reference, the names of the panel members are also recorded on the card.

Example: Gary

Consider the example of Gary presented in Figure 11. The panel consisted of two of the original assessors (Rob and Bob) plus Gary's mother, Mrs. Ibsen. The three panel members independently concluded that Gary's aggression when gathering work materials served the purpose of allowing Gary to avoid having to push a heavy wheelbarrow over to the potting bench. Therefore, the following information was entered next to *Hypothesis*: "Gary punches in this situation in order to avoid having to do heavy physical labor." (ESCAPE)

Example: Juan

Finally, consider the situation described for Juan in Figure 12. The panel consisted of two of the original assessors (Glen and Rick) plus Bill, a member of the group home staff. The three panel members independently concluded that Juan's aggression while watching television served the purpose of getting his favorite television program turned back on after it had been turned off, therefore, the hypothesis, "Juan's slapping and kicking is his way of getting staff to turn his favorite programs back on." (TANGIBLE)

So far, all our examples have all been concerned with socially mediated problem behavior. However, as we have noted, not all

NAME: Val   OBSERVER: Jacki   DATE: 11/18/87

GENERAL CONTEXT: Recess   TIME: 1:45 P.M.

INTERPERSONAL CONTEXT: The children were sitting on the grass near the playing field or walking around the courtyard. Joan was standing at the doorway talking to a male teacher.

BEHAVIOR PROBLEM: Val ran up to the male teacher and yelled, "Hey, nubbie!" in his face. When Joan tried to intercede, Val grabbed Joan's shirt sleeve and ripped it in the struggle that followed.

SOCIAL REACTION: Joan severely berated Val for about 5 minutes, telling her that she should not interrupt when people were talking to one another and that she should apologize for tearing her shirt. The male teacher repeated many of Joan's comments to Val.

HYPOTHESIS (PURPOSE): Val aggresses during the recess situation in order to get attention from those teachers who are not attending to her at the moment. (ATTENTION)

PANEL MEMBERS: Jacki, Wayne, and Joan

Figure 10. Front: Description of Val's problem behavior in one situation. Back: The first step in the categorization of Val's problem behavior in one situation showing the hypothesis formulated.

problem behavior is influenced by social factors. Thus, we have found it necessary to include a fourth category of purpose, namely, "other." This category includes a variety of nonsocial factors (purposes). Consider the situation of Juan in his bedroom described in Figure 13. Again, the panel consisted of Glen, Rick, and Bill. The three panel members independently concluded that there was no evidence of social influence in this situation. Therefore, the hypothesis was: "Juan's self-injury does not appear to serve a social purpose because it occurs when he is alone and, further, staff do not

```
┌─────────────────────────────────────────────────────────────────┐
│ NAME:  Gary            OBSERVER:  Rob            DATE:  3/10/87   │
├─────────────────────────────────────────────────────────────────┤
│ GENERAL CONTEXT:  Gathering work materials      TIME:  9:30 A.M. │
├─────────────────────────────────────────────────────────────────┤
│ INTERPERSONAL CONTEXT:  Cal asked Gary to bring over a wheelbar- │
│   row full of potting soil to the workbench.                    │
│ BEHAVIOR PROBLEM:   Gary punched Cal in the chest and tried to punch │
│   him a second time in the face but Cal ducked.                 │
│ SOCIAL REACTION:   Cal told Gary to "keep cool" and moved away from │
│   him. After a few minutes, Cal got the wheelbarrow himself.    │
│                                                                 │
│                                                                 │
│                                                                 │
└─────────────────────────────────────────────────────────────────┘
```

```
┌─────────────────────────────────────────────────────────────────┐
│ HYPOTHESIS (PURPOSE):  Gary punches in this situation in order to │
│   avoid having to do heavy physical labor. (ESCAPE)             │
│ PANEL MEMBERS:   Rob, Bob, and Mrs. Ibsen                       │
│                                                                 │
│                                                                 │
│                                                                 │
│                                                                 │
│                                                                 │
└─────────────────────────────────────────────────────────────────┘
```

Figure 11.   Front: Description of Gary's problem behavior in one situation. Back: The first step in the categorization of Gary's problem behavior in one situation showing the hypothesis formulated.

enter his room to speak with him contingent on self-injury." (OTHER)

Comment: Issues in Deriving a Hypothesis

In all of the examples given, the three panel members agreed with one another about what purpose the problem behavior served in a given situation. In practice, we used the rule that if at least two out of the three panel members agreed on the purpose, then that purpose (hypothesis) was entered on the index card. However, if each

NAME: Juan	OBSERVER: Glen	DATE: 5/18/88

GENERAL CONTEXT: Watching television	TIME: 9:30 P.M.

INTERPERSONAL CONTEXT: Juan is watching a TV program that he likes. Another resident enters the room and turns the TV to another station. Juan turns it back. The other resident turns the TV off.

BEHAVIOR PROBLEM: Juan runs into the kitchen and pulls one of the staff members into the TV room while screaming. Juan slaps and kicks the staff member.

SOCIAL REACTION: The staff member says, "You'll be all right, Juan. Calm down." Juan continues slapping. The staff member then turns on the TV and says, "Look, Juan, your favorite program. Now, will you calm down?" Juan stops slapping after about 5 seconds and watches TV.

HYPOTHESIS (PURPOSE): Juan's slapping and kicking is his way of getting staff to turn his favorite program back on. (TANGIBLE)

PANEL MEMBERS: Glen, Rick, and Dill

Figure 12. Front: Description of Juan's problem behavior in one situation. Back: The first step in the categorization of Juan's problem behavior in one situation showing the hypothesis formulated.

panel member came up with a different hypothesis for a given card, that card was eliminated from further consideration. Poor reliability of this nature was rare, occurring on the average for only 2 or 3 cards out of 100. Poor reliability makes intervention planning very difficult. Problem behavior in those few situations for which intervention planning could not proceed was addressed by using the crisis management procedures described in Chapter 2. However, as intervention progressed in other situations, we found that crises became extremely rare even in those situations for which the panel

NAME: Juan   OBSERVER: Rick   DATE: 11/20/88

GENERAL CONTEXT: In bedroom   TIME: 11:00 P.M.

INTERPERSONAL CONTEXT: Bill wished Juan a good night's sleep and
left Juan alone in his bedroom.

BEHAVIOR PROBLEM: For about an hour, audible face slaps could be
heard in the hallway outside Juan's bedroom. About 25 slaps occurred.

SOCIAL REACTION: As was the rule, staff respected Juan's privacy and
made no effort to enter his room or admonish him.

HYPOTHESIS (PURPOSE): Juan's self-injury does not appear to serve
a social purpose since it occurs when he is alone and, further, staff do
not enter his room to speak with him contingent on such behavior.
(OTHER, possibly sensory or homeostasis)

PANEL MEMBERS: Glen, Rick, and Bill

Figure 13.   Front: Description of Juan's problem behavior in one situation. Back: The
first step in the categorization of Juan's problem behavior in another situation showing
the hypothesis formulated.

members could not agree on the purpose of the problem behavior.

The category of *other* deserves further comment. First, it is
worth emphasizing that problem behavior attributed to this purpose
was uncommon, at least for the three individuals whom we are describing. Less than 2% of all situations across the three individuals
were categorized as *other*. Nonetheless, it is important to discuss
this category because in our work we have come across many individuals for whom this category was more frequent. The key feature
of this category is that it refers to problem behaviors with a nonso-

cial purpose. Since the communication-based approach that we outline is useful only for socially mediated behavior, behavior in this category must be addressed using procedures that are beyond the scope of this book. The resource materials and the discussion of nonsocial factors in Chapter 1 may be useful in planning intervention for this type of problem behavior. We can, however, provide some examples of common purposes seen in the other category. Consider Juan's situation as outlined in Figure 13. His self-injury may have been a way of generating sensory reinforcers. By hitting himself lightly, he may have been providing himself with pleasant sensations akin to a vigorous massage. Alternatively, the purpose of the behavior may have been to maintain an optimal level of stimulation (homeostasis). Too little or too much stimulation from the environment may have felt unpleasant and may have caused Juan to initiate self-injury as a way of increasing or reducing the incoming environmental stimulation in much the same way as someone turns the knob of a radio to increase or decrease the volume to a preferred level. Of course, what we have just said is quite speculative and, at present, the scientific literature on this topic is not fully developed. Nonetheless, scientists have identified homeostatic and sensory functions, and it is good to be aware of these possibilities. Interventions that address these variables are still being tested and, so crisis management procedures must sometimes be used in lieu of more long-term and educationally meaningful interventions. One possible exception to this situation pertains to self-injury that is maintained by certain organic factors, specifically, so-called self-addicting self-injury maintained by endogenous opiates. For these situations, the opiate-blocking drug naltrexone may be a useful intervention. It is important, however, to maintain a balanced perspective on the issue of purpose, because, in reality, there are many instances in which problem behavior serves social purposes most of the time. Therefore, communication-based intervention is frequently a good choice for addressing problem behavior.

One final word is in order concerning the subjective nature of arriving at hypotheses concerning the purpose of problem behavior. Many people worry that merely having a panel sit down and judge a series of index cards is no guarantee that the hypotheses derived are good ones that accurately describe what is really going on in a given situation. There are three strategies that we use to maximize the accuracy of hypothesizing. First, because all panel members are familiar with the scientific literature in this area, they are able to compare the actual situation described by direct observation with situations experimentally analyzed in the research literature. The most useful guide is when the social reaction described in the research literature is the same as the one described by direct observation. The more similar the two situations are, the more likely it is that the purpose identified in the research literature is the same as that hypothesized from direct observation. Second, as we discuss shortly, we also employ a verification procedure to determine the accuracy of an hypothesis. For example, for some situations in which attention-seeking is thought to be the purpose, we purposely give attention to the problem behavior to see if the occurrence of the behavior remains frequent. Then, we may pay attention to a nonproblem behavior to see if that behavior now increases and the instances of the problem behavior decrease. By systematically manipulating the attention given to various behaviors, we can ascertain how important attention is with respect to those behaviors. Verification, as described, is really an informal experiment. In the example just given, if the problem behavior did change systematically as a function of attention, we would have reasonably strong evidence that the purpose of the problem behavior was to obtain attention. Finally, the success or failure of the intervention based on the hypothesis about purpose provides a final check on the accuracy of the interpretation. If the intervention is successful, we have one more piece of evidence consistent with the original hypothesis. Of course, this piece of evidence (for logical and possibly practical reasons as well) is not by itself definitive, but taken together with the two other strategies already described, it provides additional assurance regarding the accuracy of the interpretation of purpose.

STEP 2: GROUPING BY CATEGORY

After the panel has formulated hypotheses, the next step is to group the cards by hypothesis category (purpose) on a large bulletin board. Figure 14 shows the results of this process for Val. The three categories that involve socially mediated problem behavior (attention, escape, tangibles) account for 134 out of the 137 cards that were developed for Val. That is, 98% of Val's problem behavior situations were socially mediated. Of the socially mediated problems, 108 cards, or 79%, were associated with attention. One card fell into the category of other and two cards were associated with no reliability because the panel members could not agree on what purpose the problem behavior served in those situations.

Similar results (not shown) were obtained for Gary and Juan. Gary had 8 cards under attention, 74 under escape, 28 under tangibles, and 2 each under other and no reliability. Again, the majority of the cards, 110 out of 114, or 96%, were related to social factors. Of these, escape accounted for 74 cards, or 65% of the total. Juan

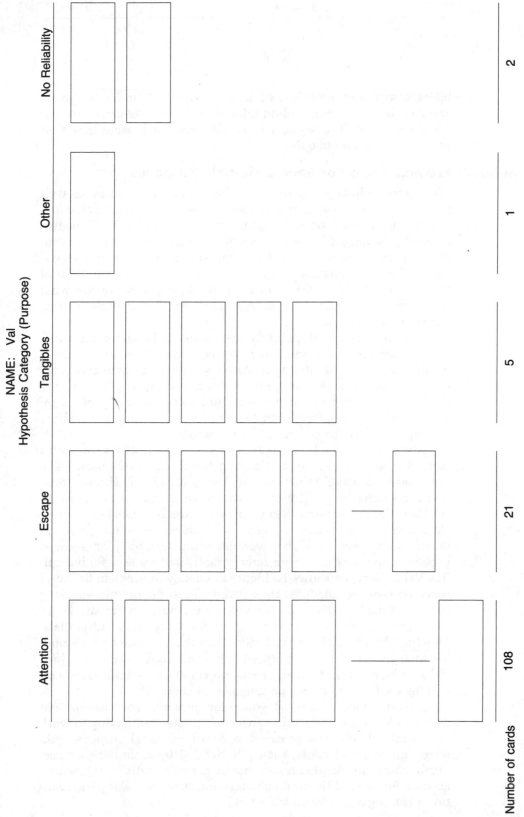

NAME: Val

Hypothesis Category (Purpose)

Attention	Escape	Tangibles	Other	No Reliability

Number of cards   108   21   5   1   2

Total Cards Across Categories: 137

Figure 14. The results of grouping the index cards by hypothesis category (purpose) for Val.

71

had 1 card under attention, 61 under escape, 41 under tangibles, and 3 each under other and no reliability. Of his 109 cards, 103, or 94%, were related to social factors. Of these, 56% were based on escape and 38% on tangibles.

Comment: Problem Behavior Serves Multiple Purposes

What is immediately apparent from Val's data in Figure 14, as well as from the results for Gary and Juan, is that the problem behaviors for each individual served multiple purposes. Thus, Val's aggressive behavior might be attention-seeking, escape-motivated, or tangible-seeking depending on the situation in which she was observed. These results support a point made earlier that the *form* of the behavior problem does not typically help you to decide what the *purpose* of the behavior is. A single form, for example hitting, served many purposes.

Another important point is that problem behavior for these three individuals was mediated by social variables in the overwhelming number of situations. Although we have come across individuals for whom sensory, homeostatic, and organic factors play a role, we typically see many more individuals whose profiles resemble those of Val, Gary, and Juan and whose problem behaviors are largely under the control of social variables.

Significantly, the three socially mediated hypothesis categories were not equally represented among the three individuals. Val's problems were largely those of attention-seeking. She showed relatively few behaviors that were motivated by escape or tangibles. In contrast, Gary's problem behaviors were largely related to escape. He showed many fewer instances of problem behavior based on tangibles and fewer still that were attention-seeking. Juan showed problem behaviors that were largely motivated by escape, but unlike Val or Gary, he showed a higher frequency of problem behavior based on seeking tangibles. He showed almost no attention-seeking problem behavior. The data for Val, Gary, and Juan are similar in two respects to those that we have seen for many other individuals. First, problem behavior served more than one purpose and, second, for each individual, one purpose stood out above the rest. Thus, Val's problems were typically based on attention-seeking, Gary's on seeking escape, and Juan's on tangible-seeking.

At this stage of the categorization process, your assessment data will have become more manageable. Instead of having to work with a pile of 100 or more cards with various social purposes, you have three piles of cards, each pile defined by a similar purpose. Furthermore, in all likelihood, one of the piles will be larger and account for most of the problem behavior, thereby making intervention planning a less formidable task.

STEP 3: FINDING COMMON THEMES
WITHIN A HYPOTHESIS CATEGORY

Example: Val

The three members of Val's panel had an additional meeting in which they reviewed the hypothesis categories that appeared on the cards. They were anxious to find ways to further simplify the intervention planning process. Val had 108 cards attributed to attention-seeking, and they knew that it was not feasible to design 108 different interventions to address each situation. Therefore, Jacki, Wayne, and Joan tried to find *common themes* among groups of cards to see if the cards would subdivide into a few groups that would require a smaller number of distinct interventions. They found that most of the situations in which Val displayed problem behavior to get attention involved four themes: independent work or activities (36 cards), teacher talks to another adult who is a male (34 cards), group activities (25 cards), and transitions (8 cards). The remaining five cards could not be categorized by these subdivisions. Figure 15 indicates the results of this process, showing how the cards were positioned on the bulletin board. These groupings meant that perhaps as few as nine intervention plans would have to be developed, one for each of the four groupings and five more for the cards that could not be grouped. Jacki, Wayne, and Joan welcomed the possibility of having to develop only 9, rather than 108, intervention plans for Val's attention-seeking behavior.

The three cards shown in Figure 16 show different situations in which Val displayed problem behavior to get attention. What is important, however, is that the three cards have something in common. In each situation, Val was required to carry out an activity independently (eating lunch, writing, painting) while her teacher Joan was otherwise occupied. The situations represented by these 3 cards and the other 33 cards with the same theme might be addressed using the same intervention. Specifically, Val could learn to signal the teacher in some appropriate way when she had finished the activity or task, for example, by saying "finished" rather than by screaming or hitting. In addition, Val could learn when Joan was able to attend to her by learning to discriminate between when Joan was busy and when she was free. As we see later, this strategy of combining communication training with specific discrimination training worked quite well in addressing the 36 cards with the purpose of attention-seeking during independent work.

The cards in Figure 17 involve the common theme or situation of Val's seeking attention when Joan began to talk to an adult male. There were 34 cards that had this theme. A plausible intervention (described later) involved teaching Val specific greeting behaviors

NAME: Val
Common Themes for Attention

Independent work or activities	Teacher talks to male adult	Group activities	Transitions	Other

Number of cards 36   34   25   8   5

Figure 15. The results of identifying common themes in the hypothesis category of attention for Val.

74

```
NAME:  Val          OBSERVER:  Jacki         DATE:  11/19/87
─────────────────────────────────────────────────────────────
GENERAL CONTEXT:  Lunch                      TIME:  12:00 P.M.
```

INTERPERSONAL CONTEXT: Val was seated at the lunch table with the other students. Joan was busy putting the finishing touches on some birthday cupcakes in honor of one of the students.

BEHAVIOR PROBLEM: Val suddenly yelled, "I'm not hungry." When Joan turned around and made eye contact, Val pulled the hair of the birthday student while staring at Joan. As Joan approached Val to protect the other student, Val spat at Joan, cursed repeatedly, and tried to scratch Joan several times.

SOCIAL REACTION: Joan pried Val's fingers off the other student and told Val that she had better start acting more grown up or nobody would want to be her friend. This theme continued for about 8 minutes.

a.

```
NAME:  Val          OBSERVER:  Jacki         DATE:  11/20/87
─────────────────────────────────────────────────────────────
GENERAL CONTEXT:  Independent academics      TIME:  10:45 A.M.
```

INTERPERSONAL CONTEXT: Val was seated around a table with other students. Each student was working individually at a writing exercise. Joan was talking to one of the students.

BEHAVIOR PROBLEM: Val screams, "F— you!" and throws a book at Joan. The book misses Joan.

SOCIAL REACTION: Joan says, "What? Did you curse? I hope I'm hearing things!"

b.

```
NAME:  Val          OBSERVER:  Wayne         DATE:  12/1/87
─────────────────────────────────────────────────────────────
GENERAL CONTEXT:  Painting                   TIME:  2:15 P.M.
```

INTERPERSONAL CONTEXT: Each student was making a painting with watercolors. Joan announced that she needed to do some paperwork and everyone should therefore continue painting.

BEHAVIOR PROBLEM: After 20 seconds, Val looked in Joan's direction and yelled, "Hey!" Joan did not answer. After 10 more seconds, Val emptied a glass of water with paint residue in it all over a large desk, causing the other students to get up and move away.

SOCIAL REACTION: Joan said, "Val, how could you? I'm sick and tired of this!" Joan continued in this vein for 2 1/2 minutes.

c.

Figure 16.   Three cards for Val grouped according to the common theme of independent work or activities in the category of attention-seeking behavior.

NAME: Val	OBSERVER: Jacki	DATE: 11/18/87
GENERAL CONTEXT: Recess		TIME: 1:45 P.M.

INTERPERSONAL CONTEXT: The students were sitting on the grass near the playing field or walking around the courtyard. Joan was standing at the doorway talking to a male teacher.

BEHAVIOR PROBLEM: Val ran up to the male teacher and yelled, "Hey, nubbie!" in his face. When Joan tried to intercede, Val grabbed Joan's shirt sleeve and ripped it in the struggle that followed.

SOCIAL REACTION: Joan severely berated Val for about 5 minutes, telling her that she should not interrupt when people were talking to one another and that she should apologize for tearing her shirt. The male teacher repeated many of Joan's comments to Val.

a.

NAME: Val	OBSERVER: Wayne	DATE: 12/7/87
GENERAL CONTEXT: Classroom desk work		TIME: 11:00 A.M.

INTERPERSONAL CONTEXT: Tom, the speech therapist, entered the classroom to talk with Joan. Val was working at a table with the other students.

BEHAVIOR PROBLEM: Val yelled, "Hey you!" at Tom. He did not respond. Val then spit at and hit the other students.

SOCIAL REACTION: Tom ran over to Val and told her to calm down. He held her arms momentarily.

b.

NAME: Val	OBSERVER: Wayne	DATE: 12/7/87
GENERAL CONTEXT: Gym class		TIME: 2:15 P.M.

INTERPERSONAL CONTEXT: Val was exercising with the other students with Joan present. Another teacher, Phil, entered the room and began to talk with Joan.

BEHAVIOR PROBLEM: Val walked up to Phil and began to stroke his hair. Joan attempted to redirect Val back to exercising. Val broke away from Joan, grabbed Phil by the hair, and screamed, "I love you!"

SOCIAL REACTION: Phil removed Val's hand from his head and talked to her for 3 minutes to calm her down.

c.

Figure 17. Three cards for Val grouped according to the common theme of Joan's talking to adult males within the category of attention-seeking behavior.

that could be used in lieu of aggression to get the attention of a male staff member. This strategy proved successful and confirmed the utility and efficiency of grouping index cards under a single theme.

Figure 18 illustrates that attention-seeking problem behavior also occurred during group instruction situations. When Val had to wait her turn before the teacher could attend to her she became aggressive. Twenty-five cards had this theme. From an intervention standpoint, these cards indicated that communication training, specifically, teaching Val to ask for attention, would be useful. However, since Val's problem also involved an inability to wait her turn, the intervention also included teaching Val to tolerate delays. In the literature, this is referred to as "delay of reinforcement." As we see later, a program combining communication training and building tolerance for delay of reinforcement was helpful for Val.

The three cards shown in Figure 19 are representative of different situations in which Val displayed problem behavior to get attention during periods of transition. In what was a familiar pattern for Val, the attention she received typically came from male staff. There were five additional cards with this theme. The similarities across the various situations made it possible to design one intervention program (described later) for Val's problem behavior in these situations. Specifically, because school policy required that all students be accompanied by an adult when moving from one location to another and because Val apparently had a strong preference for males, an intervention was designed that emphasized choice-making. Val could indicate who among several available staff (including, of course, males) she would like to accompany her to the next location. In addition, when she had chosen, Val was encouraged to also choose among conversation topics. The choice-making intervention was generally very successful and validated the grouping of the 8 cards with a transition theme.

The remaining five cards for Val could not be grouped together, and Figure 20 shows three examples. Because these cards could not be grouped together, individual interventions had to be designed for each situation. In Figure 20a., Val got attention by trying to "help" the teacher get everyone seated, but her helping behavior was aggressive. Meaningful intervention required that Joan alter her relationship with Val by teaching Val nonaggressive ways of offering assistance, for example, communication skills such as saying, "May I help you?" to the teacher. Also, Joan had to teach her how to gently prompt other children in order to be effective as a "teacher's helper." On occasion, crisis management techniques were used; for example, Joan removed Eddie from the vicinity of Val so she could not hit him. In Figure 20b., Val got attention

NAME: Val   OBSERVER: Jacki   DATE: 11/12/87

GENERAL CONTEXT: Group instruction   TIME: 10:00 A.M.

INTERPERSONAL CONTEXT: Joan was asking each student in turn to identify some pictures from a magazine and to tell a story about each one.

BEHAVIOR PROBLEM: Val knocked the magazine out of Joan's hand and yelled, "You're stupid" to the student who had been speaking.

SOCIAL REACTION: Joan angrily told Val to pick up the magazine and tried to make her apologize to the other student. When Val refused, Joan persisted for approximately 7 minutes in her efforts to get an apology.

a.

NAME: Val   OBSERVER: Wayne   DATE: 12/6/87

GENERAL CONTEXT: Gym class   TIME: 2:00 P.M.

INTERPERSONAL CONTEXT: Sue, the gym teacher, was instructing each student in turn how to roller skate. It was not yet Val's turn.

BEHAVIOR PROBLEM: Val began to roller skate by herself and plowed into two of the other students. She screamed, "Get out," and laughed.

SOCIAL REACTION: Sue turned away from the student she had been instructing and scolded Val for running into the other students. When Val then made faces at Sue, Sue told Val that she had better shape up or leave the gym.

b.

NAME: Val   OBSERVER: Jacki   DATE: 12/7/87

GENERAL CONTEXT: Neighborhood walk   TIME: 12:30 P.M.

INTERPERSONAL CONTEXT: The class was taking a lunchtime walk in the neighborhood. Joan was talking to another student.

BEHAVIOR PROBLEM: Val threw some earth at the student to whom Joan was speaking and yelled, "Watch out!"

SOCIAL REACTION: Joan explained angrily to Val how dangerous it was to throw things. She also said that Val could just stay in the classroom in the future if this is how she behaved on walks.

c.

Figure 18. Three cards for Val grouped according to the common theme of group activities within the category of attention-seeking behavior.

NAME: Val	OBSERVER: Jacki	DATE: 11/14/87

GENERAL CONTEXT: Moving from gym to   TIME: 1:15 P.M.
                     classroom

INTERPERSONAL CONTEXT: Val was told by her teacher that gym was over and it was time to go back to the classroom.

BEHAVIOR PROBLEM: Once she was in the hallway, Val collapsed on the floor and refused to move. Attempts to get her up resulted in Val's hitting and screaming at the nearest person.

SOCIAL REACTION: Several male teachers were asked to come to the hallway to help. Val responded to their requests after a few minutes and walked back to her classroom in their company.

a.

NAME: Val	OBSERVER: Wayne	DATE: 12/6/87

GENERAL CONTEXT: Moving from classroom to bus TIME: 3:30 P.M.

INTERPERSONAL CONTEXT: Joan told Val to line up with the rest of the class to go to the bus.

BEHAVIOR PROBLEM: After exiting the classroom, Val broke away from the other students and began to scream. She threw her lunch pail at Joan and ran back into the classroom.

SOCIAL REACTION: Several teachers, males and females, converged on Val and told her to calm down. After they talked with her for a few minutes, she calmed down and was accompanied by one of the male teachers to the bus.

b.

NAME: Val	OBSERVER: Wayne	DATE: 12/7/88

GENERAL CONTEXT: Moving from recess to   TIME: 2:15 P.M.
                     classroom

INTERPERSONAL CONTEXT: Joan announced that recess was over and it was time for everyone to move from the playground to the classroom.

BEHAVIOR PROBLEM: Val started giggling and screaming, "Drop dead." When Joan tried to direct Val back to the classroom, Val pulled Joan's hair and broke her necklace.

SOCIAL REACTION: Steve, another teacher, saw the episode and ran over to restrain Val. He told her to take it easy. After a few minutes of conversation with Steve, Val returned to class.

c.

Figure 19. Three cards for Val grouped according to the common theme of transitions within the category of attention-seeking behavior.

NAME: VAL   OBSERVER: Jacki   DATE: 11/13/87

GENERAL CONTEXT: Preparing for classroom work   TIME: 9:15 A.M.

INTERPERSONAL CONTEXT: Joan asked all the students to come to the table and sit down. Eddie remained standing.

BEHAVIOR PROBLEM: Val grabbed Eddie and roughly pushed him into his seat, shouting, "Sit!"

SOCIAL REACTION: Joan told Val not to push or yell at Eddie.

a.

NAME: Val   OBSERVER: Jacki   DATE: 11/27/87

GENERAL CONTEXT: Start of school day   TIME: 9:00 A.M.

INTERPERSONAL CONTEXT: Val arrived at school crying. She went to a corner of the room and sat down. Joan said, "Val, come and sit down with the rest of us."

BEHAVIOR PROBLEM: Val screamed, "Shut up," and threw some pencils across the room.

SOCIAL REACTION: Based apparently on past experiences, the teacher said, "Val, did you have a fight at home this morning?" Val said, "Yes," and began to cry again.

b.

NAME: Val   OBSERVER: Wayne   DATE: 12/5/87

GENERAL CONTEXT: Teacher left classroom   TIME: 10:45 A.M.
                 briefly

INTERPERSONAL CONTEXT: Val was sitting next to Charlie at the group table.

BEHAVIOR PROBLEM: Val put her face right into Charlie's and yelled, "Jerk!"

SOCIAL REACTION: Charlie pushed her away. Val repeated the action. Charlie furrowed his brow and began to whine. Val laughed and made faces. Charlie moved. Val repeated.

c.

Figure 20. Three cards for Val's attention-seeking behavior that could not be grouped according to theme.

when she screamed at the teacher. Joan had experienced this particular situation several times before and knew what to say to Val because Val's mother had discussed home problems with Joan, including fights to get Val to wake up, fights to get Val to eat her breakfast, and fights to get Val on the school bus. Appropriate intervention in those situations meant that Joan had to build a relationship with Val that stressed developing conversational skills (receptive and expressive exchanges described later) as a new way for Val to get Joan's attention. In Figure 20c., Val got the attention of another student by teasing. From an intervention standpoint, the teacher had no option but to remove Charlie from the vicinity of Val (crisis management). Eventually, Joan taught Val to work independently for various rewards, including attention, whether or not Joan was present in the room. This strategy (described later) minimized the inappropriate social behavior toward other students in the classroom.

Val also evidenced problem behavior for reasons having to do with escape and seeking tangibles. However, because Gary was especially prone to exhibiting problem behavior related to escape, we illustrate the process of grouping by theme for escape using Gary as an example.

Example: Gary

The three members of Gary's panel (Rob, Bob, and Mrs. Ibsen) met and reviewed the 74 cards that they had categorized as related to escape. They found that most of the situations in which Gary displayed problem behavior in order to escape involved three themes: completing a task (10 cards), response to negative feedback (48 cards), and request to perform a nonpreferred task (14 cards). The remaining two cards could not be grouped. In principle, these groupings meant that perhaps as few as five intervention plans would have to be developed, one for each of the three groupings and two more for the cards that could not be grouped. Rob, Bob, and Mrs. Ibsen welcomed the possibility of having to develop 5 rather than 74 intervention plans for Gary's problem behavior.

The situations shown in Figure 21 involve the theme that when Gary had been working on a task, he suddenly stopped working and became aggressive. Ten cards had this theme, and in each case the consequence of Gary's behavior was that another person completed Gary's work for him. Gary's aggressive behavior resulted in his not having to complete a task. A plausible intervention, described later, involved teaching Gary to ask for a break from his ongoing work. Furthermore, because Gary seldom worked for very long by himself, another component of the intervention needed to teach Gary to engage in gradually longer periods of work before his

NAME: Gary   OBSERVER: Rob   DATE: 3/24/87

GENERAL CONTEXT: Planting flower beds   TIME: 2:45 P.M.

INTERPERSONAL CONTEXT: After 5 minutes of work, Gary slowed
  down his output to the point where he was putting in about one plant
  every 2 minutes. Cal said to Gary, "We have to pick up the pace a bit,"
  and demonstrated the technique.

BEHAVIOR PROBLEM: Gary grabbed a plant out of Cal's hand and tore
  it to pieces. Then, Gary grabbed Cal's shirt and ripped several buttons
  off it in the struggle that followed.

SOCIAL REACTION: Cal disengaged himself from Gary and backed off
  about 10 feet. After 5 minutes, Gary calmed down. At that point, Cal
  finished the planting by himself.

a.

NAME: Gary   OBSERVER: Bob   DATE: 4/10/87

GENERAL CONTEXT: Home chore—vacuuming   TIME: 4:00 P.M.

INTERPERSONAL CONTEXT: Gary had been vacuuming the rugs for
  about 10 minutes. His mother was nearby providing occasional encouragement and prompting.

BEHAVIOR PROBLEM: Gary threw the vacuum at the wall and yelled,
  "No more." He then pushed his mother aside and ran to his bedroom.

SOCIAL REACTION: His mother completed the vacuuming.

b.

NAME: Gary   OBSERVER: Bob   DATE: 4/12/87

GENERAL CONTEXT: Outside chore—washing car   TIME: 4:30 P.M.

INTERPERSONAL CONTEXT: Gary had been washing the car for about
  2 minutes with help and encouragement from his brother.

BEHAVIOR PROBLEM: Gary kicked over a bucket of water, screamed,
  and then bit himself. He went inside the house.

SOCIAL REACTION: His brother finished washing the car.

c.

Figure 21. Three cards for Gary grouped according to the common theme of task
completion within the category of escape-motivated behavior.

request for a break would be honored; that is, Gary would be taught to tolerate a delay of reinforcement (the break from work). This strategy ultimately proved successful and validated the grouping of cards according to this particular theme.

Figure 22a., b., and c. present different situations in which Gary displayed problem behavior in response to negative feedback from someone about his performance on a task. Forty-five additional cards had the same theme, and in each case the social reaction to Gary's problem behavior was the same. Specifically, all negative feedback stopped. Furthermore, Gary escaped from having to complete the tasks. It is important to note that in all the examples, Gary was appropriately engaged in the task until he received the negative feedback. Only then did he become aggressive. Thus, these situations differed from those in Figure 21, in which Gary became aggressive without negative feedback but after he had been working on a task. Because task failure was a prominent feature of all of these situations, a plausible intervention involved teaching Gary communication skills to ask for help because with help, Gary's performance should improve and there would be no need for negative feedback. In other words, asking for help would ultimately make aggression unnecessary. This intervention, described in detail later, was effective in dealing with situations involving task failure.

The examples in Figure 23 all show Gary's problem behavior in response to requests to perform tasks that he did not like, and there were 11 additional cards that had the same theme. In each situation, Gary's problem behavior resulted in a withdrawal of the request to perform the nonpreferred task. Thus, Gary escaped from the task. Gary needed an intervention that would allow him to perform tasks he did not particularly like without exhibiting problem behavior. As we see later, providing individuals with choices about which tasks they will do at a given time, and embedding (alternating) task demands with preferred activities are two strategies that help keep individuals in task situations without precipitating problem behavior. Various combinations of choice-making and embedding strategies were applied with success to these situations. In short, grouping by theme once again proved to be an efficient way to undertake intervention planning.

Figure 24 shows the two cards that could not be grouped and therefore required the development of very specific intervention strategies. In Figure 24a., Gary escaped having to wait in line by screaming and by destroying property. The result of such behavior was that he was permitted to leave the store, whereupon he became calm almost immediately. This situation differed from the others in that he was not engaged in an ongoing work task, nor did he receive negative feedback, nor was he directly asked to perform a nonpre-

```
┌─────────────────────────────────────────────────────────────┐
│ NAME:  Gary          OBSERVER:  Rob          DATE:  3/10/87  │
├─────────────────────────────────────────────────────────────┤
│ GENERAL CONTEXT:  Putting seeds in pots      TIME:  11:00 A.M.│
├─────────────────────────────────────────────────────────────┤
│ INTERPERSONAL CONTEXT:  Gary was having trouble putting flower│
│    seeds in some pots. Cal said, "No, no, no, Gary. That's    │
│    not the way to do it. You're dropping them everywhere."    │
│ BEHAVIOR PROBLEM:  Gary threw down a pot on the floor and it  │
│    broke. Then he bit his hand.                               │
│ SOCIAL REACTION:  Cal remained silent and moved away from     │
│    Gary. After a few minutes, Cal cleaned up the mess.        │
│                                                               │
└─────────────────────────────────────────────────────────────┘
```

a.

```
┌─────────────────────────────────────────────────────────────┐
│ NAME:  Gary          OBSERVER:  Bob          DATE:  4/10/87  │
├─────────────────────────────────────────────────────────────┤
│ GENERAL CONTEXT:  Making bed                 TIME:  7:15 A.M. │
├─────────────────────────────────────────────────────────────┤
│ INTERPERSONAL CONTEXT:  Gary was making mistakes such as put- │
│    ting the sheet on top of the blanket. Mrs. Ibsen said,     │
│    "No, Gary, the blanket goes on top of the sheet." Gary     │
│    made more mistakes. Mrs. Ibsen said, "That's not right,    │
│    Gary. You're not paying attention."                        │
│ BEHAVIOR PROBLEM:  Gary screamed and then ripped the sheet.   │
│ SOCIAL REACTION:  Mrs. Ibsen became startled and walked out of│
│    the bedroom.                                               │
│                                                               │
└─────────────────────────────────────────────────────────────┘
```

b.

```
┌─────────────────────────────────────────────────────────────┐
│ NAME:  Gary          OBSERVER:  Bob          DATE:  4/11/87  │
├─────────────────────────────────────────────────────────────┤
│ GENERAL CONTEXT:  Sweeping sidewalk          TIME:  4:15 P.M. │
├─────────────────────────────────────────────────────────────┤
│ INTERPERSONAL CONTEXT:  Gary and his brother were sweeping the│
│    sidewalk in front of their home. Gary was sweeping the dirt│
│    back onto the clean areas. Gary's brother said, "Gary, you │
│    don't do it that way. It's no good; you're just making it  │
│    dirty all over again."                                     │
│ BEHAVIOR PROBLEM:  Gary started to jump up and down, biting   │
│    his hand, and screaming.                                   │
│ SOCIAL REACTION:  His brother stopped talking to him and      │
│    waited for Gary to calm down. When Gary was calm, his      │
│    brother said, "You're O.K. now," and finished sweeping by  │
│    himself.                                                   │
│                                                               │
└─────────────────────────────────────────────────────────────┘
```

c.

Figure 22.   Three cards for Gary grouped according to the common theme of response to negative feedback within the category of escape-motivated behavior.

84

NAME: Gary	OBSERVER: Rob	DATE: 3/10/87

GENERAL CONTEXT: Gathering work materials   TIME: 9:30 A.M.

INTERPERSONAL CONTEXT: Cal asked Gary to bring over a wheelbarrow full of potting soil to the workbench.

BEHAVIOR PROBLEM: Gary punched Cal in the chest and tried to punch him a second time in the face but Cal ducked.

SOCIAL REACTION: Cal told Gary to "keep cool" and moved away from him. After a few minutes, Cal got the wheelbarrow himself.

a.

NAME: Gary	OBSERVER: Bob	DATE: 6/25/88

GENERAL CONTEXT: Lunch   TIME: 12:30 P.M.

INTERPERSONAL CONTEXT: Gary had just finished eating his lunch. Mrs. Ibsen was very busy trying to get a number of things done so that she and Gary could keep a doctor's appointment. Because she was so busy, she asked Gary to clean the table and put away the dishes. She had to make several requests to get Gary moving.

BEHAVIOR PROBLEM: Gary responded by biting his hand, spitting, and trying to slap his mother.

SOCIAL REACTION: Mrs. Ibsen backed away. When Gary had calmed down, she quickly cleaned up the table and put the dishes in the sink.

b.

NAME: Gary	OBSERVER: Bob	DATE: 4/11/87

GENERAL CONTEXT: Shaving   TIME: 7:30 P.M.

INTERPERSONAL CONTEXT: Gary's father asked him to go into the bathroom and shave.

BEHAVIOR PROBLEM: Gary shouted, "Go away!" and bit himself.

SOCIAL REACTION: Gary's father walked away and Gary did not shave.

c.

Figure 23.   Three cards for Gary grouped according to the common theme of response to a request to perform a nonpreferred task within the category of escape-motivated behavior.

NAME: Gary   OBSERVER: Bob   DATE: 4/14/88

GENERAL CONTEXT: Supermarket   TIME: 7:30 P.M.

INTERPERSONAL CONTEXT: Gary and Mrs. Ibsen were waiting at the
checkout stand for about 5 minutes while the cashier rang up various
items.

BEHAVIOR PROBLEM: Gary suddenly screamed and started tearing up
several of the grocery items and throwing them around the checkout
area. He then ran toward the exit.

SOCIAL REACTION: Mrs. Ibsen appeared very embarrassed. She said,
"Gary, don't do that, people are looking," and she escorted Gary out of
the store into the car where he was allowed to wait. Gary calmed down
almost immediately and sat quietly in the car. Mrs. Ibsen returned to the
checkout area to wait while the cashier bagged various items.

a.

NAME: Gary   OBSERVER: Rob   DATE: 3/23/87

GENERAL CONTEXT: Potting bulbs   TIME: 1:30 P.M.

INTERPERSONAL CONTEXT: Gary was potting some bulbs. Another
worker with disabilities came up to Gary and put his face less than two
inches from Gary's face.

BEHAVIOR PROBLEM: Gary yelled, "No!" and hit the other worker in
the head.

SOCIAL REACTION: The other worker yelled, backed off, and left Gary
by himself.

b.

Figure 24. Two cards showing escape-motivated behavior for Gary that could not be grouped.

ferred task. Intervention involved teaching Gary to ask, "Can I leave now?" coupled with gradual delay of reinforcement such as, "Yes, you can, but first help me unload some of the groceries." Occasionally, a crisis management procedure was used involving a cue for nonproblem behavior such as, "Gary, while we're waiting, why don't you put on your earphones and listen to some music?" In Figure 24b., Gary escaped from being intruded on by another worker by striking that worker. The result was that the other worker left the area. Again, this situation differed from any of the other themes. The solution initially involved using the crisis management procedure of removing the intrusive worker before the situation deteriorated and, later, teaching Gary to remove himself from the situation or requesting to leave. Although these two situations contain elements common to other situational themes, the combination of intervention strategies used was unique.

Gary also displayed problem behavior related to seeking tangibles. However, Juan showed the most problem behavior with that purpose of the three individuals whom we have been describing. Therefore, we illustrate the process of grouping by theme having to do with obtaining tangibles using Juan's problem behavior as an example.

Example: Juan

The members of Juan's panel, Glen, Rick, and Bill, met and reviewed the 41 cards that they categorized as being related to tangible-seeking. They found that all of the situations in which Juan displayed problem behavior to obtain tangibles involved a single theme, namely, that other people failed to respond to Juan's rudimentary requests to obtain food or a preferred activity that was present but inaccessible or that had recently been taken away from him. (The three examples presented earlier in Figure 3 are representative.) In each situation, Juan indicated verbally that he wanted a particular item or activity or indicated nonverbally by pointing or by pulling a person in the direction of an item. Staff members often did not understand what Juan wanted and he reacted to their lack of response by becoming aggressive. Eventually, Juan either got the item or activity by himself or the staff member guessed (often after a delay) what he wanted and provided it to him. Clearly, a procedure was needed that would allow staff to respond quickly to Juan's requests thereby preempting aggression. The basic intervention that was developed had three components. First, staff who were familiar with Juan's word approximations, those who knew that "orn" meant popcorn, were told to respond to those approximations and not wait for perfect articulation of the request. Second, experienced staff would tell less experienced staff what Juan's "special" verbal approximations meant. They would tell a new staff member that when Juan said, "orn," he was probably asking for popcorn and it should be given to him if it was available. Finally, and most important, staff were taught to respond to Juan's pointing gestures as requests and to teach Juan to point in situations in which his word approximations were especially unclear. In this manner, rudimentary alternatives to aggression were strengthened. Details of this intervention are presented later, but for now we note that the intervention was successful and represented an example in which problem behavior in many different situations could be addressed by using a single comprehensive approach.

Comment: How Identifying Themes Can Guide Intervention

Recall that when the three panelists were initially formulating hypotheses about the purpose a given instance of problem behavior served, each panelist made an independent judgment and then the hypotheses were compared to see how closely the panelists agreed with one another. This strategy was feasible in formulating hypotheses about purpose because there are only four purposes from which to choose; namely, attention, escape, tangibles, and other. In contrast, there are potentially an infinite number of ways to group 100 or more cards by theme. From a practical standpoint, we have found that it is more efficient and feasible to have the three panel members meet and discuss how best to group the cards into themes as opposed to having each panel member decide independently how to group the cards. There is a fail-safe mechanism in this strategy, namely, that if the groupings are poorly made, intervention is likely to fail and the panel will know that it is necessary to reconvene and explore new ways of grouping the cards or, perhaps, even to make additional observations to gather more information.

It is worth emphasizing that since functional assessment is an ongoing and continuous process, new cards will be generated from time to time (as is apparent from the spread of dates listed on the index cards in the figures) after intervention has begun. Therefore, the panel needs to meet periodically to make decisions concerning how new cards are to be grouped and perhaps to create groupings around new themes.

The task of finding common themes within a category is made easier by having the panelists focus closely on the information concerning the interpersonal context on each card. It would be fair to say that just as social reaction was the best guide for initially judging the purpose of problem behavior, *interpersonal context* is the best guide for grouping cards into common themes related to purpose. For example, for Val in Figure 16, the panel members noticed that there was a group of situations in which the interpersonal context seemed roughly equivalent. The common elements were that the teacher was busy and that Val was therefore required to perform a task independently. With some discussion, it is usually possible for panelists to identify such similarities in interpersonal context across cards. It is fortunate that, typically, many problem situations can be grouped together around a common theme. If this outcome were not the case, intervention planning would quickly become unmanageable due to the large number of situations that would require highly specific intervention plans. Most cards do fall into a relatively small number of groups. In our work, we have noticed that there are usually fewer themes pertaining to obtaining tangibles than are associated with seeking attention or escape.

As we noted repeatedly in our discussion of the examples, the various themes that emerge within a category provide extremely helpful guides in tailoring intervention to different situations. For example, for Val, the theme of independent activities led to the intervention of teaching her communication skills coupled with discrimination training, whereas the theme related to transitions led to the very different intervention of making choices. It is worth reemphasizing that there is no one universal intervention for problem behavior. Communication training per se is not sufficient for addressing all instances of problem behavior but must frequently be combined with a variety of other procedures and sometimes crisis management as well. Even with communication training, it is clear that there is no one communicative phrase or group of phrases that can resolve all problems. Thus, for Gary, the relevant communicative phrase for addressing the theme of ongoing work involved asking for a break, whereas the relevant communicative phrase for addressing the theme of negative feedback involved asking for help.

We have seen that since different themes involve different interventions, it is almost always a mistake to think that you can deal with problem behavior by designing a single intervention to resolve difficulties everywhere. Even within a theme, you should be prepared to be flexible and open to the necessity of having to vary intervention in subtle ways. Consider the theme of ongoing work for Gary. While it is true that asking for a break represented the basic (or generic) intervention plan relevant to that theme, variations of the plan were often appropriate. For example, if Gary had been putting seeds in pots for 20 minutes, then teaching him to ask for a 2-minute break would be a reasonable strategy, but if he had been putting seeds in pots for 3 hours, then teaching him to ask for the same break would be inappropriate. He could learn to ask for a longer break or perhaps even a change in activity with the option to resume the original task at a later time. The point is that fixed cookbook recipes for intervention are generally ineffective. They do not work very well and that is why we recommend that you use the material in this book as a set of guidelines rather than as a definite sequence of steps that must be followed in a particular order and that must have a particular content. To return to our point, identifying themes can be very useful in developing generic intervention plans.

✔ CHECKLIST OF THINGS TO DO

1. Establish a panel of three people including two who have been involved in the assessments and one who is a knowledgeable direct service provider.
2. Each member of the panel should examine each index card independently and write down an hypothesis concerning the purpose (attention, escape, tangibles, or other) of the problem behavior that is described on a given card. Pay particular attention to the *social reaction* to the problem behavior since this reaction usually provides the strongest clues as to the purpose of the problem behavior.
3. Monitor for success. Success means that at least two of the three panel members agree on the purpose of the problem behavior in a given situation. Success also means that overall reliability is very high. Specifically, this means that the three panel members disagree with one another on no more than 2 or 3 cards out of 100. If the level of disagreement is higher, it is necessary to go back to the descriptive phase of assessment and make more observations in the situations in which disagreement occurred.
4. Next, arrange the cards on a large bulletin board so that cards are grouped together by category (purpose).
5. Monitor for success. Success means that the vast majority of cards fall under the socially mediated purposes of attention, escape, and tangibles, rather than other. If a large number of cards are classified other, then you will not be able to use the material presented in this book because this book focuses on socially mediated problem behavior.
6. The panel should reconvene in order to review the various categories of cards. Through discussion, panel members should try to identify common themes among groups of cards in a particular category and then post the results using the bulletin board. The panel members should pay particular attention to *interpersonal context* because it is often the best guide for grouping cards into common themes within a category. If later assessments are made (as is almost certain), the panel should meet again to categorize the new cards and to determine if the new cards fit into one of the existing themes or whether new groupings are needed.
7. Monitor for success. Success means that each category contains a relatively small number of themes, thereby making it possible to devise a relatively small number of basic intervention plans. Success also means that the thematic groupings are accurate because they lead to the construction of interventions that ultimately prove to be beneficial.

Chapter 6

Functional Assessment: Verify

Earlier in discussing functional assessment we noted that the three most commonly used assessment methods are interview, direct observation, and experiment. As we have seen, interview and direct observation are critical features of the describe and categorize components of an assessment. Experiment is the feature critical to the component of verification. In an experiment, the person doing the assessment purposely manipulates each factor thought to contribute to the problem behavior. For example, for Val, suppose that the assessor hypothesized that the reason Val displayed problem behavior during independent work was to get Joan's attention. An experimental verification would have the assessor ask Joan to assign independent work to Val for a number of consecutive days. The assessor would also ask Joan to pay attention to Val whenever she displayed problem behavior in the independent work situation. For example, Joan might say, "Val, you shouldn't scream like that!" If attention-seeking was indeed an important factor, we would expect Val to show high levels of problem behavior in this situation. On other days, the assessor might ask Joan to assign independent work to Val and ask Joan to pay attention to Val whenever she was behaving appropriately. For example, Joan might say, "Val, you are really working up a storm. Keep going and I'll check on you again soon!" If attention was important, Val would now spend a great deal of time working independently because independent work results in a lot of attention from Joan. Furthermore, because Val would be so busy working, she would show very little problem behavior. This pattern of results would make a very strong case that Val's aggression was probably related to whichever set of Val's behaviors (problem or nonproblem) Joan attended. Because attention (and only attention) was the variable that was manipulated, it is not very likely that some other variable was the real cause of Val's misbehavior. During the describe and categorize phases, the assessor did not manipulate anything. Instead, he or she simply recorded to the best of his or her ability what Val was doing and in what situation she was doing it. It is possible, therefore, that some other variable besides Joan's attention was occurring and that this variable was the real cause of Val's misbehavior. To illustrate, suppose that every time Val was given independent work to do and the teacher turned away to work with someone else, a student sitting next to Val poked her under the table or pinched her. Val might now show aggressive behavior and the teacher might respond by berating her. In this situation, it would appear as if Val became aggressive in response to the independent work assignment and that aggression had the effect of regaining Joan's attention. This outcome would lead everyone to assume that it was Joan's attention per se that was maintaining Val's aggression. In fact, however, attention would probably have very little to do with Val's misbehavior in this instance. Only when attention itself is systematically manipulated, as in our example, can we minimize the possibility that other variables besides attention are influential. Thus, if poking was indeed the important factor, then having Joan attend intermittently to Val's good behavior (independent work) would not have much effect. The other student, presumably, would continue to poke and pinch Val under the table and Val would therefore be aggressive, regardless of whether Joan was paying attention to good behavior or misbehavior. In sum, verification through experimental manipulation is the surest way to confirm that a specific factor, be it attention, escape, or tangibles, has an important influence on problem behavior.

RESULTS OF THE DESCRIBE AND CATEGORIZE PHASES ARE VERIFIED

Example: Val

Joan, Jacki, and Wayne wanted to be sure that the themes identified for Val were truly based on the interpersonal contexts and social reactions that they had identified in the describe and categorize phases. They knew from past experience that factors that seemed to be important during the describe and categorize phases sometimes were found not to be important at all because other factors had been operating that were missed by the original observers and interviewees. To rule out this possibility, the panel members carried out verification sessions in which they purposely manipulated the interpersonal contexts and social reactions found in certain situations. For example, Val had 34 cards showing that problem behavior occurred when Joan stopped paying attention to Val in order to talk with an adult male. (Figure 17b. was representative of this situation.) In order to verify whether the identified factors were accurate, the following manipulations were carried out. First, Val was assigned to work at a table with a few other students. Then, it was arranged that Tom come in at this time and talk to Joan. If Val became aggressive to Tom or one of the students, measures were taken to protect them. In addition, Tom was told to go over to Val and plead with her to calm down: "Come on Val, you know better than to hit. You wouldn't like it if someone else hit you, would you? I know you can do a lot better than this. So let's settle down, OK?" This experimental test (manipulation) was carried out on days one and three of the verification. On days two and four, everything remained the same, except that Tom was told to react in the following manner. After talking to Joan for 15 seconds or so, and before Val became aggressive, Tom was to look over at Val and say, "Oh, hi Val! How are you doing? I see you're working on a lot of good stuff. When I finish talking with Joan, I'd like to come over and talk some more with you. Keep working!" The pattern of results was very clear. Val aggressed against Tom and several other students on days one and three, the days on which Tom attended to her aggressive behavior. In contrast, on days two and four, the days on which Tom attended to Val's appropriate work behavior, Val remained calm and continued to work without disturbing anyone. Apparently, attention was indeed a powerful determinant of either aggressive or socially appropriate behavior in this situation, depending on which behavior was being attended to.

Because there were 34 index cards that were grouped by this theme, Joan and her colleagues did not want to run four verification sessions for each of the 34 cards, which would have meant conducting 136 sessions, far too many to be practical. Nevertheless, the panel members did want to check enough cards so that they could be reasonably confident that attention was indeed a critical factor in many different situations. The panel decided to verify four cards or 10% of the cards within a theme, whichever was greater. Thus, for the 34 cards with the theme of Joan talking to an adult male, the panel attempted to verify the effects of interpersonal context and social reaction for four of the cards selected at random. With a few exceptions, discussed later, all of the verification sessions conformed to the pattern described for Tom.

Joan and her colleagues repeated the process for the other cards in the attention category, including those with the theme of independent work, the theme of group activities, and the theme of transitions. Four cards were verified for each theme, bringing the total number of cards verified to 16 (including the four verified above). Recall that five remaining cards could not be grouped together, and

each of these needed to be verified as a unique instance of a problem situation. In sum, then, 21 cards were verified. Although the
verification required some effort, it did involve only 21 cards rather
than the full 108. The important result was that the panel was more
confident about the accuracy of the information presented in the
cards. Because Val exhibited escape-motivated and tangible-seeking
problem behavior as well, the verification process was also repeated
for those categories.

Example: Gary

Mrs. Ibsen and the other members of Gary's panel wished to verify
the accuracy of the information on the index cards generated for
Gary. As with Val, they decided to manipulate the interpersonal
contexts and social reactions for certain situations. For example,
Gary had 48 cards that had a negative feedback theme because he
responded aggressively when he received negative feedback following poor performance on a task. (Figure 22b. was representative of
this theme.) In order to verify whether the category and the theme
identified were accurate, the following manipulations were carried
out. First, Mrs. Ibsen asked Gary to make his bed. When Gary made
an error (e.g., placing the sheet on top of the blanket), Mrs. Ibsen
provided negative feedback: "Whoops! That's not right, Gary. You
have to pay attention to what you are doing." If Gary became aggressive, Mrs. Ibsen immediately walked out of the room and did
not press Gary to complete the task. This experimental test (manipulation) was carried out during days two and four of verification.
On days one and three, everything remained the same except that
Mrs. Ibsen reacted differently to Gary's mistakes. When Gary made
an error, Mrs. Ibsen did not provide negative feedback. Instead, she
provided assistance to Gary by saying, "It looks like you're having
a little problem, Gary. Let me help you. The sheet goes on first like
this and then you put the blanket on top." The pattern of results
was very clear. Gary aggressed against his mother on days two and
four, days on which Mrs. Ibsen provided negative feedback. In contrast, on days one and three, days on which Mrs. Ibsen offered assistance, Gary displayed no aggressive behavior and responded to
his mother's assistance by completing making his bed. Apparently,
escape from task failure and the accompanying negative feedback
was a powerful determinant of aggressive behavior. Alternatively,
an offer of assistance did not lead to aggressive behavior but to
compliance.

The panel repeated the verification process across the various
themes in the escape category. Using the 10% or four-card criterion,
the panel verified five cards with the theme of negative feedback,
four cards each for the theme of task completion and for the theme
of nonpreferred tasks, and two cards that could not be grouped by

theme. Thus, verification involved 12 cards out of the 74 in the escape category. The process was repeated for cards in the attention and tangibles categories as well. All but a few of the sessions validated the information that had been gathered during the describe and categorize phases.

Example: Juan

The members of Juan's panel, Glen, Rick, and Bill, wanted to verify the accuracy of the information on the index cards generated for Juan. They used the same procedures already described for Val and Gary. For example, Juan had 41 cards related to obtaining tangibles. All of these cards had the same theme, namely, that when other people failed to respond to Juan's rudimentary requests to obtain an item or activity, Juan displayed problem behavior. (Figure 3a. was representative of this theme.) In order to verify whether the identified purposes were accurate, the following manipulations were carried out. First, when Juan ran over to Sam and repeated, "Orn, orn," Sam asked him, "What do you want? I don't understand you. What are you saying?" When Juan responded to Sam's questioning with aggressive behavior, Sam protected himself but did not provide the popcorn. This manipulation was carried out on days one and three of the verification. On days two and four, everything remained the same except that Sam responded differently to Juan's request. When Juan asked for "orn," Sam did not wait until he became aggressive but immediately provided Juan with popcorn. Again, the pattern of results was clear: Juan aggressed against Sam on days one and three, days on which Sam failed to respond to Juan's requests with the appropriate item. In contrast, on days two and four, days on which Sam provided popcorn in response to Juan's request, Juan remained calm as he consumed the popcorn. Apparently, the failure to provide the desired items to Juan when he had requested them was a powerful factor that set off aggressive behavior. In contrast, honoring his request resulted in calm behavior rather than aggression. Seeking tangible items was thereby established as a critical factor in Juan's aggression.

The panel repeated the verification process for 4 out of the 41 cards that were grouped by the theme of failure to respond to Juan's request for tangibles. The process was repeated for cards in the attention and escape categories as well. Once more, virtually all of the experimental sessions validated the information that had been gathered during the describe and categorize phases.

Comment: The Process of Verification

In each case, the verification process involved providing attention, escape, or tangibles in response to either problem behavior or non-problem behavior. Thus, in the example discussed for Val, Tom sometimes provided attention when Val attacked him or another student, and sometimes Tom provided attention to Val when she was appropriately behaved and working independently. In one situation, Val showed a lot of aggression and, in the other situation, she showed no aggression. By purposely manipulating when attention was given to Val, the panel demonstrated the critical role that attention played in Val's behavior across a wide variety of situations involving independent work. Also important from an intervention standpoint, the panel demonstrated that attention could be used to help Val behave more appropriately. Similar findings were obtained for Gary. When Mrs. Ibsen provided negative feedback to Gary and allowed him to escape the task following his aggressive outburst, he consistently showed aggressive behavior in a variety of negative feedback situations. In contrast, offering Gary assistance rather than negative feedback following poor task performance produced almost no aggression. The verification process highlighted the important role that escape factors played in Gary's problem behavior and, just as important, how these factors could be used to encourage socially desirable behaviors. Finally, Juan's verification sessions clearly identified the central role that tangible items played in maintaining his problem behavior and, of equal significance, the role they played in maintaining Juan's appropriate requesting.

As noted previously, manipulating the factors that appear to affect problem behavior helps increase our confidence that it is these factors and not others that are really responsible for the problems. Because only one set of factors (attention, escape, or tangibles) is systematically altered at a time, it is unlikely that other factors (not manipulated and therefore not likely to be changing systematically at the same time) are critical determinants of the misbehavior.

In the verification process, we often provide unconditionally what the individual wants. That is, in Val's situation, for example, Tom gave Val a lot of attention when she was working independently. Val did not have to ask Tom to give her attention. He simply provided it when he saw that Val was working. Although the effect of Tom's "free" attention was to eliminate Val's aggression, you should not draw the conclusion that providing unconditional attention is as good an idea in intervention as it is in verification. The reason is that free attention teaches the person with disabilities to assume a very passive role. As we see throughout this book, we wish to help people with disabilities become more active in controlling their lives than they typically are. We would like them to be able to be their own best advocates. Thus, if attention from Tom is important for Val, then the best thing to do is to teach her to request attention from him rather than to wait passively for him to provide it.

We should also say a word about the importance of social reactions themselves during verification. Social reactions influence behavior in the long run. When a person with disabilities experiences many episodes in which aggression, for example, is typically followed by attention, escape, or tangibles, the person will become more likely to aggress because such behavior is reliably followed by desirable consequences. The most important thing that the person learns is that in a certain situation certain behaviors pay off in certain ways. For example, we could say that over time Val learned that attention from an adult male could be obtained in an independent work situation simply by attacking him or another student. Because Val no doubt had a long and successful history of getting an adult's attention under these circumstances, the independent work situation itself became a powerful cue for misbehavior. During verification, it is the cueing properties of the interpersonal context that have the most immediate effect on problem behavior. Thus, setting up specific interpersonal contexts is often a powerful way of demonstrating quickly what factors control problem behavior at the moment.

You will note that in verifying a given purpose we recommend at least four sessions, two in which the desired outcomes are provided contingent on the problem behavior and two in which the desired outcomes are provided in response to socially appropriate behavior. It would be easier, of course, to reduce the number of verification sessions to one each. However, we prefer the larger number of sessions to rule out chance factors that may occur on a particular day but no other day. It is less likely that chance factors would be operating in four successive verification sessions. By the same logic, we recommend that, for some of the situations, desired outcomes be made contingent on problem behavior on days one and three, and, for others, the same outcomes be made contingent on problem behavior on days two and four. This procedure should be used as well when outcomes are provided in response to socially appropriate behavior. What we have just described is known technically as "counterbalancing." The purpose of counterbalancing is to ensure that the problem or nonproblem behavior is changing because of the outcomes provided rather than because of the order in which they are being presented. Suppose, for example, you always make attention contingent on aggression on day one but never made it contingent on appropriate behavior on day one. If you always adopted this pattern, then you could not rule out the possibility that the results you got were due more to "getting off on the wrong foot" by having the person become aggressive on the very first day than to attention per se. If order is not important and attention is, then you should get the same pattern of results over the four days regardless of whether you initially respond to aggression on the first day or on the second day. Counterbalancing, then, is just one more way that we have of increasing our confidence that we have truly identified the factors influencing problem behavior.

Finally, why sample more than one situation within a theme? Recall that we recommended that you verify 10% of the cards or four cards within a theme, whichever is greater. The reason for this criterion is that we are concerned that the conclusions we draw are general. If, for instance, we verified only one card out of the 34 for Val's theme of independent work, then we would not be able to rule out the possibility that attention was important only in the independent work situation presented by that one card. To address this issue, we recommend that you verify a number of cards within each theme but, for practical reasons of efficiency and cost, not every card. Because the cards vary in terms of settings, people, and tasks, consistent verification of findings across a number of cards adds to our confidence that the important factors in a given theme probably apply to most, if not all, of the cards represented in that theme. There is one additional point: Cards that are not part of a theme and that cannot be grouped with others have to be verified one at a time. Fortunately, most cards can be grouped by various themes and, thus, the job of verification becomes feasible.

One closing comment is worthy of emphasis. Verification is the most sophisticated and technically complex procedure that we describe in this book. It is the one procedure that *does* require the use of formal data collection and analysis. Our experience has been that many service providers are intimidated by the prospect of carrying out a verification effort due to a lack of training and experience. Therefore, we recommend that at least one member of the panel overseeing the verification be a person who has extensive background and working knowledge concerning the use of the functional assessment procedures that are referenced in the Resource Materials at the end of this book. By taking this precaution, you will help to ensure that the information provided through the verification process will be accurate and revealing.

✔ CHECKLIST OF THINGS TO DO

1. For purposes of verification, randomly select 10% of the cards in each theme or four cards in the theme, whichever is greater. In the case of cards that cannot be grouped, verify each one individually.

2. For each card to be verified, carry out four sessions of assessment in which the desired outcome (attention, escape, or tangibles) is provided contingent on problem behavior for two of the sessions and contingent on socially appropriate (nonproblem) behavior for the other two sessions. Across cards, counterbalance the order in which the desired outcome is presented with respect to problem and nonproblem behavior.

3. Monitor for success. Success means that problem behavior in a particular interpersonal context is observed to occur at high levels when it is followed by the relevant outcome but occurs at low levels when the same outcome is made contingent on alternative, nonproblem behavior.

RESULTS OF THE DESCRIBE AND CATEGORIZE PHASES ARE NOT VERIFIED: SETTING EVENTS

Earlier, we noted that while verification sessions for Val, Gary, and Juan generally confirmed the results of the describe and categorize phases there were some instances in which they did not. Thus, a given interpersonal context might produce aggression on one day, but the same interpersonal context might fail to produce aggression on a different day. The fact that there are dramatically different levels of aggression occurring on different days although the interpersonal context remains the same does not mean that you are doing something wrong. It usually means that there are additional factors operating from day to day and that you need to identify these factors. Technically, factors that affect how an individual responds to a specific interpersonal context are referred to as *setting events*.

Consider the following example: A young girl with autism is presented with the task of naming vocabulary cards in answer to the question, "What is this a picture of?" On Monday, she names most of the cards correctly and does so in a calm and relaxed manner. She responds to negative feedback for errors by switching to the correct answer after she is prompted to do so. On Wednesday, she comes down with the flu. Her muscles ache, and she is feverish and extremely irritable. Despite her illness, the girl behaves appropriately as long as no demands are placed on her. However, when the teacher (who is unaware of her illness) asks her to name the cards, the girl's behavior changes. This time, when she is given negative feedback for errors, she screams and tears up several of the vocabulary cards. The interpersonal context was the same on Monday and Wednesday in that the teacher and child were interacting within the context of a vocabulary acquisition task. Why, then, did aggression occur on Wednesday but not on Monday? The obvious answer is that by Wednesday a new factor of physical illness was present. Physical illness, a setting event, affected the way in which the girl responded to the vocabulary task. Often, the presence of setting events can influence whether the results of the describe and categorize phases are verified. Therefore, it will be worthwhile to focus on these factors.

There are three general categories of setting events: physiological, physical, and social. In the example given, flu is clearly an example of a physiological setting event. However, it is also possible that the young girl (like many people with autism) is very sensitive to loud noises and tries to minimize them by placing her hands over her ears. One day, the teacher carries out the vocabulary task at a time when several of the other children are particularly raucous. The girl places her hands over her ears but is otherwise calm. However, when the teacher prompts her to put her hands down, believing that the girl is inattentive unless her hands are away from her ears, the girl's behavior changes. The girl now responds to negative feedback on the naming task by pulling the teacher's hair. One week later, the same task is repeated during a quiet period and the girl displays no aggression. In this example, noise is a physical setting event that influences whether or not the vocabulary task evokes aggression. Our third and final example involves a social setting event. On another day, the teacher again asks the girl to name the cards. While the girl is naming the cards, another student is making faces at her across the room. The young girl appears increasingly annoyed but does not show any aggressive behavior. However, the next time that the teacher gives her negative feedback for making an error, the girl pushes the table over. Yet, one day later when no one is teasing her, she completes the task without incident.

In each of these examples, a setting event influences how the individual responds to a given interpersonal context. The setting event itself does not evoke aggression but when the setting event occurs together with demands, aggression is triggered. Each of the events described (flu, noise, teasing) are unpleasant (or "aversive" in the scientific literature). Negative feedback is also unpleasant or aversive. The purpose of the young girl's aggression may have been to escape the unpleasant situation. Normally, negative feedback by itself may have been only mildly aversive to the girl and have evoked little if any aggression or escape behavior. However, the addition of the setting event was "the straw that broke the camel's back." The presence of flu symptoms, loud noises, or teasing makes the negative feedback more aversive than it would normally be. Thus, escape behavior (aggression) becomes more likely.

We have highlighted the influence that setting events can have on escape-motivated behavior. However, as we shall see, setting events influence attention-seeking and tangible-seeking behavior as well. Our experience has been that the presence of setting events is the major reason that verification sessions fail to confirm the results of the describe and categorize phases of assessment. Therefore, it is helpful to examine several examples of setting events operating for Val, Gary, and Juan.

Example: Val

It was clear to Joan and others that Val frequently sought the attention of adult males (Figure 17). When such attention was not forthcoming, Val became quite aggressive. By and large, the verification sessions confirmed this pattern of behavior, but, there were some exceptions. For example, one day a new teacher, Karl, arrived. During the first verification assessment session, when Karl talked to Joan in Val's presence, Val showed no problem behavior. During the next week, Karl and Val got to know one another, and Val now liked Karl a lot. During the next assessment session, Karl failed to pay attention to Val, and she immediately attacked both Karl and Joan. The first assessment session failed to verify that male attention was a prominent factor in Val's aggressive behavior. The second assessment session, however, did confirm the importance of male attention.

Joan and the other members of Val's panel met to discuss the different results of the two verification sessions involving Karl. They noted that when Karl and Val did not know each other, Val did not appear to care if Karl paid attention to her. However, once Karl had established good rapport with Val, she became very aggressive when he failed to attend to her. The panel concluded that previous positive experiences with a male were an important social setting event that influenced whether Val would display problem behavior in the interpersonal context in which Joan and an adult male spoke to one another to the exclusion of attending to Val. The panel decided to gather more information before proceeding further. First, they interviewed a number of other teachers and staff who regularly interacted with Val and asked them whether they noticed that Val responded differently to attention from unfamiliar males compared to males who were familiar to her. The interviewees agreed that Val did respond differently and that she was indifferent to new males until they established rapport with her. Next, the panel focused on situations in which new males arrived at Val's school and were assigned to work with her. Direct observation confirmed that when a new male staff member first interacted with Val, she appeared indifferent to the attention and she went about her

work and did not look at him. However, after the two had interacted positively for a number of days, Val was observed to become
aggressive when the staff member did not attend to her. Finally, the
panel followed up the interview and direct observation processes
by arranging for verification sessions with several new males. For
example, in one set of sessions, a new male, Kyle, was observed
interacting with Val both before he had established a relationship
with her and after he had done so. Val initially responded to Kyle's
failure to attend to her with indifference by calmly going about her
work. Later, however, Val became aggressive when Kyle talked to
Joan but not Val. In a different set of sessions, a new male, Don,
did not interact with Val over a number of days with the result that
a positive relationship was not established between Don and Val.
Instead, Don was told to talk with Joan in Val's presence on several
occasions separated by several days. Both initially and later, Val
appeared indifferent when Don attended to Joan but not her. Apparently, Don's lack of rapport with Val undermined Val's interest in
him and she did not display problem behavior in order to get his attention.

Example: Gary

It was clear to Cal and others that Gary frequently became aggressive when work demands were placed on him, and the verification
sessions confirmed this pattern of behavior. Occasionally, however,
the severity of problem behavior was not verified. Typically, Gary
would respond to work demands with mild to severe problem behavior. However, in a few verification sessions, the severity of the
problem behavior became greater than had been previously seen.

   Gary's panel met to discuss why the severity of Gary's aggression in these verification sessions was so unlike that of the other
sessions. After some discussion, it became apparent that the greenhouse had been unusually warm on those days in which Gary
showed the most severe aggression. They noted that high temperature by itself did not set off Gary's aggression. Rather, it was the
combination of work demands and heat that seemed to be the issue.
The panel decided to get more information before proceeding further. First, they interviewed other staff and family members of Gary
regarding the issue of temperature. The interviewees all agreed that
Gary was sensitive to heat. Other workers in the greenhouse, for
example, appeared able to carry out their work with no ill effects
even on warm days, but Gary appeared especially irritable on those
days. Mrs. Ibsen noted that occasionally during the summer the
home air conditioning unit would fail and when that happened,
Gary would not respond to requests to do chores at home. Instead,
he became extremely aggressive when asked to do even light work

around the house. Second, the panel made a few more direct observations of Gary on days when the temperature was warmer than usual. They noted that Gary's aggressive behavior appeared to become much more intense on those days that were warm and humid. Finally, the panel followed up on the interview and direct observation process by arranging for verification sessions to take place under more controlled circumstances. For example, they asked Gary to perform his greenhouse tasks for a short time on a few cool days and a few warm days. They noticed that, regardless of temperature, Gary was well behaved when people left him alone. However, when demands were added things changed but only during conditions of higher heat and humidity. Gary showed less intense aggression on cooler days but very intense aggression on the warm, humid days. His co-workers were not bothered by the warm, humid days, but apparently Gary was very sensitive to heat. He aggressed when demands were made of him in general but his aggression became quite severe when the same demands were made of him during warm weather conditions. The panel agreed that, for Gary, heat was an important physical setting event, one that would have to be carefully considered during the intervention planning process.

Example: Juan

It was clear to Bill and others that Juan frequently became aggressive when his access to preferred activities or foods was blocked. The verification sessions generally confirmed this pattern of behavior. As was the case with Gary, however, the severity of problem behavior was sometimes not verified, and Juan's aggression occasionally became extremely intense although no new conditions appeared to be in effect.

Juan's panel discussed this issue and made a complete search of Juan's records. His medical records indicated that he suffered from occasional bouts of middle ear infection. Furthermore, the problem behavior record kept by group home staff on the days he was sick had notations indicating that Juan's aggressive behavior was unusually intense. The panel followed up on this detective work by interviewing all relevant staff. The staff acknowledged that for some time they were aware that Juan's aggressive behavior when he did not obtain the activities or foods that he preferred became much worse when he was known to be suffering from middle ear infections. The panel continued to collect more information by arranging to observe Juan both when he was being treated for an ear infection and when he was believed to be healthy. Sick days were clearly correlated with the most intense outbursts of aggressive behavior. Normally, the panel would have continued the assessment process by arranging for verification sessions in which preferred items were intentionally withheld or provided on alternate days in the presence of ear infection and in the presence of no ear infection. However, for obvious ethical reasons, everyone decided to forego further verification because Juan appeared to be experiencing a great deal of discomfort from his ear infection. The panel members agreed that, for Juan, middle ear infection was an important physiological setting event, one for which relevant and systematic medical care would be an obligatory component of intervention.

Comment: Setting Events and Intervention Planning

It is clear from these examples that the presence of setting events can result in a failure to verify completely information gathered during the describe and categorize phases of assessment. The failure to verify can take either of two forms. First, the setting event can influence whether the problem behavior occurs at all in a particular interpersonal context. Thus, for example, before Karl had established rapport with Val she did not value his attention. Therefore, when Karl ignored Val in order to talk to Joan, Val showed no aggression. However, once Karl had established rapport with Val and she began to value his attention, the same interpersonal context of Karl and Joan talking but not attending to Val resulted in Val's becoming very aggressive. Thus, a social setting event determined whether the particular interpersonal context would produce problem behavior. Second, setting events can influence the results of the verification process by bringing about a much higher frequency and/or severity of problem behavior than is typically seen during the describe and categorize phases. This outcome was noted in some of the verification sessions for both Gary and Juan. In the examples given, Gary typically showed aggressive behavior in response to work demands and Juan, when access to preferred items or activities was blocked. However, the presence of setting events produced dramatic increases in the problem behavior, far in excess of anything seen during the describe and categorize phases. For Gary, high temperatures greatly exacerbated his ongoing problem behavior, and for Juan, middle ear infections brought about unusually severe episodes of aggressive behavior.

Setting events do not by themselves evoke problem behavior. Rather, setting events influence whether a particular interpersonal context will evoke problem behavior. For instance, whether Karl had good rapport with Val or no rapport did not matter until the specific interpersonal context occurred of Joan and Karl talking with one another and not attending to Val. Only when this interpersonal context was in place did it make a difference whether or not Karl had good rapport with Val. When he had no rapport, the context did not evoke aggression from Val, but once rapport had been established, aggression occurred. Likewise, heat did not by itself cause Gary to become aggressive. If he was left alone when it was hot, he did not show problem behavior. However, when work demands (the interpersonal context) were coupled with conditions of high heat, then and only then did Gary display extremely severe aggressive behavior. Finally, for Juan, middle ear infections did not automatically produce aggressive behavior. Instead, it was the combination of the specific interpersonal context of not being able to access a preferred activity and the presence of ear infection that brought about unusually severe problem behavior.

Physical and Medical Setting Events As we have noted, the search for setting events should begin once you encounter a failure in the verification process and you do not see problem behavior that was expected in a particular interpersonal context or when you see problem behavior in a particular interpersonal context that occurs with a frequency or severity far in excess of what you typically noted during the describe and categorize phases. A verification failure must be followed up by additional interviews with relevant people in which you ask these people why they believe the atypical results occurred during the verification session. Checking medical and staff records generated on the day on which the session was conducted may provide additional clues as to why the unusual behavior was observed. Interviews and record checks should be followed by periods of direct observation in which the presumed setting event is present as well as absent. When problem behavior increases in the presence of the presumed setting event, then you have suggestive evidence that the setting event is an important factor contributing to the display of problem behavior. Then, new verification sessions should be conducted. Some of these sessions should be conducted in the absence of the specific interpersonal context so that you can prove to yourself that it is not the setting event per se that causes the problem behavior to occur. For example, Gary was observed when it was hot outside but no work demands were placed on him; the fact that he showed no problem behavior proved that heat by itself was not sufficient to produce aggression. Some of the sessions should be carried out with both the interpersonal context and the setting event present so that you can demonstrate that it is the combination of these two factors that sets off unusual problem behavior. For example, Gary was given work demands when it was very hot and only then did he exhibit unusually severe aggressive behavior. As desirable as verification sessions are for confirming the influence of setting events, there are occasions on which they should not be carried out. Specifically, when an individual is suffering from a very uncomfortable or painful medical condition (Juan's middle ear infection), it is not ethically permissible to involve the person in repeated verification sessions that would merely compound the person's discomfort. In such circumstances, the information gleaned from direct observation will have to suffice.

Gary's situation illustrates well the important role that physical setting events can play in exacerbating problem behavior. It is not difficult to derive an appropriate intervention in this instance. Clearly, if an individual is extremely sensitive to heat, arrangements must be made to reduce heat levels or to allow the individual to avoid situations associated with high heat. At first, it would seem that the social-communicative strategies that we describe are irrelevant to physical setting events. However, even here communication strategies may play a role in reducing problem behavior. Specifically, Gary could learn to tell people when a room has become unacceptably warm. In this manner, a communication skill can be used to help remove an unpleasant physical setting event, thereby ultimately reducing the probability of problem behavior. A similar strategy could be used to address the effects of noise, another physical setting event that we described earlier. The number of possible physical setting events is very large. However, from an intervention perspective, it is generally easy to address them using the strategies that we just described. The real challenge in the area of physical setting events involves identifying them in the first place. Assessment rather than intervention is typically the most difficult part of addressing physical setting events.

Juan's situation parallels Gary's in terms of relative ease of intervention planning. When Juan's middle ear infection was identified as a physiological setting event, the relevant intervention was clearly medical. As with Gary, Juan and others who suffer from various medical conditions could learn communication skills that allow them to signal their pain or discomfort to other people who can provide appropriate medical intervention. Again, the most difficult issue here is in identifying the medical condition. Assessment is likely to prove to be the greatest challenge, especially in the case of individuals who, like Juan, have minimal communication skills to begin with. At the least, individuals who have recurrent medical conditions need to be monitored on an ongoing basis to determine if such conditions may be acting as powerful physiological setting events that make problem behavior more likely to occur. Both the scientific literature and practical experience suggest that middle ear infection is but one example of this class of setting events. Others include seasonal allergies, asthma, colds and flu, gastrointestinal upset, headache, herpes, menstrual pain, drug effects and side effects, exercise or the lack thereof, hunger, fatigue, and bad reactions to caffeine, dyes, and additives. Finding clues to accurately assess involves reviewing medical records, interviewing staff and family, and observing nonverbal behavior—for example, the individual massages his or her head during a headache, clutches his or her stomach during a gastrointestinal upset, or appears especially tired following vigorous exercise. Some individuals, fortunately, can talk and make clear when they are in a state of pain or discomfort. It is unethical to ignore such statements by failing to follow them up closely with interview and observation. Collaboration with a physician and/or nursing staff is necessary in order to perform assessment and intervention when physiological setting events are at issue. We refer the reader to the resource materials at the end of the book that note relevant references for physiological (as well as physical) setting events. These resources link setting events to problem behavior and are not meant to be medical references. As noted, medical references are best obtained by working collaboratively with medical staff.

Social Setting Events   Val's situation is particularly interesting because it underlines the great influence of social setting events in problem behavior. Generally, we tend to seek attention from people we know and care about rather than from total strangers. People with disabilities are no different in this respect, and that is why Val did not seek out Karl's attention until he had established some rapport with her. Unfortunately, the way in which she sought out his attention was to attack him physically. Superficially, this outcome would seem to suggest that *not* establishing rapport is a good idea because it prevents aggressive behavior. Obviously, that is the wrong conclusion: We want to establish positive relationships with people like Val because our relationships can become a basis for constructive interactions. In fact, in the next section of this book, we discuss the central role that rapport-building plays in enhancing social-communicative skills. We also describe how other social setting events such as the personal appearance of the individual with disabilities and the existence of shared interests with others helps to facilitate specific communicative interchanges that reduce the likelihood of (and need for) problem behavior. Indeed, throughout this book, the importance of social setting events is made apparent. Thus, in addition to the social setting events that we just described, we also discuss others including communicative interpretability, which is how well others are able to understand the communicative attempts by the person with disabilities; staff characteristics and educational philosophy, which affect the creation of appropriate contexts for communication; embedding, which is sequencing interactions to minimize problem behavior; the use of humor; staff characteristics that limit the generalization of successful interventions to new situations; and the role of social support systems in helping to maintain successful intervention effects over long periods of time. As you read about the many different types of social setting events that are examined throughout this book, you will gain a greater appreciation for how prevalent these events are as you attempt to reduce problem behavior in people with disabilities.

✔ CHECKLIST OF THINGS TO DO

1. Reconvene the panel to discuss instances in which verification sessions failed to confirm the results obtained during the describe and categorize phases. These instances may involve sessions in which problem behavior is expected but does not occur, or they may involve sessions in which problem behavior occurs at a frequency or intensity that is much greater than usual.
2. The panel should interview relevant people concerning the discrepancy and/or review medical and educational records. Based on this new information, the panel should attempt to reach consensus about whether a particular setting event is involved.
3. Next, direct observations should be made on days on which the presumed setting event is present in a particular interpersonal context and on days on which it is absent.
4. When direct observation suggests that a specific setting event is influential, new verification sessions should be carried out (when ethically reasonable) to manipulate the presence and absence of the setting event in a particular interpersonal context.
5. Monitor for success. Success means that the problem behavior is now observed to be systematically influenced by the presence of the setting event in a given interpersonal context.

PART II

THE CORE INTERVENTION

Chapter 7

Building Rapport

We say that two people have established rapport when their relationship is characterized by closeness, empathy, and mutual liking. In the absence of rapport, people may show little interest in interacting spontaneously and enthusiastically with one another. As we see next, rapport-building is a critical feature of our approach to intervention. It is an ongoing part of the intervention, not just a stage that occurs once at the beginning and is then dropped. Furthermore, rapport-building is not a mechanical set of procedures but is based on sharing, cooperation, and mutual give-and-take. Because rapport involves an *interactive relationship*, it helps to overcome the passivity that people with disabilities often show or, worse, are encouraged to show. Rapport is therefore an important part of a communication-based approach to intervention, which assumes a speaker and a listener who want to interact with one another. The presence of either the speaker or the listener acts as a signal (or "discriminative stimulus" in scientific terminology) for the other person to initiate and maintain communication. The signal or cue is effective because in the past the speaker and the listener have shared a variety of enjoyable activities and events through communicating with one another. Sometimes, however, the presence of one person does not signal to the other person that communicative behavior will pay off. There are several reasons why this situation might develop. For example, a parent may have a long history of battling with a child at meals or at bedtime. Because of this negative history, the presence of the parent in these contexts becomes a signal for problem behavior rather than a signal for communication. A second example concerns a new staff member in a group home who is just getting to know a particular resident. The two individuals have not yet established a relationship in which communication is reliably followed by pleasant interactions. Therefore, the presence of the staff member may be a signal for the resident to seek out other people and activities, in effect ignoring the new staff member rather than communicating with him or her.

In situations such as these two, it may be worthwhile to consider using the following rapport-building procedures.

MAKE YOURSELF INTO A SIGNAL FOR REINFORCEMENT

If you associate yourself repeatedly with a wide variety of activities, people, and things that the person values, then eventually your presence will become a signal that many rewarding activities and events are available with you. (In technical terms, your presence becomes a "generalized reinforcer.") The purpose of associating yourself with positive experiences is to begin reversing any hostility or indifference that the person with disabilities may feel toward you. In time, that person will view you as someone worth attending to and interacting with.

Example: Val

At first, Val had a poor relationship with Joan. Sometimes, Joan would angrily tell Val to stop spitting and cursing. Also, when Val hit others or grabbed someone's hair, Joan and her aides would have to restrain Val momentarily for protection. Because Val did not like to be held in this manner, she frequently became angrier and even more aggressive toward Joan. Over time, Joan became a person Val tried to avoid. To remedy this situation, Joan began by drawing up a list of things that she thought Val enjoyed the most. The list included singing, doing her nails, putting on cosmetics, and talking with Val about weekend activities at home as well as her art work. During the first few days of rapport-building, Joan provided these activities to Val without asking her to do anything to get them ("reinforcers were dispensed noncontingently," in scientific terms.) Joan helped Val to put on cosmetics. She turned on some popular music and sang songs with Val. Because Val liked to get strong reactions from others (such as she got whenever she displayed problem behavior), Joan made sure that whenever she and Val were talking, the conversation generated a strong reaction from her. For example, when the two were talking about Val's weekend shopping expedition, Joan was enthusiastic and animated rather than quiet and matter-of-fact. Joan knew that she was beginning to make progress when Val began to laugh regularly and make conversation spontaneously in the context of these activities.

Example: Juan

When Bill joined the group home, he was assigned to work closely with Juan in order to enhance Juan's community living skills. The other staff told Bill that Juan was for the most part indifferent to social interaction. This made it difficult for Bill to establish rapport with Juan. At first, Juan completely ignored Bill and spent most of his time sitting on the couch staring at the television. To remedy this situation, Bill found out from the other staff what sorts of things Juan liked. Also, he observed Juan for himself. Bill was able to develop a list of things that Juan liked that included food items such as ice cream, cookies, juice, and oranges. Contrary to what the other staff had said, it appeared that Juan sometimes liked people to talk to him in a friendly way although he could not talk. Bill began to build rapport by going up to Juan and handing him some cookies and orange slices. As fast as Juan ate them, Bill was there with more. While Juan was eating, Bill kept up a steady stream of talk about life in the home and aspects of life in the community that Juan had recently experienced, such as neighborhood walks and going shopping. After a few days of this type of interaction, Juan was paying attention to Bill whenever Bill entered the room and was more interested in being near Bill than in sitting on the couch in front of the television.

Comment: Some Initial Issues in Rapport-Building

Val is an example of an individual whose history of negative interactions with other people could prevent communication skills from developing further. Juan is an example of an individual whose lack of experience in interacting with another person could prevent the development of communication skills. Although Val was a rather friendly, social person and Juan was not, rapport-building was essential for both in order to provide a foundation on which to build genuine communicative interaction. Val liked to talk about her art work but Juan did not. Therefore, art work was a conversational topic in working with Val but not in working with Juan. Juan liked oranges but Val was not interested in them. Therefore, oranges were freely given out to Juan but were not part of any interaction with Val. Do not assume that what one person likes is what everyone likes. If you do, you will not be treating the person as an individual and rapport probably will not develop.

In the beginning, provide situations that the person likes without conditions (noncontingently). Do not ask the person with disabilities to earn these reinforcers or to ask for them. If you do, he or she may refuse to work and a battle will begin. Also, he or she may not yet know how to ask for the things he or she likes and may become frustrated and tantrum. In either case, any rapport-building will come to an end. The idea at this stage is for the person with disabilities to learn that you are associated with many positive, interesting, and valued experiences and are definitely someone worth paying attention to.

Rapport-building is not something that you do once and then drop in order to move on to something else. Rather, it is something that must continue as long as you have a relationship with the person with disabilities. The initial rapport-building procedure that we just described should take place many times each day. Typically, we have used this initial procedure for 2 or 3 days before adding to it. How will you know when you are succeeding? You will know when the person becomes more responsive to you. He or she will look at you more often, stay close to you, and continue to interact with you, not walk away, once you have approached him or her. He or she will seem happy to see you and smile, laugh, or, if verbal, talk to you when you are around and ask for you when you are not around. In short, the person will appear to be enjoying him- or herself when around you.

The last point, concerning enjoyment and happiness, is important and deserves further comment. Rapport-building is not a mechanical procedure. You should not become a vending machine dispensing positive experiences. The idea is for you and the individual displaying behavior problems to interact with one another within a context of sharing entertaining and rewarding activities and generally enjoying each other's company. These interactions may strike you or others as "goofing off," but that is not a problem as long as it leads to an ongoing positive relationship. Ultimately, rapport-building is intended to establish a friendship between you and the person with disabilities, a friendship that can provide a basis for teaching that person that there are other ways besides problem behavior for achieving important goals. Therefore, spontaneous, enthusiastic, and emotionally satisfying interactions are the hallmark of success in building rapport.

✔ CHECKLIST OF THINGS TO DO

1. Draw up a list of activities and items such as foods, games, and topics of conversation that are preferred by the person with whom you are working. (These are known as "individualized reinforcers.")
2. Provide these reinforcers for free. Do not ask the person to work for them and do not make the person request them. The aim is not just to carry out technical procedures but rather for both parties to enjoy themselves. Rapport-building should continue throughout the entire intervention process described in this book.
3. Continue to provide the activities and items for several days until successful. Success means that the person looks at you when you are nearby, tries to stay close to you, continues to interact with you after you have approached, and talks to you if he or she can. Success also means that he or she will smile and laugh when you are around and otherwise seems to enjoy your company.

MAKE YOURSELF INTO A SIGNAL
FOR APPROACH AND SIMPLE COMMUNICATION

Now that the person with disabilities is consistently paying attention to you, it is time to ensure that he or she will initiate interactions. You want the person to approach you when appropriate and ultimately to communicate with you in any way that he or she can. In this phase of intervention, the person begins to learn that he or she can influence you in order to get things of value (reinforcers) without resorting to problem behavior.

Example: Juan

When Juan had learned to attend to Bill whenever Bill entered the room, Bill decided that it was time for Juan to learn to initiate interactions. Until now, Bill had initiated all the interactions. Now when Bill entered a room, he would stand 5–10 feet away from Juan and wait for him to approach. At first, Juan looked eagerly at Bill but did not move toward him. After 1 or 2 minutes, Juan became impatient and made some grunting sounds. Bill still did not move. At this point, Juan got out of his chair and walked over to Bill. Bill immediately responded by giving Juan some coffee and cookies and talking to him about the day's events. Over the next two days Bill repeated this procedure at least a dozen times using a variety of items. When Juan was reliably approaching Bill, they went on to the next step: when Juan approached Bill, Bill did not offer any reinforcers. After a minute, Juan said, "Orngy," a word that Bill recognized as "orange." Bill immediately gave Juan an orange slice and began talking to him. Since Juan had almost no speech, Bill was constantly on the lookout for word approximations to which he could respond. Another opportunity came an hour later when Juan approached Bill and asked for "keem," an approximation of ice cream. Again, Bill gave Juan what he wanted and started talking to him about his favorite flavors of ice cream. During the next three days, Bill repeated the procedure several dozen times. By the end of this phase, Juan was reliably approaching Bill and using all of his word approximations, at various times, to request desired foods and activities. Juan was on his way to learning that there was a direct relationship between saying specific words ("orngy") and obtaining specific consequences (getting an orange to eat).

Example: Gary

Gary's mother, Mrs. Ibsen, had been successful in getting Gary to attend to her and now she wanted to move on to the next stage of rapport-building. She had taught Gary to approach her using the

procedure just described for Juan. When approach was established
in this way, she decided it was time to encourage simple communication. Because Gary, unlike Juan, could talk, Mrs. Ibsen now required that Gary talk before she would give him what he wanted.
When Gary approached her and looked at his tape recorder up on
the shelf, Mrs. Ibsen smiled at him but did not provide the recorder.
After less than a minute, Gary said, in a loud voice, "Music, please,"
and Mrs. Ibsen immediately handed him the recorder, allowing him
to put in his favorite tape and play it. While the tape ran, Mrs.
Ibsen sang along with Gary and later talked to him about the songs
to which they had listened. A few hours later, Gary approached his
mother in the kitchen while she was preparing food. Mrs. Ibsen
repeated what she had done earlier, waiting for Gary to say something. When Gary remained silent for about 30 seconds, Mrs. Ibsen
looked at him and said, "Sandwich?" When Gary repeated this
statement, Mrs. Ibsen said, "Sure, Gary," and handed him the
bread, mayonnaise, lettuce, and turkey so that Gary could make a
sandwich for himself. The next day, in the same situation, Mrs.
Ibsen did not have to cue Gary to ask for a sandwich. He spontaneously requested one. Over the next few days, Gary began to request
many different things after he approached his mother and she honored all of his requests.

Comment: Linking Rapport-Building and Communication

People with developmental disabilities are often not encouraged to
take an active role in controlling their own lives. It is sometimes
easier to do things for them and this approach encourages them to
be passive. To counteract this passivity, it is important not to be
satisfied when your child, student, or group home resident, for example, simply pays attention to you and appears happy to see you.
You must move beyond this beginning level of rapport-building
and make yourself into a signal for approach and communication,
a signal that works because you are associated with many positive,
valued, and interesting things.

    When you are establishing this part of intervention, you may
find that behavior problems continue to occur. If this happens, ask
yourself if you are demanding too much of the person. For example,
Bill could have withheld oranges when Juan said "orngy" and
made him pronounce the word better. That would have been a
pointless strategy because it would have delayed his getting what
he wanted for too long, causing him to become frustrated and possibly aggressive. Later in intervention you can make more demands
on the person, but for now the idea is to encourage him or her to
use whatever communication he or she has in order to influence
you. This strategy teaches the person that positive approach and

communication pay off and therefore problem behavior is not necessary.

Sometimes, as with Gary, the person does not ask for what he or she wants, although you know that the person knows how to ask. If this situation develops, do what Gary's mother did. That is, help (prompt) the person to make the request. Do not use this procedure every time, however, because then the person may always wait for you to provide prompts and become too passive. Instead, wait up to 60 seconds before providing the prompt, or prompt only every second or third time that the person fails to make the request. If you adopt this strategy, the person will soon learn that it is better to communicate right away because not communicating simply means that one has to wait until one's mother or teacher decides to give a prompt and that could mean waiting a long time.

Communication takes many forms. Clearly the way that Juan communicated was very different from the way that Gary communicated. If the person with whom you are working does not speak, you can still carry out this phase of rapport-building. However, instead of waiting for the person to use speech, you may have to accept grunts accompanied by pointing, or perhaps simple sign language or picture cards, or perhaps allow the person to lead you by the hand to where the desired object or activity is. The important thing is to honor whatever type of communication the person is able to use.

How will you know if you are successful? The answer is that the person will nag you a lot by approaching you frequently and making requests. You will probably find this development annoying at times because it prevents you from doing other things. But ask yourself this question: Would you rather be nagged or punched in the face? Would you rather be nagged or have the person bang his or her head in front of you until he or she is bloody? Most people learn to tolerate the nagging because it is short term and decreases problem behavior. If the nagging is too much for you, try to break up the day so that other people are available to assume part of the responsibility. In any case, remember that this phase of intervention lasts only a few days and soon you will have an opportunity to use additional interventions that will sharply reduce nagging.

✔ CHECKLIST OF THINGS TO DO

1. Wait for the person to approach you before providing free reinforcers, and continue this procedure for a few days.

(continued)

2. Once the person is reliably approaching you, wait for up to 1 minute for him or her to make a request and then provide the reinforcer. The form of the request does not have to be speech; it can be sign language, gesture, picture cards, or any communication means that the person has at his or her disposal.

3. If the person does not make a request within 1 minute, use a prompt. Do not overdo prompting, but prompt intermittently as necessary and/or wait up to 1 minute before providing the prompt.

4. Monitor for success. Success means that the person is frequently approaching you to make requests. Remember, nagging can be annoying but it is temporary and better than self-injury and aggression.

HELP THE PERSON WITH DISABILITIES TO BECOME LIKEABLE TO YOU

We have been focusing on ways to make yourself likeable to the person with disabilities. An equally important point, frequently overlooked, is that the person with disabilities should be likeable *to you*. In order for you to encourage communication, you must be a responsive listener. You are not likely to be responsive if you do not like the other person. Instead, you may avoid him or her whenever possible and try to keep your social interaction to a minimum. The result is that neither communication skills nor friendships are being built.

In reality, many teachers and direct support staff find some people with disabilities physically unattractive, boring, or fearsome. It is not good to deny these feelings when they exist by assuming that one ought not to have them. When these feelings exist, they often lead to a pattern of avoidance and even rejection. Therefore, it is better to be honest and acknowledge the feelings by actively confronting them. In our culture, friendship formation often depends on considerations of personal appearance and shared interests. Therefore, we will concentrate on these two factors.

Example: Personal Appearance. Juan

Juan was physically unattractive to most people in his group home. His clothes had a disheveled, institutional appearance and did not reflect community standards of how a person his age should dress. His face was covered with acne and his hair was unkempt. Juan frequently had body odor and sometimes bad breath as well. His table manners were poor and he frequently got food on his clothing and in his hair. At several meetings, some staff admitted that although they had been successful in getting Juan to approach them ρand communicate, they were uncomfortable when Juan did come near because of his appearance and personal hygiene. Staff were assured by the group home manager that their reactions to Juan were natural given societal values and that they should not feel ashamed. Instead, the manager said that the staff members should ask themselves what expectations they had for physical appearance and personal hygiene for people who did not have disabilities, for example their friends and relatives. The expectations that the staff had for persons without disabilities became the basis for developing a program for Juan to ensure that whenever possible he would be held to the same standards as people who did not have disabilities. The program that was developed for Juan had several elements. First, many of his clothes were given away for recycling. Then, Juan was taken periodically to the shopping mall, and staff presented him with a number of plausible options for clothing. If Juan indicated a preference for an item, that item was purchased. If not, the staff made the choice. The goal of these outings was to select clothing that would evoke positive comments from the people with whom Juan interacted daily. A competition ensued among the staff to see who could help Juan select the most socially admired wardrobe. Second, Juan was taken to the dermatologist who prescribed medication for his acne, which subsequently cleared up. Third, a program was put into effect that systematically monitored and taught Juan to brush his teeth several times a day as well as to floss. Showering skills were another target of intervention as was the application of deodorant. Grooming intervention also included regular visits to a barber who focused on giving Juan a stylish but subdued haircut. Juan learned to brush and comb his hair as needed and his progress in this area was also monitored. Finally, a schedule was developed for improving Juan's table manners and cleanliness.

Comment: Personal Appearance Is a Serious Consideration

Some people may reject the focus on grooming or clothing as shallow and beneath the dignity of anyone who is serious about trying to help individuals with disabilities. That attitude is a mistake. That attitude implies that we ought to have lower expectations for certain individuals just because they have disabilities. It is equivalent to making excuses for these individuals based on the notion that in some basic way they are different. Making excuses is demeaning, counterproductive, and unnecessary. It is demeaning because it sets people with disabilities apart from the rest of us and is therefore a form of rejection. It is counterproductive because making excuses ensures that nothing is done about the impact the individual has on others and therefore new learning experiences and the possibility of forming friendships with others is denied. It is unnecessary because many programs can effectively teach an individual with disabilities how to fit in better with community standards and, therefore, to make that individual more likeable to others.

Of course, an improvement in physical appearance does not by itself guarantee likability and there are some aspects of appearance that cannot be changed. Nonetheless, addressing this issue can sometimes start the process of helping the person to be accepted by others. For example, staff enjoyed the shopping outings with Juan, and he became a center of attention when he put on his new clothes and when he was later seen by others in them. His clothing became a topic of conversation and, although he could not speak, Juan appeared to enjoy being the star attraction. We would like to also note that when the staff took Juan to the shopping mall to buy new clothes, they were effectively beginning the process of broadening his life. Juan had previously been excluded from most community outings. Now, he was provided with the experience of shopping in the community mall, of going for haircuts, and of being seen in public as the well-groomed, well-dressed man he had become. Furthermore, Juan experienced an increase in personal control since he was asked to indicate, for instance, what his clothing preferences were and which aftershave lotion he liked best. Juan's stylish haircut, the scent of his aftershave lotion, and his improved complexion had a positive effect on the attitude of others toward him. These factors as well as the dramatic gains he made in the area of personal hygiene changed the way people viewed him. He now seemed much more like other people in the community, and staff became more responsive to his approaches and his communicative overtures. Indeed, based on the example of Juan, you may want to consider improving likability *before* you try to enhance approach and communication. If you feel that an individual's personal appearance is so unacceptable by community standards that few people would want to interact with him or her, then you may want to address acceptability as your first priority, only later focusing on approach and communication.

✔ CHECKLIST OF THINGS TO DO

1. Draw up a list of reasons why you do not want to interact more with the person with disabilities. The list may include many things such as personal hygiene, grooming, style of clothing, and physical condition.

2. For each reason, write down what would need to change in order for you to feel like interacting more with the person, for example, eliminating body odor.
3. Draw up a plan to achieve each goal, for example, to teach the person to shower more effectively and to use deodorant on a regular basis.
4. Maintain all programs and monitor for success. Success means that you no longer feel uncomfortable about the person's physical appearance and more readily accept approaches and communicative overtures from the person. In addition, the focus on improved physical appearance provides opportunities for additional community outings and a more varied life.

Example: Shared Interests. Gary

Gary's family often looked forward to respite care for Gary so that they could leave the house and pursue their independent interests. For years, they had viewed Gary as someone they had to take care of rather than someone with whom they could enjoy life. Gary's mother, Mrs. Ibsen, had spoken of this problem openly and with some guilt. One day, the behavior consultant with whom Mrs. Ibsen was working pointed out that perhaps the family found Gary boring. After some discussion, everyone in the family agreed that it was more fun to be with someone who had the same interests, and each member of the family thought about what activities *both* they and Gary enjoyed and could share. Gary's brother loved rock music and so did Gary, so several times a week Gary and his brother listened to rock music together. Gary's brother did not see this activity as a burden since it was something that he liked to do anyway. Gary and his brother shared a common interest and enjoyed singing together, collecting rock posters, and occasionally going to concerts. Gary's father did not like rock music, but he was an avid jogger. Gary's father noticed that his son would sometimes imitate him when he saw his father jogging. Therefore, it seemed reasonable that Gary and his father would go to the neighborhood park several times a week and run around the track. To everyone's surprise, Gary liked this activity and seemed happy whenever his father invited him to go to the park. Gary and his father shared a common interest and Gary frequently asked to go jogging. He developed curiosity about the equipment that went along with jogging (running gear, stop watches, water bottles) and his father and he would sometimes talk about these things. Mrs. Ibsen and her daughter were not interested in either rock music or jogging but enjoyed weekly expeditions to the pizza parlor. Because Gary loved pizza too, it seemed reasonable that he would accompany his mother and sister to the pizza parlor and eat there as part of a family outing. While there, Gary talked about the food a lot and gradually learned about all the many topping possibilities.

Comment: Shared Interests Serve Many Positive Functions

Shared interests are the basis for liking and friendship among people who do not have disabilities and there is no reason why they should not also be the basis for developing liking and friendship for people who do have disabilities. It is unreasonable and unnecessary to expect parents, teachers, or residential staff to befriend a person with disabilities who does not share any interests with them. With a little effort, it is frequently possible to identify several activities that are mutually enjoyable and that can serve as a basis for genuine liking and spontaneous interaction. In addition, as the example makes clear, common interests also serve as a springboard for developing communication skills because there is something that both partners want to talk about.

Shared interests also provided a springboard for enhancing Gary's lifestyle. In the past, Gary spent most of his time sitting at home, not participating in community activities. Now, he attended concerts with his brother, jogged in the neighborhood with his father, and frequented the local pizzeria with his mother and sister. People in the community began to recognize Gary and there was greater variety in his social circle. His brother's friends talked to him about music. The regulars in the park greeted him as he jogged with his father and asked him how his training was going. Occasionally, other people would join Gary and his father, jogging along with them, and adding further opportunities to socialize. The staff at the pizzeria as well as some of the other customers made small talk with Gary, especially as they got to know him better. In general, Gary experienced greater personal control. For example, he helped choose new tapes with his brother and was involved in planning concert outings. He got to pick the jogging route each day and was in charge of the jogging gear. He chose half of the toppings at each pizzeria visit, ordered the food, and began learning to count money and pay for the food. As with Juan, rapport-building provided an early opportunity in intervention for people around Gary to enable him to expand his life and to allow him to experience more control over his life.

✔ CHECKLIST OF THINGS TO DO

1. Draw up a list of activities that are of common interest to the person with disabilities and the person without disabilities.
2. Whenever possible, try to match the two people so that they frequently engage in activities that are mutually enjoyable.
3. Continue the procedure on an ongoing basis and monitor for success. Success means that the person with disabilities frequently requests that the other person join him or her in the desired activity, and that the person without disabilities frequently initiates the activity spontaneously, appearing happy to do so. In addition, the focus on shared interests provides opportunities for additional community outings, greater personal control, and, in general, a more varied life.

Chapter 8

Choosing Communication Forms

Most of the procedures for building rapport that we have just described continue throughout the course of intervention. You should continue to pay attention to issues related to personal appearance and sharing common interests. Also, you should keep encouraging approach and simple communicative behavior. Communicative behavior is particularly important because by teaching the person with disabilities that communicating with you pays off in general, you are paving the way for successfully teaching specific types of communication that are designed to replace problem behavior.

CHOOSE COMMUNICATION FORMS THAT SERVE
THE SAME PURPOSE AS THE PROBLEM BEHAVIOR

We do not view problem behavior as random, or psychotic, or as maladaptive. We view problem behavior as being useful to an individual and that is why he or she displays it so often. Because problem behavior serves a purpose for the person performing it, it is very difficult to eliminate unless we provide that person some alternative means for achieving the purpose currently served by the problem behavior. Teaching the individual specific forms of communication that serve the same purpose as the problem behavior is one way of providing an alternative to problem behavior. When a problem behavior such as head banging and a communicative behavior such as saying, "I have to go to the bathroom," serve the same purpose and both are successful in getting the individual displaying the behavior to the toilet, then we say that the two behaviors are functionally equivalent. The technical term, "functional equivalence," simply means that two behaviors serve the same purpose (function) and are therefore equivalent to one another. Sometimes, you may hear the term "reinforcer" as a synonym for function or purpose. In that case, these two behaviors are functionally equivalent because they are maintained by the same reinforcer: An individual may either head-bang or ask to go to the bathroom but both behaviors serve the same purpose or are maintained by the same reinforcer, being taken to the toilet.

Example: Val

Joan had carried out a functional assessment of Val's problem behavior and had learned that most of her misbehavior was related to seeking attention. A major signal for problem behavior appeared to be the withdrawal of teacher attention. When Joan had paperwork or was instructing another student, Val responded to this withdrawal of attention by screaming, striking another student, or grabbing Joan's clothing. Joan decided to teach Val a new behavior that served the same purpose as the problem behavior. The functionally equivalent behavior that she chose was a simple form of communication: Joan taught Val to tap her on the shoulder whenever she wanted Joan's attention. Joan decided to begin with a tapping response rather than speech because Val had very poor articulation. Whenever the signal for problem behavior occurred, the assistant teacher prompted Val to communicate with Joan by saying, "Val, tap Joan on the shoulder." Joan would turn around and say, "Yes, Val, what do you want? Do you want to show me something?" Because of all the communication training that occured during rapport-building, Val quickly understood that tapping was worthwhile. Both aggression and tapping served the same purpose of getting the teacher's attention. Consequently, Val did a lot of tapping and showed very little aggression.

Joan noticed that on some days Val seemed to give up on tapping and went back to being aggressive. This situation puzzled Joan because she thought that tapping was functionally equivalent to aggression and therefore should have replaced that behavior. Joan decided to look more closely at what was happening. She noticed that on days when she responded to Val's tapping with enthusiasm saying, "Wow, Val, what's happening? Do you have something to tell me?" Val did a lot of tapping and showed almost no aggression. On days when Joan was distracted by the other students or was feeling a bit tired, she responded in a more matter-of-fact way saying, "Yes, Val, what is it?" On these days, Val soon stopped tapping and went back to being aggressive. Joan realized that not all forms of attention were the same. Joan realized that whenever Val was aggressive, Val evoked strong reactions from other people. Therefore, to make tapping truly equivalent to aggressive behavior, Joan understood that she had to make sure that her response to tapping was as vigorous and noticeable to Val as the response Val typically got for her aggression. When Joan became more consistently animated in her reaction to Val's tapping, Val rarely showed aggressive behavior and did a lot of tapping.

Sometimes, even a vigorous response from Joan did not do much to encourage Val's tapping and to limit her aggression. Again, Joan took a closer look at what was happening. She discovered that whenever Tom, the speech therapist, entered the classroom to talk with Joan, Val was not satisfied with tapping Joan and regaining her attention. Instead, Val would yell, "Hey you," at Tom, bang her fist on the table, and shout, "Whoa!" If Tom failed to respond to this outburst, Val began to spit, curse, and hit the other students. At that point, Tom began to talk with Val, trying to get her to quiet down. Apparently, the presence of Tom was a signal for aggressive behavior. Val had learned that she could get Tom to talk to her by becoming disruptive and dangerous to others. Once again, Joan realized that not all forms of attention were the same. Joan now understood that in order to make tapping functionally equivalent to aggressive behavior when Tom was around, it was Tom and not Joan who needed to provide the attention. Joan taught Tom how to get Val to tap rather than attack, and Tom carried out the procedure. Soon, when Tom entered the classroom to talk to Joan, this situation became a signal for Val to tap Tom in order to get him to talk to her, and Val's aggressive behavior disappeared. In fact, tapping was now functionally equivalent to aggression. Therefore, aggression had become unnecessary.

Example: Gary

Mrs. Ibsen had carried out a functional assessment of Gary's problem behavior using the procedures described earlier in this book. From this assessment, she learned that her son's aggression and self-injury served two major purposes: escape and tangible-seeking. For example, when she asked Gary to make his bed, he would usually begin the task correctly but would soon make mistakes such as putting the sheet on top of the blanket. When he was told that he had made a mistake, "No, Gary, the blanket goes on top of the sheet," he would typically respond by biting himself and hitting his mother. This behavior frightened Mrs. Ibsen and she did not pressure Gary to make his bed. Thus, Gary's aggression and self-injury allowed him to escape the task of bedmaking. Gary's mother also noticed that when he wanted a tangible item that was inaccessible—for example, a bag of potato chips located in a cabinet out of his reach—he would stamp his feet, bite his hands, and hit people.

At this point, some family member would guess what he wanted and get the potato chips down for him. Thus, Gary's self-injury allowed him to obtain some of his favorite foods.

Because Mrs. Ibsen now understood the purposes that her son's problem behavior served, she was in a position to teach Gary new behaviors that he could use to get what he wanted. Specifically, she decided that whenever Gary began to get upset while making the bed, she would teach him to say, "Help me, please." This behavior served the same purpose as aggression and self-injury because whenever Gary requested help, Mrs. Ibsen would provide assistance thereby reducing Gary's frustration with the task. Just as aggressive and self-injurious behavior reduced Gary's frustration by allowing him to escape from having to correct all of the mistakes that he made in making his bed, so too did asking for help, by allowing him to receive assistance thereby dramatically decreasing the number of mistakes he made as well as decreasing the length of the task and the amount of negative feedback he received. Both the aggressive behavior and the requesting behavior served the same purpose of reducing the frustration involved in making the bed, and escaping an unpleasant situation.

Mrs. Ibsen followed a very specific plan in teaching Gary alternatives to his problem behavior. By carefully watching Gary over time, she knew that certain signals set him off. For example, during bedmaking, and with many difficult tasks in general, Gary responded to negative feedback such as, "No, Gary, you didn't do that right," or "Gary, that's wrong, let's try it again," with aggression and self-injury. Therefore, Mrs. Ibsen decided that she would try to make negative feedback into a signal for Gary to communicate rather than to display problem behavior. Whenever she had to give her son negative feedback, she immediately prompted him to request help by saying, "That's wrong, Gary. Say, 'Help me Mom.' " When Gary imitated the prompt, she provided assistance, saying, "No problem, Gary. What we need to do is put the sheet on first, then the blanket. Here, I'll show you." Gary needed few prompts to catch on because, as a consequence of all of the rapport-building procedures described previously, he was used to communicating with her and having communication in general pay off. Therefore, he acquired the specific communication skill very rapidly. Mrs. Ibsen applied the same strategy to Gary's seeking tangibles. She had learned through careful observation that desired objects that were out of reach constituted a signal for Gary to display problem behavior. Therefore, she prompted Gary to request these items whenever she saw him looking at them and attempting to reach them. For example, she would say, "Gary, it looks like you want the potato chips. Say, 'Mom, potato chips, please.' " As before, Mrs. Ibsen had to use only a few prompts before Gary was requesting items and she was able to fade out the prompts. In a short time, the two signals for misbehavior (negative feedback and desired objects out of reach) were transformed into two signals for communication ("Help me, Mom," and, "Mom, potato chips, please."). Now, Gary talked a lot and showed little problem behavior.

Comment: Issues in Teaching the Functionally Equivalent Behavior

These examples show how important it is to carry out a thorough functional assessment. Without such an assessment, it would be impossible to know the purposes that various instances of problem behavior serve. Information on purpose is vital to choosing an alternative communication form to replace the problem behavior.

By now, it is clear that we do not regard problem behavior simply as something undesirable to be eliminated as quickly as possible. In fact, we regard problem behavior as providing a critical clue about what is important to an individual. After all, if a person is willing to bang his or her head against a wall in order to get attention from others, that surely demonstrates that attention is important to that person. The existence of problem behavior is sometimes the only clue that we have to help us find out what is important to an individual. Therefore, your first goal should be to understand the problem behavior and not simply to eliminate it. With understanding comes the possibility of choosing a functionally equivalent behavior to replace the aggression or self-injury that you find undesirable.

Once a functionally equivalent behavior has been identified, the question becomes when to teach that behavior. The general strategy used is the one chosen by both Mrs. Ibsen and Joan. They identified the specific signal that set off problem behavior, which was negative feedback for Gary and withdrawal of teacher attention for Val. After the signal had been identified, Gary and Val were taught to use the functionally equivalent communicative behavior each time that the signal occurred. Because Gary and Val had extensive general communication training as part of the rapport-building process, they were accustomed to having their communication attempts work and, therefore, prompts could be faded rapidly.

True functional equivalence means that the communicative behavior produces an effect that is close to or the same as the problem behavior it is intended to replace. Parents and teachers sometimes make the mistake of assuming that if aggression, for instance, is a form of seeking attention, then it is necessary only to give the person with disabilities a general way of asking for attention, such as, "Play a game with me, please," and the aggression will disappear. If you think about this strategy for a moment, however, you will realize why it cannot work. Consider your own need for attention. If you want attention from your spouse, you will probably not be satisfied with getting attention from your neighbor instead. Furthermore, if the type of attention you want is warm, expressive, emotional support, you will probably not be satisfied with a brief, matter-of-fact interaction with your spouse. People with disabilities are the same as you are. Not all forms of attention are equal. If a person with disabilities wants the attention of the speech pathologist and not the teacher, then it makes no sense to teach that person how to get the teacher's attention. If a person is used to getting a dramatic reaction from others as the result of problem behavior, then he or she will probably not be satisfied to get a low-key reaction from others as the result of communicative behavior. These points were made clear in the discussion of Val. Only when Joan responded to Val's communication with enthusiasm and only when she taught Val how to get Tom's attention as well was true functional equivalence achieved. At that point, the problem behavior became unnecessary because Val could use communicative behaviors that produced the same effects as aggression.

Our examples also make clear that the same problem behavior can serve more than one purpose for an individual. For example, Gary's aggressive behavior sometimes helped him to get potato chips, but at other times the same aggressive behavior helped him to get out of having to make his bed. Thus, aggression served the dual purpose for Gary of obtaining tangibles and of escape. This situation is very common and it means that you will have to identify many different functionally equivalent forms of communication in order to address the multiple purposes that problem behavior can serve. If you assume that you can teach one general form of communication, then you will not be successful. Mrs. Ibsen had to teach several different communication forms before she was able to eliminate Gary's aggressive behavior.

How Will You Know If You Are Succeeding? As with communication training in rapport-building, success means that the person will nag you a lot. He or she will ask you frequently (and appropriately) for attention, assistance, and a variety of tangible items in situations that formerly set off problem behavior. Signals for aggression and self-injury are now signals for communication. The more signals that are present, the more communication will occur. In fact, communication becomes an automatic response to signals that used to evoke problem behavior. By automatic, we mean that the person produces the communicative response to the signal quickly and consistently. Because of the growth and success of communication, problem behavior will decrease or disappear altogether. If all the nagging bothers you, remember that this phase of intervention is temporary and you will soon be carrying out procedures that reduce the nagging. Also, you should try to break up the day so that many different people are available to respond to the communicative requests and so that no one person is unduly burdened. In any case, try to keep in mind that nagging, unlike aggression and self-injury, is annoying rather than dangerous.

✔ CHECKLIST OF THINGS TO DO

1. Carry out a functional assessment to determine the various purposes that the problem behaviors serve.
2. Based on the results of the functional assessment, choose functionally equivalent communication forms, which are forms that serve the same purpose (produce the same effect on others) as the problem behavior. Carefully consider the exact nature of the consequences provided for communication, who delivers these consequences, and in what situation they are delivered. If there is not an exact or close match between the consequences for problem behavior and the consequences for communicative behavior, then functional equivalence may not be achieved and the problem behavior will continue.
3. Teach the person with disabilities to respond with the new communicative behavior in situations that formerly set off the problem behavior.
4. If the problem behavior serves more than one purpose (as it often does), make sure to teach multiple communication forms that address each of the purposes served by the problem behavior.
5. Monitor for success. Success means that the person with disabilities asks you frequently (and appropriately) for attention, assistance, and tangible items and does this quickly and consistently in situations that used to signal problem behavior. The problem behavior will decrease or be eliminated.

CHOOSE COMMUNICATION FORMS THAT ARE MORE EFFICIENT THAN THE PROBLEM BEHAVIOR

Functional equivalence is not the only factor to consider in choosing communication forms to replace problem behavior. It is also critical that the new communication forms are more efficient than the problem behaviors that they replace. "Efficiency" is a term that refers to how readily a specific behavior achieves a specific purpose. (Recall that we have been using "purpose" as a synonym for the technical term "reinforcer.") One behavior is more efficient than another if it is able to fulfill a purpose more readily. For example, consider a woman who bangs her head in order to get attention from others. Head-banging may cause others to run over immediately to care for her and to talk to her at length every time she bangs her head. Suppose that the woman is taught the functionally equivalent communication form of saying, "How are you today?" whenever she wants to get attention from others. Suppose too that other people generally ignore her question and only occasionally answer her and when they do, just briefly. Although both the problem behavior and the communicative behavior serve the same purpose, the problem behavior is more efficient because it results in attention from others on a very reliable basis in contrast to the communicative behavior. Although the two behaviors are functionally equivalent, the woman continues to bang her head because this behavior is a more efficient way of getting attention. Apparently, functional equivalence is not enough. If communicative behavior is to successfully replace problem behavior, it must be more efficient than the problem behavior as well as functionally equivalent to it. Two factors seem to be especially important in determining behavior efficiency: ease of performance (effort) and ease of interpretability. We illustrate the role that these two factors play by discussing Val and Juan.

Example: Effort. Val

Early in the school year when Joan began teaching Val, she noticed that Val seemed particularly interested in getting the attention of several male teachers, and she would frequently become aggressive to get their attention. Joan's first attempt at selecting functionally equivalent communication forms was to teach Val the sentence, "Hi (Rob, Phil, Bob, or Bill), how are you?" Unfortunately, Val became confused very easily and began to refer to Rob as Phil or Bill as Bob. She also began to use similar names, such as Rob and Bob, interchangeably. When she did this, the male teacher often did not respond to Val because he assumed that she was addressing someone else. Joan then stepped in and corrected Val, "No, Val, that's not Rob. Do you know who that is?" Val frequently required several tries before she said the correct name. To speed things up, Joan interrupted Val repeatedly in order to prompt her, but these interruptions annoyed Val and she began to refer to all males as Rob and became resistant to prompting. Getting attention by using people's names required a lot of effort for Val at this stage of intervention. When she used her new communication form to get attention, she made many mistakes and required much prompting. The result was that there was a long delay between communicating and getting attention. In contrast, when Val hit one of the other students or threw her work table over, all teachers in the vicinity, including the male teachers of interest, rushed over to Val and talked to her at length about her behavior. Soon, Val stopped communicating when she wanted attention and instead aggressed. At this point, Joan realized that although the sentences that she had been teaching Val were functionally equivalent to Val's aggressive behavior because the sentences and the aggressive behavior were both means for getting attention, something else had to be done. Specifically, Joan saw that getting attention through the use of sentences was too much effort for Val. Val had to try out many different sentences before she got the right one and the result was that attention was very delayed. In other words, the sentences, although functionally equivalent, were inefficient compared to the problem behavior. To remedy this situation, Joan taught Val to tap the shoulder of any male from whom she wanted attention. Although this strategy seemed to be a step backward from the more sophisticated communication form of the sentences, Joan felt it was necessary to give Val an alternative that would be quickly and consistently honored. In any case, she planned to reintroduce teaching sentences when Val had a number of successful experiences with tapping and aggression had been brought under control. Because of her previous experience in tapping to get the attention of Tom, the speech pathologist, Val quickly learned that she could use tapping to get the attention of all of the male teachers. Val got attention immediately from the other person whenever she tapped. Tapping not only produced the desired outcome quickly, but it also required a fraction of the effort involved in getting attention by attacking others or damaging property. In other words, not only was tapping functionally equivalent to aggression, it was also more efficient than aggression. Soon, Val was doing a lot of tapping and exhibiting almost no aggression.

Example: Interpretability. Juan

Interpretability is an issue because the speech of many people with developmental disabilities is sometimes very difficult for others to understand. Consequently, the person with disabilities may make an appropriate request only to find that other people fail to respond to the request, either by treating it as if it were nonsense and not responding at all or by responding but not providing what was requested. Juan provides a good example of this.

Although Juan had a few word approximations in his vocabulary, most of his speech was poorly articulated. Nonetheless, Bill, who worked with Juan, hoped to reduce Juan's aggressive behavior by teaching him a functionally equivalent communicative alternative. Because Juan was frequently aggressive during his morning exercise routine and because Bill had determined that the aggressive behavior served the purpose of ending the exercises, Bill decided to teach Juan to say, "Take a break," after a few exercises had been completed. In this way, Juan could end the exercise period appropriately without becoming aggressive. However, Juan had difficulty pronouncing the words, and soon he was saying, "Takee," as an approximation for "Take a break." Bill decided to accept this approximation because he was anxious to strengthen communication as an alternative for aggression during exercises. In fact, after only a few days, Juan stopped kicking and slapping Bill during the exercise routine and used the word "takee" frequently. Unfortunately, an undesirable pattern emerged. Whenever Bill was on his day off or was otherwise absent, Juan again became aggressive during his exercises. This situation was reported to Bill who investigated the matter more closely. He asked other staff members to substitute for him occasionally and participate in the exercise routine. On the first day, Dave asked Juan to do a few sit-ups. Juan complied and then said, "Takee." Dave replied, "What?" and Juan repeated, "Takee." Dave could not understand what Juan wanted and he replied "Okay. Let's do some more exercises." At that point, Juan said, "Takee, takee, takee!" Dave answered, "I see. You want me to take you outside. We'll go outside but let's finish up here first." As Dave approached Juan to continue the exercise, Juan slapped Dave with force. Dave persisted a few more times but Juan slapped him repeatedly. At this point, Dave backed off and said, "We're going to wait until you calm down." Dave waited a long time and eventually got called away to his other responsibilities in the home. Bill interviewed Dave later and told him that "takee" meant "take a break." Dave admitted that he would not have guessed the meaning of that word for a very long time, if ever. Other staff members who had tried the exercise routine said that they agreed with Dave. Bill now saw that although "takee" and aggression were functionally equivalent behaviors, only aggression worked to get Juan out of the exercise situation quickly and consistently. In other words, "takee" was less efficient than kicking and slapping. Bill and the other staff decided to choose a new functionally equivalent communication form that would be easy for everyone to interpret including new staff, visitors, volunteers, and anyone else who might interact with Juan in the future. A keychain was purchased that was hooked to Juan's belt loop. The staff attached a laminated cardboard circle with the words "I want a break" written on it to the keychain. Through prompting and fading of the prompts, Juan learned to grasp the keychain and display the break symbol after he completed each series of sit-ups, toe touches, or jumping jacks. Each time he asked for a break this way, staff allowed him to sit down for a few minutes. When new people came to work with Juan, his break request was understood and quickly and consistently honored. Now, everyone reported that Juan reliably asked for breaks using his keychain and completed his exercises without aggression.

Comment: Response Efficiency

In both examples, communication forms were chosen initially that were functionally equivalent to the problem behavior that they were intended to replace. For Val, the sentences "Hi, (Rob, Phil, Bob, Bill), how are you?" and for Juan, the sentence "Take a break" were each equivalent to the various forms of aggression in terms of function or purpose. Unfortunately, neither of the sentences was as efficient as aggression in helping the individual to get what he or she wanted.

Val's sentences were less efficient than her aggressive behavior because they involved more effort. She had difficulty remembering all the names of the male staff with the result that she had to try out many different sentences before she stumbled onto the right one. Because of her confusion, the attention that she wanted from a specific male teacher was greatly delayed. This delay became a signal for Val to return to her aggressive behavior because that behavior produced attention almost immediately. Although Joan's prompting would have resulted eventually in Val's learning everyone's name, teaching her this would have taken a long time. Also, the prompts themselves became a signal for aggression in the short run, because the prompts actually delayed attention. At this stage of communication training, it is important to teach the person with disabilities that communication is more efficient than problem behavior. When this lesson has been learned, the teacher can always go back to introducing sentences again gradually. Joan was therefore wise to begin teaching a new communication form (tapping) when she saw that the sentences were inefficient. Tapping involved considerably less effort than hitting other students and throwing the work table over. Tapping also produced attention with almost no delay. This explains why Val learned this new form of communication quickly and why aggressive behavior all but disappeared in this situation.

Juan's behavior presented a somewhat different example of response inefficiency. Although "takee" was interpretable by Bill, no one else knew what Juan meant. Some people believe that when a person with disabilities communicates in a way that is difficult for others to understand, then the only thing that a teacher or parent needs to do is to tell others what the various strange-sounding words mean. This might be a good strategy if the individual always encounters the same people again and again. However, a broad goal for people with disabilities involves ensuring that the person has as many different social experiences and meets as many different people in as many different community situations as possible. That means that it is virtually certain that people like Juan encounter many individuals who do not understand strange words such as "takee." In this situation, what happened with Dave is likely to be repeated. Recall that Dave misunderstood Juan's request and thought that "takee" meant that Juan wanted to be taken outside. Worse still, most of the time Dave simply ignored Juan's request, treating it as if it were nonsense. From Juan's perspective, speaking became a very unreliable way of getting a break. Some people offered him an option he did not want. Other people offered Juan what he did want. "Takee" was a communication form that produced inconsistent and/or delayed results. In contrast, slapping was more efficient because most people would back off quickly after Juan had slapped them several times. For all these reasons, Bill and the rest of the staff were right to switch to the new communication form of the keychain with the written sentence that was readily interpretable by all people who might be in contact with Juan. Because the sentence was easy for others to understand, interpretability was no longer an issue. Display of the keychain produced consistent results after minimal delay. Now at last, Juan had a response that was not only functionally equivalent to aggression but was more efficient than that behavior. Consequently, aggression decreased and was soon eliminated altogether.

There is one additional strategy that you might consider. As we noted, both Val and Juan became aggressive when their newly learned communication skills proved ineffective. Val's aggression resulted in male teachers rushing over to her and paying much attention to her. Juan's aggression resulted in others allowing Juan to escape his exercise routine. Although these reactions were all understandable given the danger involved, they had the effect of teaching Val and Juan that their problem behavior was still very efficient and could be relied on to generate attention or escape when all else failed. We recommend that you minimize your reactions to problem behavior to help teach the person with disabilities that such behavior is no longer a very efficient means for producing desired outcomes. If you must respond to problem behavior, then use the crisis management procedures described earlier in this book and, if at all possible, simply ignore the problem behavior. More likely, however, you will need to respond by using the other crisis management strategies: protecting others from aggressive attacks, momentarily restraining the aggressive person, or removing others from the vicinity of the aggressive person. In any case, whatever you do, try not to pay a lot of attention to the person who is engaging in attention-seeking problem behavior, and try not to allow the person who is exhibiting escape-motivated problem behavior to consistently get out of the situation that he or she dislikes. If you make this extra effort, you are providing the person with disabilities an additional incentive to use his or her new communication skills because you are teaching that person that problem behavior is not as efficient as it used to be.

✔ CHECKLIST OF THINGS TO DO

1. After you have chosen a functionally equivalent communication form, monitor the person with disabilities to see whether problem behavior decreases to an acceptable level.
2. If problem behavior persists, then you need to assess if delay in obtaining the desired outcome is a factor. You need to determine if the delay in obtaining the desired outcome that typically follows communicative behavior is longer than the delay in obtaining the desired outcome that typically follows the problem behavior.
3. If delay of reinforcement is a factor, then observe the person to see if the communicative behavior involves too much effort. You will know that effort is an issue if the person requires a long time to perform the communication form correctly and/or requires many prompts from other people in order to respond correctly. Also, check to see whether the communicative behavior is readily interpreted by others. You will know that interpretability is an issue if others fail to respond to the communicative behavior or appear confused by it (by repeatedly asking, "What do you want?" or saying, "I don't understand.") or frequently offer the person the wrong reinforcer.
4. If either effort or interpretability is an issue, choose a new functionally equivalent communication form that is more efficient than the one that it is intended to replace. (Choosing efficient forms is detailed in the following two sections of this chapter.) After teaching the new form, repeat Steps 1–3.
5. Minimize your reactions to problem behavior to help teach the person with disabilities that such behavior is no longer a very efficient means for producing desirable outcomes.
6. Monitor for success over a period of weeks. The new form should produce reinforcement reliably and with little delay. The person should display the new form consistently in all appropriate situations. Finally, problem behavior should decrease or disappear altogether in the targeted situations.

CHOOSING A COMMUNICATION SYSTEM

Many of the examples that we have been discussing involve the use of speech as a system of communication. Clearly, speech is the preferred system because it is used by almost everyone. Unfortunately, not all people with disabilities can talk or talk very well. For these people, other systems of communication need to be considered. For example, Juan had trouble making himself understood through speech, so he was taught to communicate instead using the printed words. Printed words are not the only alternative. Sign language, gestures, and picture boards can also be used as functional equivalents for problem behavior. Although sign language has been used traditionally only with people with hearing impairments, there is some evidence that people with disabilities who have not acquired speech, despite participating in well-designed speech programs, are able to learn to communicate with signs instead of speech. Picture boards can also be helpful, particularly for people who may lack the fine motor skills that are important in expressing oneself in sign language. Using this system, an array of pictures is placed on a large board, each picture representing a desired activity or tangible item. The person can communicate simply by pointing to the relevant picture. A variation of this communication system involves using picture books in which representations of each desired activity or item are pasted on a separate page. Gesture systems can also be used, which can be as simple as teaching people to lead you to the object or situation that they desire. Alternatively, they may be taught to achieve the same goal by pointing. In any case, much of what we have just discussed was implicit in many of the examples pertaining to response efficiency. Since choosing a communication system is such an important consideration for parents, teachers, and everyone involved with a person with disabilities, it is worthwhile to elaborate on this issue more explicitly.

Example: Juan

As part of the rapport-building process, Bill had been responding for many months to Juan's requests for various tangible items. For example, when Juan said, "Orngy," Bill recognized this request as an approximation of the word "orange" and provided Juan with one, and Juan learned that communication in general was a worthwhile activity. Also, and most important, this strategy paved the way for teaching Juan later that specific forms of communication (the keychain with the message) could be substitutes for problem behavior. Although most of Juan's problem behavior served the purpose of allowing him to escape from unpleasant tasks, some problem behavior served the purpose of getting him desired items. For example, he might tantrum in order to gain access to coffee or television. Bill was able to decrease these tantrums by accepting Juan's word approximations for these items, specifically, "kee" for coffee and "tee" for television. As long as Bill was present, Juan appropriately requested "kee" and "tee" and Bill provided them immediately. Thus, the word approximations were more efficient than, and functionally equivalent to, the tantrums. Unfortunately, Bill was not always around and when he was not present, there were many times that people could not understand what Juan wanted. Juan reverted to tantrums and even became aggressive, and this situation was the result of the interpretability problem discussed earlier. Fortunately, Bill and others were aware that there are many communication systems from which to select functionally equivalent forms to replace tantrums and aggression. They chose pointing as a new alternative and taught Juan through prompting and fading procedures to point to either the coffee or the television when Bill was not around to interpret Juan's word approximations. If words failed, Juan immediately shifted to pointing as a means of expressing his desires. Other people were able to interpret this gesture easily and respond to it quickly with the result that problem behavior disappeared. By the end of this phase of intervention, Juan was using elements of three communication systems: printed words, speech, and gestures. He used printed words (the keychain) instead of the problem behavior that served an escape function, speech (in the presence of Bill) instead of the problem behavior for the purpose of obtaining tangibles, and gestures (pointing in the presence of everyone but Bill) instead of the problem behavior that served the same tangible function.

Comment: Alternatives to Speech

You must be flexible in choosing a communication system. For people like Juan whose speech is difficult to understand, you must be prepared to work with alternatives to speech. If you insist that everyone talk because talking is what we all do, then you may be setting yourself up for failure. Primarily, you are being unfair to the person with disabilities because you are forcing him or her to communicate using a system that he or she has not mastered. Other people will therefore have difficulty interpreting the speech, and poor interpretability, as we have seen, leads to low response efficiency. The person with disabilities is thus likely to go back to exhibiting problem behavior as a way of getting what he or she wants. The cardinal rule in choosing a communication system is to consider how much skill the person with disabilities has in using the system. The person must be able to use the system to make him- or herself readily understood by other people who can then respond quickly and consistently, thereby limiting frustration and preventing a return to problem behavior. As we saw with Juan, this may mean that you have to give the person more than one communication system to use and to match each system with the context in which it is most efficient.

✔ CHECKLIST OF THINGS TO DO

1. For each person, make a list of communication systems that you think he or she can learn quickly or that he or she has already shown some skill in using. The list can include systems such as speech, sign language, gestures, pictures, and printed words as well as anything else you think may be useful.

2. After you have chosen functionally equivalent forms from a particular system to replace problem behavior, ask yourself whether the chosen form is at least as efficient as the problem behavior. You will know that it is not efficient if many people have difficulty understanding (interpreting) the form.

3. If interpretability is an issue, then you must decide whether to choose an equivalent form from the same system or to try a different system. You will know that it is time to move to a different system if the person has general difficulties with the system currently in place. For example, if the person has poor articulation overall, then merely picking a new form from the speech system probably will not help. If the person is using signs but has poor fine motor skills overall, then picking a new form from the sign system probably will not help. If you choose a new system, repeat Step 2.

4. If the form chosen in Step 3 is interpretable in one situation but not in others, ask yourself whether you are trying to force the person to communicate using only one system when he or she might better use several different systems, each matched to a particular setting. You will know that you are forcing the issue if the person can make himself or herself readily understood in one setting with a particular communication system but cannot do so in other settings.

5. If one communication system is inadequate to meet all situations, then work with several systems and try to match each communication system with the demands of each situation in which the person has to function. This step is an extended repetition of Steps 2 and 3. You will know that you are successful if the person is able to switch from one communication system to another depending on the situation.

CHOOSING THE FIRST COMMUNICATION FORMS

We have seen that choosing the right communication system is important because this ensures that a person's communication is interpretable by others and is therefore more efficient than the problem behavior it replaces. Effort is also involved in determining communication efficiency, and effort is an important consideration in choosing the first communication forms. If you begin by trying to teach a person with disabilities many different phrases for different situations, you will often find that you have overloaded the person's learning ability. In this situation, communication training requires too much effort and the person reverts to "easier" ways of achieving goals, such as problem behavior. A better plan is to begin by teaching a general communicative phrase or gesture that can be used in many different situations. Learning a single initial phrase or gesture involves far less effort than learning multiple phrases or gestures and is therefore more likely to be successful in replacing problem behavior.

Example: Val

Joan realized that Val had difficulty learning the names of all the male teachers, and, at first, Joan and several of the other teachers thought they could solve the problem by teaching Val to say, "Hi, how are you?" without mentioning anyone's name. That way, Val would not have to systematically learn all the names of the male teachers. However, the teachers were concerned that "Hi, how are you?" was not a sufficiently general way of getting people's attention. For example, if a male teacher who had been working with Val had to turn away from her to work with another student, and Val responded by saying, "Hi, how are you?" then people could rightly say that Val's method of getting attention was inappropriate for the situation. People who did not know her very well might be tempted to ignore such a strange statement. Some of the teachers proposed that Val be taught several different statements to get other people's attention, each statement appropriate for a specific situation. Thus, when the male teacher turned away, Val could learn to say, "I want to talk to you some more." Several teachers felt that although the idea was good in principle, in practice Val would be forced to learn a large number of different sentences for each attention-seeking situation that she encountered every day. Val would not only need to learn each sentence and articulate it correctly, but she would also need to learn to match each sentence with the appropriate situation. This new communication task did not seem very feasible because she had trouble enough remembering the names of just a few male teachers. Joan and several other teachers worried that the proposed communication forms would involve a lot of effort and frustration, and it would be more convenient for Val to get attention by becoming aggressive again. After some reflection, Joan and the other teachers decided to teach Val to tap a person on the shoulder to get attention. There were two reasons for their decision. First, tapping was an appropriate way of getting attention in almost any situation. Second, and just as important, tapping was already in Val's repertoire. From time to time she had been observed to tap other people and, therefore, training would not take very long. In summary, the teaching staff felt that tapping was a good choice as a communication form because it could be used in many situations and could be taught very quickly. Therefore, without too much effort, Val acquired an efficient and general means for getting other people's attention, thereby making aggression unnecessary.

Example: Juan

When it had became clear to the staff who were working with Juan that few people could understand that "takee" meant "take a break," some suggested that Juan be taught a variety of different sentences, each corresponding to a different escape situation. For example, Juan could say, "No more exercises," when he needed a break from exercising; "No more cleaning," when he was tired of cleaning the bathroom; and "No more walk," when he wanted to stop his evening walk in the neighborhood. Some staff felt that the use of different sentences would help people to determine what Juan wanted in each situation. After some discussion, the staff decided that the proposal was not feasible for two reasons. First, Juan had poor articulation and he was likely to mispronounce the words so much that no one could understand him. Second, and much more important, they felt that, even if Juan could learn to articulate well, it would require a great deal of effort on his part to learn the different words. This meant that Juan would make many errors and he might learn that words were inefficient compared to problem behavior. The staff felt that early in communication training, it was critically important for Juan to have as many successful experiences as possible with minimal effort. Therefore, they decided to adopt the keychain strategy described earlier. This strategy provided Juan with a quick way of terminating virtually any frustrating situation. Unlike sentences, each of which could be used in only a specific situation, the keychain could be used universally and gave Juan an immediate and general way of dealing with many situations that typically acted as signals for aggression.

Comment: Use General Communication Forms Initially

As with choosing a communication system, choosing the first communication forms to replace problem behavior is important because it influences response efficiency. In the examples given, the initial speech forms chosen for Val and Juan were quite inefficient and in each case had to be replaced with alternative forms that were more efficient. It is important to emphasize that choosing an alternative form was *not* simply a matter of switching to a different system of communication of gestures for Val and the printed word for Juan. There were two critical considerations that led to the new choices, both of which reduced effort, thereby increasing efficiency. The first consideration was generality: Each of the new forms could be used by the individual in a wide variety of situations right from the start. Neither Val nor Juan had to participate in a lengthy and frustrating training period in which many new forms had to be mastered. The use of a general form, at least initially, allows the person with disabilities to experience many successes in difficult situations without having to resort to problem behavior. After a period of time, parents and teachers can begin to replace the general communication form with a number of more specific forms, and communication becomes more precise and sophisticated. In the beginning, however, the emphasis is on generating successful experiences rather than on polished communication skills. The second consideration, also related to effort, is that the first communication forms, whenever possible, should already be in the person's repertoire. In Val's case, tapping was already in her repertoire although she did not use it consistently. Because Val had occasionally used tapping in the past, her teacher had merely to strengthen and encourage a behavior already present rather than build a new one. The amount of effort on Val's part to learn the general use of tapping was minimal. Therefore, she was able to acquire quickly a highly efficient alternative to aggression.

✔ CHECKLIST OF THINGS TO DO

1. When choosing a functionally equivalent form of communication to replace problem behavior, begin by choosing a form that can be used in a wide variety of related situations rather than in only a few specific situations.
2. If possible, begin by choosing a communication form that is already in the person's repertoire.
3. Monitor for success. Success means that the form you have chosen requires little effort to execute. The person with disabilities should

(continued)

> be able to learn the new form quickly with relatively few prompts and to display that form appropriately in many related situations. Problem behavior will decrease greatly or be eliminated in those situations.

STRENGTHENING RECEPTIVE LANGUAGE

Expressing oneself (using expressive language) is not the only aspect of communication. It is also important to understand others, a skill referred to as receptive language ability. Consider the following. Expressive language might involve a person with disabilities requesting a sandwich by saying, "I'd like a cheese sandwich now." Receptive language involves understanding what others say when the request is met with the response, "Sure, you can have a sandwich. The cheese is in the refrigerator. The bread is on the top shelf. The knife is in the bottom drawer." If the person does not know the difference between top and bottom, or between refrigerator, shelf, and drawer, then he or she will not be able to get what he or she asked for and will continue to be dependent on others. Expressive communication is often hindered by poor receptive language skills, which is illustrated in the following example.

Example: Gary

Mrs. Ibsen had been working on strengthening Gary's expressive language skills for many months. Gary was asking for various items routinely rather than exploding into aggressive behavior as he had done in the past. Mrs. Ibsen was pleased with the progress that her son was making but was concerned that he was too dependent on her. When Gary asked for a cheese sandwich, Mrs. Ibsen had to gather all the food together while Gary waited passively. She decided that from now on when Gary requested something, she would give him permission when appropriate and then Gary would have to obtain it independently. The next time that Gary asked, "May I have a cheese sandwich, please?" Mrs. Ibsen replied, "Sure, Gary, the cheese is in the refrigerator. Help yourself." Gary stood near Mrs. Ibsen, staring at her and waiting for something to happen. Nothing happened. Gary soon began to get agitated. Mrs. Ibsen became fearful that Gary was about to return to his old ways. Then she realized that Gary may not know what the word "refrigerator" meant. She led Gary over to the refrigerator and placed her hand on it, saying, "Refrigerator." In response to her question, "What is this?" she prompted Gary to answer, "Refrigerator." When he repeated the word, she said, "That's right, Gary. Open the door."

When he did, she pointed to the cheese and had him take it out. Through many repetitions of this interaction, Gary began to respond to Mrs. Ibsen's statement, "Sure, you can have a sandwich. The cheese is in the refrigerator." Mrs. Ibsen wisely decided to teach Gary that several other items of interest (jelly, turkey, mayonnaise, and milk) were in the refrigerator. Gary was able to respond to many statements that Mrs. Ibsen made about what was available in the refrigerator. However, Mrs. Ibsen was not content to let Gary's receptive language skills remain at this improved level. Over time, she prompted Gary to respond to statements such as, "The bread is on the top shelf," and "The knife is in the bottom drawer." Through prompting, she also taught Gary to ask questions when he did not know where things were. Gary learned to ask, "Where are the potato chips?" Mrs. Ibsen once replied, "Your brother has them. Go ask him." After several months, Gary and his mother were having conversations such as this:

Gary: *I'd like some pea soup and chicken.*

Mrs. Ibsen: *OK, Gary. There's a can of pea soup next to the spices, and the cooked chicken is in the refrigerator.*

Gary: *[Gets the soup and the chicken.] Where's the can opener?*

Mrs. Ibsen: *Ask your father. He had it last.*

Gary: *[Gets the can opener from his father. He proceeds to warm the soup in a pot and the chicken in the oven.] I can't find the plates.*

Mrs. Ibsen: *There are clean ones in the dishwasher.*

Gary: *[Gets a soup bowl and a plate and puts his food on them.]*

Mrs. Ibsen: *How's the food, Gary?*

Gary: *Good.*

Comment: Why Develop Receptive Language Skills?

When Mrs. Ibsen told Gary that the cheese was in the refrigerator and he should help himself, Gary failed to respond to the invitation. His receptive language skills were poor and he did not know the word "refrigerator." This problem is very serious because, as Gary showed, a lack of understanding can make expressive communication less meaningful and efficient. Nothing happened after Gary made his request for cheese because Gary did not understand his mother's response. Therefore, a delay occurred between his request and his receiving the cheese. If Mrs. Ibsen had not acted to reduce this delay by improving Gary's receptive language skills, Gary would probably have reverted to aggressive behavior because in the past this behavior frequently got him what he wanted. It is often the case that people with disabilities fail to understand what others are saying to them. When this confusion produces a delay in getting what is wanted, as it did for Gary, a lack of receptive language skills can contribute to the development of problem behavior. The solution is to teach receptive language skills that make the problem behavior unnecessary. Although Mrs. Ibsen was able to teach Gary quite a few skills on her own, not every parent and teacher is able to determine what are relevant receptive skills and when to teach them. We recommend that parents and teachers consult with a communication specialist to develop receptive skills because it is beyond the scope of this book to present a receptive language curriculum.

An additional advantage to developing receptive language is that this skill makes conversational exchanges possible. In the early stages of intervention, it is appropriate to emphasize expressive language so that the person with disabilities learns that he or she can actively influence others to achieve specific goals without having to resort to problem behavior. However, if you do not move beyond developing expressive language skills, you may find yourself behaving more like a vending machine and less like a person involved in a relationship. For example, if your child has few or no receptive skills, then he or she may make a demand to which you respond. Once you have responded, the interaction is over. It is as if the child has put some money in a vending machine and once the product is dispensed, the child walks away. This scenario is not what most people would label as a conversation or a social relationship. Receptive language skills, as the example of Gary and his mother illustrate, make it possible for two people to have a prolonged exchange. Over time, the exchange begins to approximate a conversation. Conversation, in turn, helps further the broader goal of building rapport, which itself reduces the likelihood of problem behavior.

✔ CHECKLIST OF THINGS TO DO

1. Make sure that you have taught the person with disabilities an appropriate form of expressive communication for each situation that has previously signaled problem behavior.
2. Check to see if you have become a vending machine, that is, a person whom the individual with disabilities approaches and communicates with briefly in order to get something and then leaves as it is obtained.

3. If you have become a vending machine, determine whether this has developed because the person with disabilities has poor receptive language skills. In general, you need the help of a communication specialist in order to make this assessment.

4. If receptive skills are poor, provide instruction, particularly in relation to situations in which problem behavior has been frequent.

5. Monitor for success. Success means that you and the person with disabilities are having longer and longer conversational exchanges in general, as well as in specific situations that used to signal problem behavior.

A NOTE CONCERNING HOW TO EVALUATE THE INTERVENTIONS DESCRIBED IN THIS BOOK

If you were a researcher, you would evaluate the effectiveness of the interventions that we have described through formal and systematic data collection. For example, you might count the frequency with which Val aggressed against other people each day before the intervention and then compare it with the frequency of her aggression each day after the intervention. Rigorous data collection and analysis is a hallmark of good research and, over the years, has helped us to identify effective interventions. We have listed a number of scientific articles that describe the intricacies of formal data collection in the Resource Materials and in the references in Chapter 3. The interested reader can obtain more information on formal data collection by consulting these sources. In our field tests, however, we found that families and service providers were generally not able to carry out formal data collection procedures. Even professional consultants associated with the interventions were reluctant to embark on extensive data collection. Therefore, we had to implement a more user-friendly approach to evaluation. The key to this approach was the question: Were the people (parents, teachers, residential staff, and job coaches) who carried out the intervention procedures satisfied with the results? For instance, in evaluating the functional equivalence procedures that we have described, we would tell each service provider, family member, or consultant who was directly involved to evaluate the intervention for themselves by asking themselves, "Did the functional equivalence intervention dramatically reduce or eliminate the problem behavior?" The answer to this question was made with reference to a scale ranging from 1 to 7 where 1 meant "I strongly disagree" and 7 meant "I strongly agree." If the evaluators expressed dissatisfaction by a rating of 4 or less, we arranged for additional functional assessments and, if necessary, redesigned our intervention, perhaps by adding other procedures described in this book. If the evaluators were satisfied and gave a rating of 5 or more, we considered our intervention effort to be successful.

Several points are worthy of comment. First, we have come to believe that formal data collection is generally not needed when you are using procedures that already have a strong scientific basis such as the ones that we describe in this book. There is no need to ask parents and teachers to reinvent the wheel, and, in any case, it is not a practical request. Even when professionals are consulting about an individual, there is usually no need for formal data collection. However, we cannot emphasize enough that it *is* critical to evaluate outcomes in some manner. After all, even a scientifically valid intervention may fail if it is used in the wrong situation or inappropriately. Our user-friendly approach to evaluation is, in essence, a consumer satisfaction survey that is described in the scientific terminology as demonstrating social validity. Poor social validity (low consumer satisfaction) should sound an alarm to all concerned that something is not quite right with the intervention plan and more assessment is needed.

Second, a decrease in the frequency of problem behavior does not by itself guarantee consumer satisfaction. For example, a child who hits other people 10 times a week but produces no bruises or tissue damage may be viewed as a minor annoyance by adults whereas another child who aggresses only once every 2 months but hospitalizes the teacher involved may be viewed as a dangerous individual. In other words, any statement concerning the severity of problem behavior is often a subjective judgment that involves considerations of frequency, intensity, and the patience level of the service providers involved. For all these reasons, consumer satisfaction ratings are a meaningful and practical way of knowing how effective an intervention ultimately is.

Finally, the positive field test results (see Appendix) provide confirmation that close attention to consumer satisfaction throughout the course of assessment and intervention pays off. The field tests summarize and validate that the interventions, taken as a whole, were effective in day-to-day situations.

Chapter 9

Creating an Appropriate Context for Communication

In order for communication skills to be truly useful to the person with disabilities, many different individuals need to work with the person to strengthen and practice newly acquired skills in a variety of settings. At this point, you need to consider if there is an appropriate environment for expanding the person's communicative repertoire. We will discuss three important considerations of such an environment.

SUFFICIENT, MOTIVATED, AND COOPERATIVE STAFF

Regardless of legal regulations, situations arise in which a single teacher may be responsible for eight or more children, or one group home staff person is responsible for a similar number of adults. Sometimes these poor staffing ratios are the result of high rates of employee turnover, frequent absenteeism, or inefficient administrative structures. Regardless of the specific reasons, the practical effect is that not enough staff are available for adequate programming. This situation jeopardizes the communication-based interventions that we have been describing. Communication requires an active and receptive partner. When staff are unavailable or otherwise engaged, then no one is around to respond consistently and promptly to newly emerging communication skills. At best, then, these skills are used only in the presence of those few staff who are able to respond adequately. At worst, the new skills prove inefficient and the person with disabilities reverts to problem behavior as a way of achieving goals. If you wish to expand the communication skills of your child or student, you must ensure that adequate staff are available to respond to him or her. What is "adequate" varies according to the skills being strengthened and the particular person being in-

structed. However, there is one general rule. Because more intensive interaction is required early in intervention, more staff need to
be available at this time. This means that you may need to secure
administrative support to provide adequate staff, typically on a ro-
tating basis, to interact with the person acquiring the skills. The
personnel-intensive nature of the early phase of intervention typically does not last long. Therefore, it is possible to return to a more
normal staffing pattern after a short period of time. Although this
phase of intervention is brief, it is intensive and unless plans are
made to ensure adequate numbers of staff in the beginning, there is
a good likelihood that intervention will not be effective. If this happens, parents and teachers become frustrated and, just as seriously,
so does the person with disabilities.

Sometimes, an adequate number of staff are present but the
person with disabilities still does not receive a sufficient amount of
attention. There are a number of reasons for this situation. Staff
may not agree on the best approach to handling problem behavior.
Some staff may feel that the proper approach to serious problem
behavior is reactive, that is, waiting for the problem behavior to
occur and then following it with punishing consequences. These
staff may have tried positive approaches in the past without success. As a result, they are now skeptical of all positive approaches,
including the ones that we are discussing. In contrast, other staff
may be strongly committed to a communication-based approach.
These individuals may feel constant frustration at the lack of cooperation from the other staff. Do not attempt to expand an intervention program before there is consensus among staff about proper
strategy. It may be possible for a parent or teacher to persuade relevant others to give the approach a fair try, in which case intervention can proceed. It may be necessary for administrators to reassign
staff on a volunteer basis so that only those people who are committed to an intervention strategy are asked to implement it. Forcing
people to carry out procedures about which they are skeptical never
works. Cooperation must be voluntary.

There are instances in which staff are not motivated to implement new interventions, but it is not a question of cooperation.
Some staff may view their roles simply as caretakers. As long as
they provide a safe environment for the person with disabilities
and look after that person's basic needs, they feel they are doing
their job. Of course, we all hope that by now most staff have been
trained so that they view their role as educators rather than as simply caretakers. Before attempts are made to expand intervention, it
is important to ensure that additional staff are selected whose approach is educational and not merely caretaking. These motivated

individuals can then facilitate expanding communication training beyond its initial level.

A cooperative and motivated staff, whether in a school, group home, or workplace, can help the individual learn that communication skills are useful in a variety of situations with a variety of people beyond those who initiated the intervention. These multiple successful experiences help prevent any return of serious problem behavior.

COMMITMENT TO COMMUNITY-ORIENTED INTERVENTION

A communication-based intervention approach assumes that there are things worth communicating about. However, if a person has to function in a barren, segregated environment, then there may be very little about which to communicate. A case in point concerns children attending a segregated school. The children are placed in a classroom with others who also have disabilities. If some or all of these children exhibit severe behavior problems, as is not uncommon, the teacher may have decided to child-proof the classroom. Any objects that could pose a hazard during episodes of aggression or self-injury are removed. Although this concern for safety is admirable, it often results in classrooms and living situations that are sterile and institutional in character. Few activities or materials are available that evoke communication. Furthermore, because the teacher must often attend at the same time to several individuals who have problem behaviors, the teacher may be engaged constantly in crisis management and lack the time and energy to respond effectively to communication attempts. Also, because the classroom is segregated, the child's peers, who may also have severe communication deficits, may be unable or unwilling to provide support for newly emerging communication skills. The environment that we have been describing is one in which communication is unlikely to pay off and such an environment may come to be a signal for problem behavior.

The difficulties that we have been describing are often overcome by adopting a more community-oriented philosophy of intervention, one that focuses on creating a more varied lifestyle for these children. At a minimum, this philosophy means that there are daily structured attempts to bring children into direct contact with the wider community in which they live. This community orientation must include systematic attempts to teach children with disabilites how to interact with peers who have no disabilites, as well as instruction in how to function in a variety of neighborhood settings such as supermarkets, shopping malls, recreational facilities, and restaurants. Older individuals need to be taught in a work environment as well so that they can learn independent work skills in addition to skills involving social interactions with other workers. The community constitutes an environment that is rich in activities and objects that are worth communicating about. In this environment, the person with disabilities has greater opportunities to use communication skills with peers who are responsive to communication attempts. Of course, success in the community often depends on the support of a knowledgeable teacher, job coach, or parent who is prepared to prompt and reward desirable behavior while at the same time encouraging other members of the community to do the same. Coordination of home, school, and work activities becomes essential in a community-oriented model of intervention. There must be agreement among all concerned that this approach has the highest priority of personnel and resources. In the absence of a community orientation, communication skills are not likely to expand and be truly functional. Therefore, problem behavior may remain as the individual's main strategy for achieving social and personal goals.

FUNCTIONAL EDUCATION AS THE PRIMARY GOAL

Functional education means that the primary goal of intervention is to provide individuals with disabilities with a wide range of skills that will enable them to live as independently as possible and participate to the greatest extent possible in community activities. However, not everyone shares this goal. A clear sign that this is so is if functional activities involving communication training are permitted only after other objectives have been addressed. For example, a priority objective may require sessions in which the individual with disabilities rubs a rough sponge against his or her arms because of claims that he or she will thereby develop a greater sense of self; or if an individual must string beads, supposedly to gain fine motor skills that can be later used in work situations; or he or she must go on a field trip to visit Santa and his elves despite the fact that the individual is 15-years-old. None of these situations is relevant to achieving functional educational or vocational goals. Not one involves the acquisition of communication skills that promote independent living and greater community participation. If nonfunctional goals are a priority, then parents and teachers must lobby to have these goals changed. Only then is it possible to extend communicative competence so that the individual acquires skills that benefit him or her throughout life. Only then are individuals in a position to learn communicative alternatives to problem behavior in those real-life situations from which they would otherwise be excluded.

✔ CHECKLIST OF THINGS TO DO

1. Determine if there are adequate staff available to be responsive to newly emerging communication skills. If not, work with those responsible to ensure increased staffing, particularly for the initial phases of communication training.

2. Make sure that all staff involved in the intervention share the same values regarding the importance of communication-based intervention and are willing to cooperate with one another to implement this approach. Also, make sure that the staff view themselves primarily as educators (not just caregivers) and are motivated to carry out strategies aimed at strengthening and extending communication skills.

3. Take steps to guarantee that the intervention has a strong community-oriented focus that strives to bring people with disabilities into direct contact with the wider community in which they live.

4. Assess whether the primary program goal is to promote independent living and maximum participation in the community. If not, change the programming to meet this goal or work with people who share this goal.

CREATING COMMUNICATION OPPORTUNITIES

When you have created an appropriate context for communication, you are in a position to strengthen and extend the communication repertoire of the person with disabilities. A common obstacle to strengthening and extending newly acquired communication skills is the lack of opportunities to practice them. Sometimes the situations that signal problem behavior do not occur very often. If you wait for these situations to occur naturally, then you may be slowing down the intervention process. The following examples illustrate how you can avoid this difficulty.

Example: Val

Val was making some progress in learning to tap other people to get their attention rather than getting it by being aggressive or screaming. However, progress was slower than Joan liked. Many of the situations in which Val had displayed problem behavior in the past simply did not occur frequently, so there were not enough opportunities for Val to get much practice in getting people's attention through tapping. However, Joan had kept a complete list of problem situations identified earlier by the functional assessment. Because these situations were known to set off aggression and screaming and would occur sooner or later, Joan decided that she would not simply wait for them to occur. Instead, she purposely arranged for those situations to occur on a regular basis so that Val would have many more opportunities to learn how to cope with these situations with her communication skills rather than problem behavior. One situation identified in the functional assessment involved problem behavior that occurred whenever Joan was called away from working with Val to work with someone else. Joan decided that in order to provide enough opportunities for Val to strengthen and extend her communication skills, she would arrange for a number of other staff to interrupt her, many times each day, while she was working one-on-one with Val. For instance, Joan arranged to have the speech-language pathologist, Pete, come to her classroom when Val and Joan would be working together. When Pete arrived, he called Joan to the doorway of the classroom and pretended to confer with her about something. After 20 seconds, Val began to look upset. At that point, the assistant teacher prompted Val to approach Joan and tap her. When Val complied, Joan said, "Yes, Val, I'll be right back. You wait for me in your seat." After a few more seconds, Joan returned and said, "Thanks for waiting, Val. Now where were we?" This strategy was repeated several times a day with the speech-language pathologist. After about a week, Val no longer got upset when Joan was called away by Pete. Instead, she approached Joan and tapped her, thereby reminding Joan that she wanted to continue working with her as soon as possible. When the situation with Pete was under control, Joan began to add many similar situations to create more communication opportunities. For example, she arranged that the gym teacher, the psychologist, the music teacher, and the school nurse come by the classroom to call her away from working with Val. She had various people in the school call her on the phone, and she left Val supposedly to have a telephone conversation. She also left Val many times to go to her own desk to do paperwork. She had the assistant teacher prompt some other students in the classroom to ask for attention so that Joan would stop working with Val to work with them. Over time, Val had many opportunities to regain Joan's attention through tapping rather than aggression. These frequent opportunities also involved many different people. Because of all this practice, Val was almost never aggressive when Joan was called away to attend to someone else. When Val was able to control her behavior in this situation, Joan decided that she could gradually reduce the number of practice opportunities that she arranged for Val. Eventually, the opportunities that occurred during the normal daily routine were sufficient to maintain Val's appropriate communicative behavior.

Example: Gary

Gary was learning to ask for help rather than becoming aggressive in situations that he found aversive and wished to escape. Unfortunately, days went by in which there were few opportunities for Gary to strengthen and extend this important communication skill. Mrs. Ibsen decided that she would use the list of problem situations identified by the functional assessment to create more practice opportunities for Gary. For example, the functional assessment had shown that Gary did not like to vacuum the carpets in his house. Since vacuuming was an activity that occurred only once per week, Gary did not have much opportunity to practice asking for help when he began to find this task aversive or boring. Mrs. Ibsen decided that for a while she would ask Gary to vacuum carpets twice a day, and she created 14 practice sessions per week. When Gary began to get agitated, Mrs. Ibsen used the prompting and fading procedures described earlier to get Gary to ask for assistance or to ask for a break. When Gary asked for help or a break, Mrs. Ibsen helped him or allowed him to rest for a while. Gary was soon able to tolerate vacuuming with few or no problem behaviors. When this goal had been reached, Mrs. Ibsen scheduled extra sessions with other activities that normally did not occur very often, for example, shaving, raking leaves, washing the car, and sweeping the sidewalk. Because of the extra practice that Gary was getting, his communication skills became stronger and more reliable across a wide variety of situations that in the past had signaled problem behavior. Mrs. Ibsen gradually reduced the number of extra practice sessions when Gary's proficiency had improved. Eventually, situations that were part of the normal daily routine were adequate for maintaining Gary's communicative efforts, as well as keeping problem behavior at a very low level.

Comment: Communication Opportunities and Functional Assessment

Communication, like any skill, needs to be practiced in order for an individual to become better at it. At the beginning of training, it is generally enough for one teacher or one parent to provide instruction in a small number of situations so that the person with disabilities can begin to experience success in influencing others with communication rather than problem behavior. For a skill to be truly useful, however, it must be applied in a wide variety of circumstances, some of which may not occur often enough to promote rapid learning. For this reason, Val's teacher and Gary's mother were both right in taking steps to ensure that as many opportunities as possible were available for practicing communication skills. Rather than waiting for these opportunities to occur naturally, both Joan and Mrs. Ibsen purposely arranged for situations to occur that formerly signaled problem behavior. This is where functional assessment continues to contribute to intervention planning. All of the situations identified by the functional assessment as evoking aggression and other undesirable behaviors can be cues for helping parents and teachers to set up the home or classroom to strengthen and extend the communication skills that have been acquired. By purposely setting up these situations many times each day, a parent or teacher is in a position to teach alternatives to problem behaviors more quickly and more widely. Thus, Val learned to tap in the presence of many different people in many different situations, and Gary quickly learned to request help across a variety of different tasks, many of which would not normally have occurred often enough to make such quick learning possible.

Both Joan and Mrs. Ibsen realized that it would take too much effort to continue to arrange for extra practice opportunities indefinitely. Also, since these extra opportunities were somewhat unnatural (vacuuming carpets 14 times per week), it was not desirable to have so many sessions in the long run. Joan and Mrs. Ibsen were therefore wise to decrease gradually the number of extra opportunities when Val and Gary had clearly mastered the appropriate communication skills. The goal, which they achieved, was to return to the normal, day-to-day routine in the living situations experienced by Val and Gary. At this stage, the communication skills were strong enough to be maintained without extra practice opportunities.

✔ CHECKLIST OF THINGS TO DO

1. Review the list of situations previously identified by the functional assessment as signals for problem behavior. Assess whether these situations are presented with sufficient frequency to ensure that communication skills can be acquired quickly and widely enough to be useful.
2. If the frequency is not adequate to ensure that communication skills can be strengthened and extended, arrange for the relevant situa-

tions to be presented more often to provide greater numbers of opportunities for mastery of the skills.

3. When the skills have been mastered, gradually reduce the number of extra opportunities and return to the level normally experienced by the person in his or her daily living situation.

4. Monitor for success. Success means that the person with disabilities displays the relevant communication skills in each situation identified by the functional assessment and does so reliably and without being prompted.

PART III

ADDITIONAL PROCEDURES AND PROGRAMMING FOR GENERALIZATION AND MAINTENANCE

Chapter 10

Building Tolerance for Delay of Reinforcement

We have mentioned several times that following successful communication training the person with disabilities may begin to nag other people by overusing communication skills. We have suggested that nagging is a temporary problem and is, in fact, a good sign because it typically means that the person with disabilities has learned a new method for getting what he or she wants and therefore no longer has any need to resort to aggression or self-injury in order to obtain desired goals.

We have also suggested that in the short run parents and teachers should accept a certain amount of nagging. However, once communicative alternatives to problem behaviors are well established, then the time has come to teach the person with disabilities to tolerate some "delay of reinforcement" (in technical terms), that is, to learn that not every request will be honored immediately. There are at least three reasons why it is important to teach the person to tolerate a delay and stop nagging others. First, nagging is a behavior that most parents and teachers sooner or later find annoying. If you are busy trying to carry out various obligations, it can be very frustrating to have someone nag you every few seconds. You may also find nagging particularly annoying if you are ill, distracted, or just feeling tired. Second, nagging is not a very mature or socially acceptable way of interacting. Most interactions have a give-and-take quality and are conversational in nature. Therefore, overwhelming someone with a lengthy series of requests is not acceptable because it violates social norms. Third, if the person with disabilities spends all of his or her time nagging others, then he or she may get very little done. Nagging may interfere with vocational tasks, academic work, and home chores. It is important not to allow this outcome to occur because we do not want the person with disabilities to lose out on the opportunity to participate actively in normal daily living routines.

In the following, we describe several strategies and procedures for reducing nagging so that the person learns to tolerate delay of reinforcement without engaging in problem behavior and without decreasing active participation in daily living routines. The basic tactic for building tolerance for delay requires the person with disabilities to complete some task before honoring his or her request. Because the activity takes some time to complete, the result is that there is a delay between requesting and receiving the object of the request. You can gradually increase the quantity and quality requirements of the activity in order to produce, within appropriate limits, longer and longer delays, thereby effectively reducing the level of nagging. Finally, you can teach the person with disabilities when it is appropriate to make requests, for example, only after a chore has been successfully completed and only when the person who is in a position to honor the request is not too busy with his or her own activities. The various guidelines that we just described can help the person with disabilities learn to tolerate delays of reinforcement without becoming frustrated. The guidelines also help to promote mutual respect among all the people involved. A parent or teacher, for example, must learn to treat a request seriously and honor it when feasible. The person with the disability, in turn, must become aware that other people cannot be expected to gratify all needs immediately since they too have their own lives to lead and may be too busy at a given moment to honor a request. In the end, more equal and socially sensitive relationships can emerge.

LEARNING TO TOLERATE DELAY

Example: Val

Val had gotten very good at tapping other people in order to get their attention. However, Joan noticed that Val often was seeking attention before she completed her work. When Val was directed to return to her work, she frequently responded by screaming, spitting, and throwing materials around the room. Joan had decided that the time had come for Val to learn to stop nagging other people and instead to request attention after she had completed a reasonable amount of work. To accomplish this goal, Joan began working with Val in folding and putting away the laundry. Joan said to Val, "Please put away the laundry and let me know when you're finished, then we can talk." Val responded by folding two shirts and then tapping Joan. Joan told Val that she was not finished and had to do more work before they could talk. Val became upset. Joan changed her strategy in order to avoid making Val aggressive. She handed Val only three items of clothing and said to her, "Val, I'd love to talk with you but you have to do some work first. Please put away the laundry and let me know when you're finished." Val quickly folded the three items and tapped Joan. Joan said to Val, "Finished?" and Val said, "Finished." Joan complimented Val and made sure that she was finished. Joan then rewarded Val by engaging her in a conversation. After a while, Joan repeated this procedure by giving Val four items of clothing. When Val had completed her chore, Joan prompted her to say "Finished," and then engaged her in a conversation. Over a period of weeks, Joan increased the number of articles of clothing so that Val was folding several dozen items, and she was working for 15–20 minutes at a time before announcing that she was finished. Joan gradually stopped prompting Val to say "Finished." Instead, the completion of the laundry task (neatly folding all the articles of clothing) became a natural signal for Val that she had completed her chore and could announce that she was finished, thereby earning the right to engage Joan in a conversation. Joan sometimes noticed that Val would rush through the folding and make several errors. When Joan noticed this, she would respond to Val's "Finished," by saying, "Okay Val, let me check your work. Whoops, here's a few pieces that aren't done very well. Do these over and let me know when you're finished." Val would then redo the work, being prompted if necessary, and then announce that she was finished. Joan would respond by saying, "You fixed all of the mistakes, Val! Good job. What should we talk about?" Over time, Val learned that errors and sloppy work only delayed further her conversations with Joan, and she became more and more careful with her work. After about 2 months, Val was no longer a nag. She worked carefully for 20 minutes or more and then announced that she was finished, thereby getting Joan's attention. Joan was so satisfied with this result that she applied the delay procedure to many other chores such as cleaning the kitchen, vacuuming the rugs, and making lunch. Val learned that she could always get Joan's attention by asking for it but only after she had completed her assigned work.

Val became quite proficient at seeking out the attention of other people when she completed her work. A new difficulty arose that troubled Joan. Val did not seem to understand that other people were sometimes busy with their own duties and obligations and were not available for conversation even if Val had completed her work satisfactorily. For example, Joan might be seated at her desk writing on a pad and obviously busy. Nonetheless, as soon as Val was finished working, she would announce, "Finished," and expect Joan to begin talking with her. If Joan said, "I'm sorry, Val, but I'm busy right now. I'll be with you in a minute," Val would become angry and start cursing. Joan realized that Val had to learn when it was acceptable to seek out the attention of others and when it was not. Therefore, the next time that Val announced that she was finished and Joan was busy, Joan had the assistant teacher say to Val, "Not now Val. Joan is *busy*. She's writing at her desk." After about 10 seconds, Joan put away her writing pad. At that point, the assistant teacher said to Val, "It's okay now, Val. Joan is *finished*." When Val announced again that she had finished her work, Joan responded by saying, "You're finished too, Val! Thank you for waiting. What should we talk about?" Joan gradually lengthened the amount of time that she was engaged in writing on her pad. Each time, the assistant teacher prompted Val by telling her that Joan was "busy" and then prompted Val again when Joan was "finished". After several weeks, Joan's writing on her pad became a natural signal for Val to wait and not interrupt. Just as important, Joan's putting her pad away became a natural signal for Val to announce that she had finished her chores and wanted to interact with Joan. The assistant teacher was able to fade out the prompts for "busy" and "finished" because the situation itself was a cue to Val as to when it was and was not appropriate to seek Joan's attention. At this point, Joan asked a number of other adults to be busy writing on a pad. Val was therefore able to practice and extend her new skill of not interrupting others. Because Joan wanted Val to learn not to interrupt people in a variety of situations, she provided additional opportunities for Val to learn when people were "busy" versus "finished" and available for interaction. For example, using the procedures just described, Val learned that adults were also "busy" if they were talking to others, working with other students in the class, or talking on the telephone, as well as in a number of other circumstances. By providing so many different opportunities, Joan was able to teach Val the general concept of "busy." Soon, Val was waiting patiently (after she had finished her work) until other people were not busy. Only then did she announce that she had finished her own work and only then did other people give her attention. All the members of the staff now agreed that Val was no longer a nag and that she had successfully learned to tolerate a delay in getting attention from others.

Example: Gary

Mrs. Ibsen was pleased that Gary was able to request a wide variety of things and no longer engaged in aggression to get them. However, Mrs. Ibsen was not always able to provide Gary with what he wanted immediately. For example, Gary asked her where a particular videotape was while she was busy cleaning in another room.

When she responded by telling him that she could not look for the tape at the moment but would help later, Gary bit his hand and started screaming. Apparently, Gary had not learned to tolerate any delay in getting what he wanted. His constant nagging and need for immediate gratification was very annoying to his mother, who began to complain of being drained and tired when Gary was around. Mrs. Ibsen decided that she needed to teach Gary to wait for what he wanted, at least occasionally. The next time that Gary asked for the videotape and Mrs. Ibsen was busy, she told him, "Sure, Gary, you can have the tape *later*. First, please take out the garbage. When you come back, we'll look for the tape together." Gary was used to carrying out the garbage and he complied. While he was doing this, Mrs. Ibsen used this time to finish her own work. When Gary returned and repeated his request, Mrs. Ibsen said, "Okay, Gary, we've both finished our work. Let's look for the tape." Over the next few days, Mrs. Ibsen repeated this scenario and each time asked Gary to do a little more work. Over a period of several weeks, she added delays to other requests that Gary made by asking him to perform different chores. Eventually, Gary learned that whenever his mother told him that he could have what he wanted *later*, she would honor his request when he finished the chores that she had asked him to do. The word "later" became a natural signal for Gary to complete any work he was asked to do, and the completion of his work became a natural signal for him to approach his mother and make requests. Mrs. Ibsen was very happy with these results because it meant that she did not have to respond immediately to every request that Gary made. Instead, she could ask Gary to work for a period of time (eventually 15 minutes or more) and she could get her own work done. Other members of the family also carried out these procedures. Gary no longer responded aggressively when he had to wait for what he wanted, and just as important, his family did not view him as a nag anymore.

Example: Juan

At first, Bill was pleased when Juan extended his key chain to request a break from doing exercises. Juan was rarely aggressive anymore and his requesting had become very reliable. Soon, however, certain patterns began to develop that bothered Bill. Juan got into the habit of requesting a break after doing only one push-up or one sit-up. Worse, Juan sometimes requested a break while he was being accompanied to the exercise area before he had done any exercises. Juan's frequent requests for breaks were beginning to prevent any exercises from taking place. Bill also found it annoying when Juan requested one break after another because it meant that Bill had to be constantly available to respond to Juan's requests. Be-

cause Juan had clearly mastered the skill of requesting a break
(rather than aggressing), Bill decided that the time had come to
teach Juan that not every request that he made would be honored
immediately. The next few times when Juan requested a break following, for example, a single toe touch or no exercises at all, Bill
responded by saying, "Sure, Juan, you can have a break but let's do
a couple of toe touches first." Bill then modeled the exercise activity and when Juan imitated, Bill paused at the end of three toe
touches and waited for Juan to initiate a request. After about 5 seconds, Juan requested a break and Bill said, "Sure, Juan, you can
have a break because you did your exercises." After the break was
over, Bill resumed the exercises, again asking Juan to complete
three toe touches before pausing for Juan to request a break. This
procedure was repeated many times over the next few weeks. Bill
gradually increased the number of exercises that Juan had to complete before a break request was honored. Eventually, Juan was able
to complete 30 or 40 push-ups, sit-ups, or toe touches before he
asked for a break. Bill made sure that he did not increase the exercise requirement too quickly because he discovered that whenever
he did so Juan would begin to get agitated again. By increasing the
requirement very slowly over several days, Juan was able to remain
calm and learn that requests always paid off, although not necessarily right away. Juan adapted to this new routine and began to make
fewer break requests. The end of each group of exercises was followed by a pause by Bill. Soon, the combination of completing a
group of exercises and Bill's pausing became a natural signal for
Juan to initiate a request for a break. Because these requests paid
off, Juan was able to tolerate the longer exercise periods. Bill and
other staff who were involved in the exercise routine noted that
Juan did not seem very much like a nag anymore. Instead, he did
his exercises and took his breaks in a pattern that resembled a normal workout. Juan had learned to tolerate a delay of reinforcement
(a delay in getting a break) without becoming aggressive.

Comment: Steps in Building Tolerance for Delay of Reinforcement

The main strategy for teaching an individual that he or she must
wait, at least occasionally, to receive what he or she wants involves
teaching the individual that he or she must first complete some
assigned activity before requests are honored. For example, Juan
had to engage in a period of exercise before getting a break. Juan,
whose behavior was often motivated by getting out of having to do
things, could not simply get breaks for free, which would result in
his sitting around the house doing nothing all day. He could get
break periods and free time on a reliable basis, but he had to do his
exercises or some other activity first. Likewise, Val was not allowed
to solicit immediate attention from others all day long whenever

she wanted it, which was too disruptive to her class. Instead, she had to finish a variety of chores before she could receive attention following appropriate communication. Gary, too, was not permitted to obtain all the items that he wanted on demand, which was too exhausting for his mother. Instead, he had to help out around the house before his requests for items were honored.

It is very important to ensure that periods of work become associated with subsequent periods when the individual gets to do what he or she wants. If work periods simply signal to the individual that he or she will be prevented from obtaining what he or she wants, then when the individual is asked to do something, problem behavior is likely to occur. In contrast, if after satisfactory completion of work, communicative requests are *reliably* and *consistently* honored, then work itself becomes associated with eventual access to reinforcement. In this environment, many people with disabilities soon come to look forward to carrying out a variety of home, school, and vocational tasks because these tasks are followed predictably by periods in which individuals get to do what they want.

Sequence of Steps   The procedure that we have described involves the following sequence: 1) the individual makes a request; 2) in response to the request, the parent or teacher asks the individual to carry out some constructive activity with a promise that reinforcement will occur afterward; 3) when the activity is completed, the individual makes the request again; 4) the parent or teacher acknowledges that the activity has been satisfactorily completed and proceeds to honor the request to provide items, breaks, or attention.

Some comment is in order concerning Step 3. It may initially be necessary to prompt the individual to make his or her request again when the work activity is completed. Over time, it is possible to fade out the prompt because various cues associated with work completion became natural signals for making the request again. For example, for Juan, when a set of exercises was completed, Bill paused and stopped issuing exercise instructions to him. This pause became a natural signal for Juan to ask for a break. For Val, the folded laundry and the absence of other items to be folded became a natural signal for her to request attention. For Gary, the empty garbage can, for example, was a natural signal for him to return to the kitchen and once again make a request to his mother.

The quantity and quality of the work required are also important considerations in planning how to respond to a request. Work requirements must be increased *gradually*. Increases that are too rapid can set off a new round of problem behavior. Lengthy periods of work effectively delay reinforcement and unless the individual has had enough experience with delay to know that reinforcers will eventually be available, then the delay period could become a signal for aggression and self-injury, behaviors that in the past were often associated with the reinstatement of reinforcers. Bill, Joan, and Mrs. Ibsen were careful to make sure that work requirements were increased slowly over time. If the person with disabilities suddenly becomes agitated or disruptive following an increase in the work requirements, it should be a cue for the parent or teacher to go back a step and *temporarily* require less work. When the problem behavior no longer occurs, then the work requirement can be increased again but at a slower rate than was attempted initially. If Juan became aggressive when he was required to increase his sit-ups from five to 10, then Bill would decrease the requirement to five again. When Juan had calmed down and could do five sit-ups without a problem, then Bill would immediately increase the requirement but to only six or seven sit-ups rather than the 10. Over time, Bill worked up to even higher requirements but at a slower rate of increase.

During this procedure, there is often a tendency for people with disabilities to rush through a work requirement, often performing at substandard levels. This tendency is understandable given that the person is learning that the delay is ended when the work requirement has been met. The key to solving this problem is illustrated by Joan's behavior towards Val. When Val was very sloppy in completing the laundry task, Joan asked her to fix her mistakes. Because it took Val additional time to redo the laundry, mistakes and poor quality work became associated with even greater delays of reinforcement. In time, the person with disabilities learns that the shortest delay in obtaining what he or she wants is associated with high quality work performance.

A person is typically asked to return to work when the reinforcement period is over. For example, early in the intervention when Juan had completed five sit-ups, he was allowed to rest on the couch and watch television for 5 minutes. Then he was asked to perform the next part of the exercise routine. At first, he balked and started to become agitated. One approach to solving this problem is to extend the break period. Bill might have chosen to let Juan watch television for 10 minutes instead of 5 minutes. A parent or teacher needs to experiment with different durations of breaks to see which is best. If the break is too short, then the person with disabilities may learn that doing work is not very rewarding because the breaks are too short for resting or for generating a change of pace, and he or she may engage in problem behavior again. If the break is too long, the person may not get much accomplished during the course of the day. It is necessary to balance these two considerations of avoiding problem behavior and of not getting enough work done. In general, however, once a person has adjusted (no longer shows problem behavior) to a longer break period than was initially used, the parent or teacher should *slowly* begin to reduce the length of the break.

As we have seen, adequate breaks are especially important when the person's problem behaviors are based on escape. If a person's problem behaviors are based on getting attention, then the reinforcer for satisfactory work must involve an adequate amount of attention. For example, if the person has worked for 20 minutes and has done a good job, it is not enough to give him or her 10 seconds worth of attention. How much time is adequate needs to be determined on an individual basis, but generally at least several minutes of conversation is reasonable. If problem behavior is related to obtaining tangibles, then the number of tangibles presented following satisfactory work completion must be sufficient. For example, if Gary's mother had allowed him to watch only 2 minutes of a videotape, then Gary would have probably become agitated. Instead, his mother allowed him to watch an entire segment of the tape just as she would have done for herself or for one of her other children. To summarize, the reinforcement that is provided following satisfactory work completion must be acceptable to the individual, and that is true whether the reinforcers are related to escape (breaks), attention, or tangibles.

Sometimes, it is not possible to honor a request even when work has been satisfactorily completed. For example, a teacher or parent may be busy doing something else at the time the work requirement has been met. Thus, when Val finished folding the laundry, she requested attention from Joan. This request posed no difficulty as long as Joan was free but not when Joan was busy working with another student or talking to another adult. The person with disabilities needs to know *when* to make a request and determining the appropriate time involves two considerations. First, the work requirement must have been met. Second, the parent or teacher must be free at the time the request is made. The second consideration means that you must teach the person with disabilities to learn the difference (watch for the signals) between when an individual is busy and free. Joan taught Val that "busy" meant that Joan (or another adult) was writing on a pad, talking to another adult, working with another student, or talking on the telephone. Val also learned that Joan was also busy in a number of other situations. At all other times, Joan was not busy and therefore free to honor Val's requests. Teaching Val not to interrupt was important because it reduced her nagging, but it also obligated Joan to respond to Val when she was free. When you, as a parent or teacher, are not busy, then you too have an obligation to respond to legitimate requests. If you do not, then you will be teaching the person with disabilities that communication no longer pays off and therefore you can expect that problem behavior will return.

Teaching a person to tolerate delay may not be sufficient if a child, for example, requests a reinforcer that is unavailable, for example, "I want to make a snowman" when it is July, or dangerous, for example, "I want to play with the can" when the can contains lye. In such situations, we can recommend a supplementary strategy so that you negotiate a compromise with the person who has the disability. Begin first by acknowledging the request, for example, "I know you like to build snowmen but it's very hot today and there is no snow." Then, offer a substitute, related reinforcer such as, "I have a great idea. We can go to the beach and build a snowman out of sand." It is often possible to offer a substitute reinforcer of equal or greater value such as, "You like this can but it's bad for you. Look what I found—a big empty can. Let's fill it with these soap bubbles, shake it up, and see what happens!" Generally, people accept interesting, substitute reinforcers. On occasion, you may not be able to come up with a substitute. In those rare circumstances, the person with disabilities may act up and you will probably have to resort to crisis management procedures. However, our experience has been that these circumstances are quite uncommon and compromise or substitution is effective the vast majority of the time.

It is neither necessary nor desirable for a parent or teacher to delay reinforcement for every request. If a person with disabilities, for example, is very hungry, or has to go to the bathroom, or is in pain, then obviously any request based on these needs must be responded to immediately just as you would if the request were made by a person without disabilities. Also, if you are free when the person makes a request, then you need not make him or her carry out an activity just for the sake of delaying reinforcement. The idea is to teach the person that *sometimes* (but not every time) it is necessary to perform some chores or school work or vocational activity or, perhaps, some appropriate recreational activity before a request is honored. This situation is true for people without disabilities and therefore it is also true for people who have disabilities.

✔ CHECKLIST OF THINGS TO DO

1. When the person with disabilities has learned to request breaks, attention, or items using appropriate communication skills rather than problem behavior, then it is necessary to teach him or her that reinforcement may not always occur immediately. The person must learn to tolerate at least occasional delays in getting what he or she wants.

2. When the person makes a request for a particular reinforcer, the parent or teacher should acknowledge the request and tell the person that he or she can have what he or she wants after a specific work activity (chores, school work, or vocational tasks) has been completed. If necessary, prompt the person to carry out the work activity and over time fade out the prompts.

3. The person should be prompted (if necessary) to request what he or she wants again when the work has been satisfactorily completed, and the parent or teacher is not busy and is therefore available to honor the request.

4. If the work is of low quality, then the parent or teacher should ask the person to correct his or her mistakes. Following appropriate correction, prompt the person to request what he or she wants again.

5. The parent or teacher should set up situations that teach the person to recognize when others are busy and not able to honor a request and when they are not busy and therefore able to honor a request.

6. Gradually increase the work requirement over time. If problem behavior begins to reoccur, then temporarily decrease the work requirement. When behavior problems are under control again, then increase the work requirement at a slower pace than you originally used.

7. Fade out the prompts that you employed to get the person to request reinforcers following work completion over time. Natural signals should now cue the person to recognize when the work requirement has been satisfactorily completed and when others are available to honor his or her request.

8. Make sure that the reinforcement that follows satisfactory work completion is something the person wants.

9. To extend the skill of tolerating delay, repeat Steps 1–7 using many other people, including parents and teachers, in many different situations.

10. When it is not possible to provide what the individual wants, consider offering a related substitute reinforcer of equal or greater value.

11. Monitor for success. Success means that the person with disabilities does not engage in problem behavior when his or her request for a reinforcer is not honored immediately. Success also means that the person is able to complete high quality work during the delay period, a period that may last 15–20 minutes or more. Eventually, the person is able to respond to relevant natural signals by requesting the reinforcer again after the work has been completed.

Chapter 11

Embedding

ESTABLISHING A POSITIVE CONTEXT FOR DEMANDS

In this chapter, we describe a procedure called "embedding" that is especially helpful in situations in which demands set off problem behavior. Embedding is a procedure that involves placing demands in a positive context, which is any situation that puts the person with disabilities in a good mood. The main idea behind embedding is to identify stimuli that evoke behaviors such as smiling, laughing, and being attentive and enthusiastic that would indicate that the person is in a good mood. If the person is in a good mood, he or she will be much more likely to carry out work demands without showing behavior problems than if he or she is in a bad mood.

Because embedding involves additional effort, you clearly would not use this procedure unless other procedures, for example, functional equivalence training, are not working very well. Generally, you reserve embedding for two special situations. First, you should employ all necessary procedures, including embedding, to ensure compliance when the demand you are presenting is critical for the health and safety of an individual. Second, when a pattern of problem behavior develops in response to demands that are important for living successfully in the community, you should consider embedding as an intervention option. We illustrate the procedure with several examples.

Example: Val

Joan had learned that most of Val's problem behavior was a form of attention-seeking. However, there were also occasions when Val responded to demands with aggression. For example, when Joan would say, "Val, let's sort your dirty clothes," in preparation for doing the laundry, Val sometimes responded by screaming, "No!" as well as cursing, spitting, and hitting Joan or other students. Because these behaviors frightened Joan and posed a danger to others, Joan decided to apply an additional strategy for dealing with demand-related problem behavior. Joan had discovered during the ongoing rapport-building process that Val loved to joke around. When Joan would joke with Val, not only was the joking a signal for Val to listen carefully to Joan but it also functioned as a signal for smiling and laughing. In other words, humor was a signal for nonproblem behavior. Therefore, Joan decided that whenever Val responded with problem behavior twice in a row to demands, she would begin the next demand with humor. At the beginning of the third episode, Joan did not say, "Val, let's sort your dirty clothes." Instead, Joan began by saying in an animated and silly voice, "Val, look at all the dirty clothes! They're going to attack us! Help, they're chasing me!" At this point, Val would laugh and pretend to fend off the dirty laundry. Joan would then continue, "Val, let's fight back against the gross clothes! Get over here, gross darks! Get over there, gross lights!" While Joan spoke, she put a few dark items on one side of the counter and a few light items on the other side of the counter. Val watched closely, laughing all the while. Joan continued, "Val, don't let them gang up on me! Separate the lights and the darks! Hurry, they're about to attack again!" Val immediately joined in and quickly began to put lights and darks into the two piles. Joan responded, "Val, we're defeating the enemy! Victory is ours! The gross things are under control! I'm going to turn on the washing machine now. You grab the darks and dump them in!" Throughout the entire encounter, Val was in an extremely good mood. In fact, she looked for additional things to do. Joan was so pleased with the outcome that she applied the procedure, as appropriate, to many other demand situations as well. She would sometimes add in other signals for nonproblem behavior that had been identified during the rapport-building process, such as singing with Val, playing popular music, and conversing about weekend activities. Eventually, Joan taught many of the school staff to use the new procedure. After several weeks of using it, Joan and several other teachers agreed that embedding demands among signals for nonproblem behavior was an effective way of putting Val in a good mood and minimizing the likelihood that she would become aggressive when she was asked to carry out a task.

Example: Gary

Mrs. Ibsen noticed that occasionally when she would make a demand of Gary, he would exhibit problem behavior although he had been requesting help whenever he needed it. For example, when it was time for him to clean up after lunch and throw away the trash, put the dishes in the dishwasher, and clean the table, Mrs. Ibsen would say, "Okay, Gary, you're done. Time to clean up." Gary would on occasion and for no obvious reason respond to his

mother's request by biting his hand, spitting, and sometimes slapping family members. Mrs. Ibsen realized that teaching functionally
equivalent responses to problem behavior was no guarantee that
problem behavior would not arise again in response to demands.
Therefore, she decided that she would use an additional intervention strategy whenever Gary responded with problem behavior
twice in a row to demands. She remembered that during rapport-
building, music had been a powerful signal for nonproblem behavior. Whenever she had allowed Gary to play his favorite tapes, not
only was the music a signal for listening but it also functioned as a
signal for Gary to pay attention to her, smile, and laugh, especially
when she sang along with him and talked with him about the music. Gary's good mood was apparent when he listened to music.
Mrs. Ibsen believed that if she could get Gary in a good mood, he
would be much more likely to comply with demands and not show
problem behavior. To test this idea, Mrs. Ibsen asked Gary to clean
up after lunch. When he responded to this request twice in a row
with problem behavior, Mrs. Ibsen switched to her new strategy.
Instead of asking Gary a third time to clean up, she turned on one
of his favorite tapes and began singing along with the music. Soon,
Gary was singing too. After a few minutes, she turned the tape off.
Gary immediately said, "Music, please," and his mother turned the
music on again. During the next few minutes, Gary and his mother
sang together and talked about the music. Mrs. Ibsen then turned
the music off again. Gary requested that it be turned on and Mrs.
Ibsen honored his request, and repeated the sing-along for several
more minutes. Gary was smiling and laughing and appeared to be
in a wonderful mood during this time. Mrs. Ibsen turned the music
off again. When Gary asked that the tape be turned on again, his
mother replied, "OK, Gary. You can turn the music on again but
you have to clean up now." Gary turned the music back on and
he and his mother sang together while each carried out his or her
respective tasks. If Gary stopped cleaning for 30 seconds or more
before he was finished, his mother stopped singing along with him.
She said, "Gary, if you want to sing together, we have to work together." Gary started working again, and he and his mother continued their duet. Gary gradually learned that working was associated
with the opportunity to listen to music and sing along with his
mother and so he rarely stopped until he finished his task. When
he did finish, his mother let him keep the music on for as long as
he liked. Over many weeks, Mrs. Ibsen introduced other signals for
nonproblem behavior that she had used to build rapport, such as
conversing with Gary about favorite topics such as jogging or eating
pizza. She used this embedding strategy whenever Gary showed
repeated aggression in response to demands. She did not use the

additional procedures unless Gary had shown problem behavior twice in a row in response to a demand. Mrs. Ibsen taught other members of the family to used the embedding procedures when necessary. All the family members agreed that embedding demands among the signals for nonproblem behavior and allowing those signals to continue during the work period was an effective way of putting Gary in a good mood and keeping him in a good mood while he worked.

Mrs. Ibsen was very pleased with how effective the embedding procedure was at home. Therefore, when Rob, the supervisor of the supported employment program, contacted Mrs. Ibsen about structuring a work schedule for Gary, she carefully went over with Rob the key elements of the embedding strategy that she had found so successful. Rob was receptive to this input because he wanted to minimize problem behavior in the greenhouse so that Gary could retain his job there. Many of Gary's co-workers occasionally listened to music while working and so this feature of the embedding program was easily incorporated into the greenhouse work routine. Thus, if Gary had shown problem behavior twice in a row in response to the demand that he pot bulbs, Cal, Gary's job coach, used the embedding procedure with music as a way to induce good mood. Cal also embedded demands using such naturally occurring events as sharing a soda with Gary, eating doughnuts together, or simply joking around. Embedding demands in a positive context dramatically reduced Gary's problem behavior, helping him work effectively in the greenhouse without disrupting his co-workers. The embedding procedure contributed to the goal of achieving a broader lifestyle for Gary by enabling him to continue to work in the community where he could interact with co-workers who did not have disabilities as well as with the customers.

Example: Juan

Occasionally, when Bill would ask Juan to do his exercises he would exhibit problem behavior. This difficulty was most likely to occur when Bill increased the number of exercises that Juan had to perform before taking a break. As Juan was learning to tolerate a delay in reinforcement, he would from time to time start to scream and kick when Bill increased the exercise requirement. Bill decided that whenever demands set off problem behavior in two consecutive episodes, he would change the way he presented demands in the third exercise episode. It had been clear to Bill for some time that demands were often a signal for problem behavior. Bill also remembered that in building rapport with Juan, he had identified many signals for nonproblem behavior. When he gave Juan ice cream or oranges, not only were these items a signal for eating but they were also a signal for Juan to become very attentive, stay close to Bill, and often smile or laugh. It seemed to Bill that the items that he gave to Juan to build rapport put Juan in a very good mood. Later in rapport-building, when Juan learned to approach Bill and ask him for the same items, Bill noticed that Juan seemed to be in a good mood when the items were given. In short, these items given unconditionally following a request constituted signals for a variety of nonproblem behaviors that could be summarized by the term "good mood." Bill felt that it was reasonable to assume that if Juan was in a good mood at the time a demand was given, then he would be less likely to display problem behavior in response to the demand. To test this idea, Bill waited until Juan had exhibited problem behavior in two consecutive teaching episodes in response to a demand. Bill adopted a new strategy for the third episode. If, for example, the upcoming demand was, "Juan, do five toe touches," Bill held off making the demand right away. Instead, he showed Juan a bowl of ice cream at the start of the exercises and then offered him some. If Juan accepted the ice cream, Bill waited until he had finished eating and then showed him the bowl again, waiting for Juan to make a request. When Juan requested "keem" (ice cream), Bill let him have some more. Bill continued this process a few more times, occasionally with other items such as oranges. When Juan had received four portions of an item, he seemed to be in a very good mood. Juan then requested a fifth portion. This time, however, Bill did not provide the reinforcer right away. Instead, he said, "Sure, Juan, you can have some more ice cream but let's do five toe touches first." When Juan completed the exercises, Bill waited for him to make the request again and then provided the ice cream. After Juan ate the ice cream, he requested a break and received one. In the next teaching episode, Juan did not respond with problem behavior when Bill asked him to do five more toe touches. Therefore, Bill did not repeat the embedding procedures. In fact, Juan generally complied with Bill's exercise demands. However, on those few occasions when Juan showed problem behavior during two episodes in a row, Bill repeated the rapport procedure at the start of the third episode. Bill and the other group home staff who were watching agreed that embedding demands among the signals for nonproblem behavior was an effective way of putting Juan in a good mood and preventing him from responding to demands with problem behavior. The staff were so encouraged by his progress that they began to take him to the local gym for exercise workouts. Thus, what started out as an effort to reduce Juan's problem behavior at home facilitated regular community outings. Juan's life became more interesting as he encountered the many people and activities associated with a community gym.

Comment: The Importance of Rapport to Embedding

As the examples make clear, embedding can be a very useful procedure for preventing problem behavior signalled by demands. It is usually not necessary for you as a parent or teacher to use this procedure because functional equivalence training and attention to response efficiency are generally sufficient to manage aggression, self-injury, and other difficult behaviors. That is why in the examples the parent, teacher, or job coach did not introduce embedding until there were two consecutive teaching episodes in which a particular demand set off problem behavior. You do not want to overuse this procedure because it does involve additional time and effort. It is important to remember that people without disabilities respond from time to time with anger when confronted with the demands of daily living. Therefore, we ought not to have a special, higher standard for people with disabilities because they are entitled just as we are to blow off a little steam now and then in response to an unwelcome demand. If the demand is not vital to the person's welfare, you may even want to wait awhile until the person has shown general compliance in several situations before presenting the demand again. However, if you wait too often you could then be teaching the person that problem behavior pays off because it ends task demands. Responding twice in a row with problem behavior to the same demand when the demand is important is another matter and embedding may be necessary. It is also a necessary procedure if the person with disabilities begins to get into a pattern where several times a day he or she responds with aggression or self-injury when a specific demand or set of demands is presented. Such a pattern does not only limit the person's involvement in daily living but might also pose a threat to other individuals who live or work in close proximity.

In order to use the strategy of embedding, you need to identify signals for problem behavior and signals for nonproblem behavior. It should not be difficult at this stage to develop a list of signals for problem behavior, because this list already exists as a part of the functional assessment conducted earlier. In the examples given, functional assessment had identified doing laundry as a signal for Val's aggression, cleaning up and greenhouse tasks as a signal for Gary's aggression, and exercise demands as a signal for Juan's aggression. The main source of information regarding signals for nonproblem behavior is the rapport-building process itself. Recall that during rapport building a variety of items and outcomes are provided for free (early stages) or after the person with disabilities has requested them (later stages). The effect of providing these tangible items, activities, conversation, and shared interests is that the person with disabilities becomes attentive to you, tries to stay close to you, approaches and communicates with you, and initiates activities with you. All of these behaviors are nonproblem. Just as important, the positive context created by rapport-building generates certain emotional responses such as smiling, laughing, and other expressions of enjoyment. That is why parents and teachers who are successful at building rapport with a person who has disabilities often describe the person as being in a good mood. This observation, however, raises an important point. The intention of embedding is to make use of the good mood that follows the establishment of rapport between two people in order to minimize problem behavior. It follows that unless rapport has been established and is continually being maintained, it is unlikely that embedding will work. For example, as long as Joan was joking with Val, she carried out her chores without being aggressive or disruptive. However, when Joan was not there, the substitute teacher was unable to get Val to do the laundry even when she tried to use humor. The problem was that the new teacher had not established rapport with Val. Val for the most part tried to ignore or distance herself from the new teacher, preferring instead to interact with other people with whom she had already established rapport. The solution to this difficulty, of course, would be for the new teacher to follow the various rapport-building procedures described earlier. As a result of this process, humor would be more likely to be effective and the new teacher would be able to get Val to do the laundry without displaying problem behavior. To summarize, rapport needs to exist to increase the likelihood that embedding will work. Furthermore, the rapport-building process itself helps identify what signals will be most effective in producing nonproblem behavior.

When signals for problem and nonproblem behavior have been identified, the embedding procedure itself becomes relatively straightforward. As illustrated in the examples, the various items that signal nonproblem behavior are provided a number of times for free or following a request from the person with disabilities. In each example, the presentation of these items (signals) reliably produced a good mood in the person. Good mood is the primary indicator of likely success and demonstrates that the choice of signals for evoking nonproblem behavior was a sound one. If you do not see any evidence that behaviors associated with good mood are present, it probably means that you need to use different signals or you need to build rapport so that the signals will produce nonproblem behavior and good mood. For example, when Val's substitute teacher tried to use humor, that teacher noticed that Val seemed indifferent and sometimes cranky, a sure sign that humor was not evoking a good mood and an indicator that embedding would not decrease aggression, which is, of course, what happened. Only after the substitute teacher carried out the necessary rapport-building procedures did humor evoke a good mood and result in the elimination of aggression in response to demands.

When you have presented the signals for nonproblem behavior several times and have observed that the person with disabilities is now in a good mood, you may present the demand again because the demand is embedded in the context of reinforcers that have evoked a good mood. A variation of the procedure, illustrated by Joan and Mrs. Ibsen, is to continue presenting the signal for nonproblem behavior while the person is working. Joan kept joking while Val was doing the laundry, and Mrs. Ibsen left the music on while Gary was cleaning. In general, there is no harm in continuing to present reinforcers while work is being done as long as the reinforcers do not interfere with work performance. For example, listening to music clearly did not prevent Gary from cleaning up, but if a videotape had been chosen as a signal for nonproblem behavior, then Gary might have spent a lot of time looking at the television screen and very little time cleaning. Clearly, then, videotapes would be a bad choice and music would be a good choice.

✔ CHECKLIST OF THINGS TO DO

1. Using information from the functional assessment, compile a list of demands that are signals for problem behavior.
2. If you have already established rapport, then compile a list of tangible items, activities, conversation, and shared interests that were part of the rapport-building process and that signal nonproblem behaviors indicative of a good mood, including smiling, laughing, and other behaviors indicating enjoyment and interest.
3. If you have not yet established rapport, then do so using the procedures described earlier in this book. When rapport is established, carry out Step 2.
4. If the person with disabilities responds to a demand with problem behavior on two consecutive episodes, then begin the third episode by presenting signals for nonproblem behavior at least three or four times. Following the final presentation of the nonproblem signal, present the demand again (because the demand is now embedded in a positive context). You can continue to present the nonproblem signal while the person with disabilities is responding appropriately to the demand. If, however, the nonproblem signal appears to

distract or interfere with the person's work, then do not continue to present the signal.

5. Monitor for success. Success means that the person with disabilities reliably shows behaviors that indicate good mood following presentation of the signals for nonproblem behavior. Success also means that when the demands that have been evoking problem behavior are presented again, the person complies with those demands and does not exhibit problem behavior.

Chapter 12

Providing Choices

Many people with disabilities are not provided with opportunities to make significant choices in their daily lives. They are often told what tasks they must perform, with whom they may interact, where they must be, when they may do certain activities, and what rewards they may have. This creates situations that encourage the person to be passive. The individual soon learns that he or she has little control over his or her life and few ways to influence others. While a case can be made that considerable control is appropriate for very young children, it is much less appropriate for older children and adolescents, and generally inappropriate for adults. The mentality of total control is a leftover from previous times in which it was common to view people with disabilities, even adolescents and adults, as being perpetual children. We now understand that this attitude is actually a form of discrimination. We assume that adolescents and adults who do not have disabilities should have some breathing space and be allowed to make choices for themselves rather than having decisions forced upon them. When we view our own personal lives, we often become resentful and angry about the extent to which others force decisions upon us. Yet, when we interact with persons who have disabilities, we sometimes forget our own negative reactions to being controlled and instead attempt to control every facet of the lives of these people. It is the discrepancy between how we treat people without disabilities and how we treat people with disabilities that leads us to refer to an excessively controlling attitude as a form of discrimination. A nondiscriminatory attitude involves providing a person with disabilities with as many opportunities to make choices as possible, within the limits imposed by considerations of safety as well as personal growth in the form of education and life experiences. We do not ignore the necessity for controlling situations in which a person poses a danger to him- or herself or others. Nor do we give up so much control that the person avoids receiving education associated with acquiring independent living skills or avoids participating in the community and its many social and personal options.

SHARED CONTROL

Providing people with disabilities with opportunities to make choices is another way of teaching them that they can influence others without having to resort to problem behavior. If, for example, an individual is given the choice of working with one teacher or another, or on one task or another, then that individual experiences a situation in which his or her choices significantly influence important aspects of daily living. Furthermore, the individual learns that social influence is possible without problem behavior. Of course, some people object to providing choices and do not want to give up control because they feel that it is their job as a parent or teacher to be in control. This thinking is unrealistic. In reality, parents and teachers who must interact with a child or adult who exhibits severe self-injury or aggression often have little or no control, which is why they call in outside experts and consult intervention books. The important point to bear in mind is that what we are advocating is not giving up control but rather *sharing control*. Shared control is something that people without disabilities commonly experience in their daily lives. Therefore, if we are serious about fully integrating people with disabilities into a normal life routine, then we must attempt to share control of their lives with them. Shared control does not mean that we let the person with disabilities do anything that he or she wants to do. Rather, it means that we permit individuals to make choices as part of an intervention approach that stresses functional education and a commitment to life in the community. Parents, teachers, and residential staff provide the menu but the person with disabilities, whenever possible, makes the final selection.

Scientific data now exist demonstrating that when a person with disabilities is provided opportunities to make choices, problem behavior decreases. Because the person must often communicate in order to express a preference, choice-making can easily become part of the communication-based interventions that we have been describing.

Example: Val

Joan was concerned that Val's daily routine provided almost no opportunities for her to make decisions and become less passive. Although embedding and other procedures were useful ways of reducing problem behavior, Joan began to look for opportunities that would enable Val to learn that choice-making could be associated with getting what she wanted even in situations that formerly evoked problem behavior. Joan hoped that Val would be a more active participant in her daily routines and learn that she could get what she wanted directly through choice-making rather than indirectly through problem behavior. An opportunity soon presented itself. Joan had seen that Val, like many people with disabilities, had difficulty in making transitions. For example, when it was time to leave the gym following a workout and return to her classroom, she would frequently collapse on the hallway floor outside the gym and refuse to move. Several school staff would gather around her and plead with her to get up. If any of the staff touched her, she would grab their hair or clothing, spit, and scream. Joan realized that transitions had become yet another signal for Val to engage in attention-seeking problem behavior. Obviously, something had to be done to aid the transition to the classroom. Joan reasoned that because Val's behavior was a form of attention-seeking, then Val might stop if she could obtain specific and preferred types of attention through some means other than aggression. Because Val would leave the school building if she was unsupervised, an adult was always assigned to accompany her back to the classroom after gym. Val had strong preferences with respect to with which adults she enjoyed interacting (and from whom she received attention). She also had strong preferences regarding topic of conversation, conversation being another way that Val received attention. Keeping these facts in mind, Joan instructed staff to give Val a choice as to whom she would like to accompany her back to the classroom. Thus, when the gym period was over, the gym teacher asked, "Val, would you like to walk back to your classroom with me or with Tim?" Although Val had established a good relationship with each of these adults (they were strongly preferred over other adults), her preferences shifted from day to day. Therefore, when she indicated her choice by pointing or saying the adult's name, that choice was always honored. On the walk back to the classroom, the adult provided choices of conversational topics. For example, the adult would ask, "Well, Val, what should we talk about today? Do you want to tell me about what happened in gym or what you did over the weekend?" These were among several topics of conversation Val liked. When she made her choice, for example, by an indirect statement, "We shopped at the mall on Saturday," the adult immediately engaged her in conversation on that topic. Sometimes, things did not go smoothly. Val would refuse to make choices and become aggressive, and, in this case, a back-up crisis management procedure was used. For example, Val would be momentarily restrained by two adults and escorted back to her classroom. These forced escorts initially occurred several times a day at various transitions. After a few weeks, however, these incidents decreased to fewer than once per month. Joan believed that Val was learning the value of making choices. When a forced escort was necessary, Val did not get to choose the adult who would escort her nor was she able to talk about her favorite topics. In contrast, she was able to have both of these when she responded to choices offered her. Although Val received some attention during the forced escort procedure, this was not a preferred form of attention. Val learned over time to use her communication skills to make choices. Choice-making became a powerful and consistent way for Val to get attention, especially the specific forms of attention that she most preferred.

Example: Gary

Mrs. Ibsen was very pleased with the progress Gary made as a result of using embedding to reduce his problem behavior in chores. As Gary behaved more appropriately in a variety of situations, Mrs. Ibsen began to use embedding less frequently. However, she noticed that Gary would occasionally hit or bite himself when asked to do certain chores. Although this behavior was much less serious than it had been in the past, all members of the family agreed that something needed to be done to prevent the aggression and self-injury from returning to former levels of intensity. Mrs. Ibsen also felt that Gary needed to be more independent as well as behaving appropriately, so she decided to use chores as opportunities to strengthen choice-making. Rather than telling Gary that he had to do a particular chore, Mrs. Ibsen decided to offer him choices between several chores that needed to be done around the house. She felt that because Gary often displayed problem behavior as a way of getting out of and escaping from tasks that he did not like, offering choices was one way of assuring that Gary could control the work situation somewhat by picking the least unpleasant out of several alternatives. Gary could learn in this way that he could influence the work situation to his advantage without having to resort to problem behavior. As the time for work grew near, Mrs. Ibsen asked Gary, "Do you want to vacuum, wash the car, or sweep the floor?" If Gary indicated a preference, Mrs. Ibsen honored his choice. However, Gary sometimes displayed problem behavior in the middle of the task that he had chosen. Mrs. Ibsen added embedding procedures when this happened. Sometimes, Gary refused to make any choice at all. In this situation, Mrs. Ibsen picked the task and, if problem behavior began to occur, she added embedding procedures. On many occasions, Gary picked one of the tasks and completed it without incident and without his mother having to use other procedures such as embedding. Because Gary's mother knew that her son's preferences changed over time, she always offered several alternatives and always honored the one chosen. Mrs. Ibsen had learned that Gary might refuse to vacuum on Monday morning but on Monday afternoon he might choose to vacuum and carry out that chore with enthusiasm. Gary sometimes did not choose a task for many days. When this happened and Mrs. Ibsen felt that the task had to be done, she would ask Gary to do it, but she would make sure to use embedding. As choice-making became a common feature of his daily life, Gary generally would pick one of the alternatives offered and complete his work without problem behavior.

Mrs. Ibsen also knew that when Gary had to wait a long time in line at the supermarket checkout stand, the resulting aggressive behavior was probably motivated by his desire to escape. Mrs. Ibsen and Bob, the parent trainer, agreed that because people without disabilities are able to choose among a variety of time-killing activities while waiting in line, Gary too should be afforded the opportunity to choose among such activities. People without disabilities read magazines while waiting, eat snacks that they are about to pay for, and talk to one another. Therefore, Gary was asked, "Do you want to look at a magazine, eat [name of item], or talk about [specific topic of conversation]?" Almost always, Gary would make a choice, engage in the activity, and show no problem behavior. In the few instances in which Gary showed problem behavior, Mrs. Ibsen carried out one or more of the crisis management strategies described earlier.

Cal, Gary's job coach, decided that choice-making could also be useful in the greenhouse. Gary carried out a number of different tasks such as potting bulbs, planting flower beds, working on the seed beds, fertilization, watering, and harvesting flowers. These tasks often did not have to be carried out in any particular order. What was important was that all tasks were completed in a 2- or 3-day period. Given this flexibility, it was possible to offer Gary choices: "Gary, what do you want to do next: pot bulbs, fertilize, or water?" Cal had learned that, although Gary's preferences did change from day to day, on any given day he preferred some tasks over others. By accommodating Gary's preferences through choice-making, Cal was able to get Gary to carry out many different tasks without any display of problem behavior. If Gary refused certain tasks day after day, or if a specific nonpreferred task had to be carried out right away, Cal used embedding procedures. In general, Gary made many choices each day and completed a significant majority of the required tasks without needing the additional embedding procedures.

Example: Juan

Bill was worried that because Juan had very little understanding of language and almost no speech, people tended to do things for him rather than letting him act independently. It was very difficult for staff in the group home to communicate with Juan in order to discover his preferences and, unfortunately, many staff gave up trying with the result that Juan remained quite passive. Juan did, however, actively indicate his preferences through his use of the keychain to request breaks, the speech approximations he used with Bill, and his ability to point to items he desired when all other means of communication failed. These various forms of communication helped Juan to be less passive. Bill wanted more, and he was always looking for new opportunities to get Juan involved. Bill felt that it was important to teach Juan to make choices, partly to reduce Juan's passivity but also as a way of encouraging the staff to view Juan as a person who, whenever possible, should be offered choices. The staff were accustomed to giving Juan one or more of a small group of items that they knew he liked. This activity helped build rapport and was an important part of embedding. However, it put Juan in a rather passive position. To counter this problem, Bill encouraged all staff to allow Juan, whenever possible, to choose among things he liked. For example, rather than simply giving Juan a cup of coffee, which he liked, the staff showed several items to him at the same time and asked him to point to the one he most wanted at the moment. Juan might be shown a cup of coffee, some oranges, a bowl of ice cream, and a bag of potato chips and asked, "Juan, point to the one you want." When he pointed, he was given the item. If he did not point, no item was given to him. He seemed confused by the new procedure at first, but after being prompted to point a number of times, he was able to express his preferences without being prompted. The staff tried hard to include new items in an attempt to identify additional items Juan liked. Within a week, Juan was choosing items rather than simply being given them. More important, when staff learned that one or two items were most desired at a particular time, they made sure that it was those items, not others, that were used if a situation called for embedding. For example, at 2 P.M., staff asked Juan to choose among several items. Juan chose some orange slices. Ten minutes later it was time for Juan to exercise. If he became disruptive during the exercises, the staff used the embedding procedure but made sure that oranges, for example, rather than some other reinforcer were used to put Juan in a good mood before continuing the exercise routine. Both Bill and the staff agreed that embedding was most effective when the reinforcers that were part of the procedure were ones that Juan had recently chosen rather than ones the staff chose. The staff also learned that because Juan's choices changed from day to day and even within a day, it was important to offer him frequent opportunities to express his preferences. By being aware of Juan's changing preferences, staff were able to improve the effectiveness of the embedding procedure and they saw fewer and fewer problem behaviors in task situations.

Comment: Choosing Among Options

In each of the above examples, parents, teachers, and group home staff offered the person with disabilities a number of different options from which to choose. Val's teacher arranged for a choice between several adult escorts as well as a choice of conversation topics. Gary's mother offered her son a choice among home chores and supermarket activities, and Gary's job coach offered him a choice of greenhouse tasks. The group home staff provided Juan with a variety of items from which to choose. Since parents, teachers, the job coach, and group home staff defined the list of alternatives that they offered, they retained some control over the situation. Likewise, since the person with disabilities was not forced to accept a specific alternative but was free to choose, he or she too retained some control over the situation. Shared control is therefore evident in all the examples given. Two points are worth emphasizing. First, parents, teachers, the job coach, group home staff, and others must retain some measure of control to avoid situations in which a person with disabilities always chooses the same task and avoids other tasks that may be beneficial for him or her to perform, always chooses the same person which whom to interact and limits his or her social exposure, and always chooses the same reinforcer and fails to experience an array of items that may be useful later in building rapport and motivating performance of worthwhile activities. Second, one should not be rigid in implementing shared control. It is sometimes appropriate for the person with disabilities to choose an alternative not offered by the parent, teacher, job coach, or group home staff. For example, when Gary's mother offered her son a choice between vacuuming, washing the car, or sweeping the floor, he would sometimes choose a fourth alternative that had not been offered, such as raking leaves. If this new chore needed to be done and there was no need for any of the other chores to be carried out right away, then it would be desirable for Mrs. Ibsen to allow her son to rake leaves. By rewarding his initiative, Mrs. Ibsen would be teaching her son to participate actively in home life rather than encouraging him to wait passively for someone to tell him exactly what to do next.

Choosing Not to Choose   The person with disabilities may not always make a choice. That is not a problem and when this situation arises, the individual should not be forced to choose or be reprimanded as part of a punishment approach as opposed to being prompted by way of an educational approach. To do so is to make a mockery of the idea of choosing as a behavior that is performed in the absence of coercion. If it is essential for a specific task to be performed and that task is never chosen, then a parent or teacher could present the task using embedding procedures. In general, it is important to provide natural consequences for failure to make a choice. The natural consequence for people with disabilities as well as those without disabilities is that someone else chooses for you. In Val's case, failure to choose meant that her teacher selected the adult who would escort her back to the classroom and Val would not be able to engage in conversations about her favorite topics. In Gary's case, Mrs. Ibsen or the job coach selected the specific chore that Gary had to perform and Gary missed the opportunity to work on something he liked or at least one that was minimally objectionable. For Juan, failure to choose simply meant that the staff did not give Juan any of the items that they offered him. That was fine if Juan did not want anything at the moment but if he did, he lost the opportunity to obtain it. In each example, individuals who did not take advantage of the opportunity to choose were subsequently confronted with a less desirable situation than they might have had if they indicated a preference. This natural consequence for failing to choose contrasts sharply with the very positive consequences often available from making a choice and is an additional incentive for encouraging individuals to make choices.

The choices offered to individuals were in many instances directly related to the factors that had been identified as important in maintaining their problem behavior. For example, since much of Val's aggression and screaming during transitions was a form of attention-seeking, Joan made sure that the choices given to Val involved the same reinforcers that controlled the problem behavior, namely, attention from specific adults and attention in the form of preferred conversation topics. Choice-making therefore provided Val with a new way of getting the attention that had previously been given to her as a result of her problem behavior. If Joan had allowed Val to choose among a variety of tangible items instead, it would probably have been an ineffective strategy because Val's behavior was not motivated by obtaining tangible items. Similarly, because Gary's aggression and self-injury in demand situations was a form of escape behavior, Mrs. Ibsen and the job coach were careful to provide Gary with choices that involved a variety of tasks. Therefore, choice-making provided Gary with a new way of avoiding task situations that were aversive to him at the moment. Alternatively, choice-making also allowed Gary to select preferred tasks. In either case, the aversiveness of the home and greenhouse chores was reduced as a consequence of Gary's being allowed to make selections and, therefore, the motivation for problem behavior was also reduced, resulting in far fewer instances of aggression and self-injury. If, for example, Mrs. Ibsen had instead provided Gary with choices relating to attention, it would probably have been an unsuccessful strategy because Gary's problem behavior was not related to attention-seeking.

As we noted, choice-making procedures are also useful in increasing the effectiveness of other procedures, especially embedding. Thus, when staff had used the choice-making procedure to discover the tangible items that Juan most preferred at a given time, they were in a position to incorporate those reinforcers, when appropriate, in the embedding procedure. Because the items chosen were the most desired ones available at the moment, using them in the embedding procedure was especially effective in putting Juan in a good mood and that in turn resulted in fewer problem behaviors during the exercise routine.

Providing individuals with opportunities to make choices works well with a communication-based intervention approach because choice-making is itself a form of communication. That is, Val pointed or used speech to indicate her preferences; Gary used speech to select a specific task from the array of tasks presented to him; and Juan pointed to express his preference for one item over another. If needed, other communication forms such as sign language or picture boards can also be used for making choices. No individual with disabilities should be deprived of the opportunity to make choices simply because he or she has poor speech skills, since there are so many different communication forms available.

A focus on choice is an important additional way that you have of enhancing the lives of people with disabilities. A passive lifestyle in which the individual with disabilities simply waits to be told what to do, when to do it, and with whom to do it is exchanged for a life in which there is an emphasis on personal control, taking the initiative to make choices, and influencing others.

✔ CHECKLIST OF THINGS TO DO

1. Whenever appropriate and feasible, provide the person with disabilities with an array of options with respect to the tasks on which he or she needs to work, people with whom he or she may interact, tangible items, and social activities.
2. Try to create options that are related to the factors that control problem behavior. For example, if a person's aggression is motivated by escape from task demands, provide an array of tasks from which

(continued)

the person can choose. If a person's aggression is motivated by attention, make available a variety of individuals (teachers, group home staff, family members) with whom the person can choose to interact. If a person's aggression is motivated by tangibles, offer an array of tangible items from which the person can choose.

3. Allow the person to choose one of the options provided and honor that choice. Choices can be communicated through speech, sign language, gestures (pointing), picture boards, or any other means available.

4. If the person chooses an option not offered, honor that choice unless it is disruptive or prevents important goals from being met.

5. Provide natural consequences for failure to make choices. For example, if the person with disabilities does not choose one of the task options offered, you will need to choose a task for him or her. You may need to prompt performance of the task that you have chosen and you may need to use embedding procedures as well. In the case of attention (social interaction preferences), you will need to choose the other individual with whom the person with disabilities will interact. In the case of tangible items, do not provide any of the reinforcers but, after a short time, offer the options again.

6. When appropriate, incorporate the chosen option into the embedding procedure.

7. Monitor for success. Success means that when the person with disabilities is provided with options, he or she will typically choose one. When choices are honored within the context of situations that are associated with problem behavior, such behavior will become less frequent or be eliminated altogether. Finally, the effectiveness of embedding procedures will improve when these procedures are based on options chosen by the person with disabilities.

Chapter 13

Generalization

Consider the situation of a young girl with autism who exhibits self-injury and aggression at home whenever her mother asks her to make her bed. After her mother carries out the interventions that we have been describing, the girl stops that behavior and makes her bed without creating a fuss. The mother is very satisfied with this outcome. However, when the girl's father asks her to make her bed, she becomes severely aggressive again. Apparently, the intervention success achieved by the mother did not transfer to the father. When an intervention success does not transfer from one person to other people, we say that "generalization" has failed to occur. Generalization is the transfer of intervention success from one situation to many other situations. Unless generalization occurs, few people will regard the intervention as successful. In the example described, we would hope that following intervention the young girl would stop her problem behavior in the presence of a wide variety of other people in addition to her mother. That is, we expect generalization across people. We also desire that the girl will no longer display self-injury and aggression in other settings besides the home such as in the classroom, in the shopping mall, on the school bus, in a restaurant, or at the beach. This is called generalization across physical settings. We also expect the girl to stop displaying problem behavior not only in response to a request to make her bed but also in response to many other requests such as making her lunch, cleaning her room, taking a shower, dressing herself, completing school work, or helping to shop for groceries. This is called generalization across tasks. Sometimes (but not often), when intervention is carried out in a limited situation, intervention gains occur in a wide variety of new situations in which intervention did not take place. This positive outcome is called unprogrammed generalization because the intervention program was not instituted in the new situations and yet gains were observed in those situations. Thus, in our example, if following the mother's intervention in the bed-making situation the girl no longer displayed problem behavior in the presence of her father, or at school, or when asked to make her lunch, then her improvement in all the new situations is an example of unprogrammed generalization because no intervention had taken place in those situations. However, unprogrammed generalization is the exception rather than the rule. It is usually necessary to program generalization. If you want behavior improvements (intervention gains) to occur across people, physical settings, and tasks, then you must institute interventions across people, physical settings, and tasks. That does not mean that you have to carry out interventions with every person, setting, and task that the individual with disabilities might encounter. It does mean that, typically, you will have to conduct intervention in a variety of situations in order to see widespread improvement in behavior. Fortunately, if you program generalization in enough carefully chosen situations, you will after time begin to see instances of behavior improvement in new situations that were not involved in the initial intervention. Unprogrammed generalization does occur when enough programmed generalization has been carried out. Thus, in our example, if the mother had taught her daughter how to behave appropriately in several different task situations such as bedmaking, taking showers, dressing, and making lunch, then appropriate behavior might also be seen in new task situations such as toothbrushing, room cleaning, and exercising although the mother did not provide instruction in those situations. Many examples of programmed generalization were implicit in earlier portions of this book, and we now consider generalization explicitly.

SUCCESSFULLY PROGRAMMING GENERALIZATION

Our approach to programming generalization has two major components. First, we begin in a controlled situation and then gradually move to less controlled situations. Second, we choose teaching environments carefully so that they represent a broad range of naturalistic situations, which are situations that commonly occur or may be expected to occur in the daily community life of the person with disabilities.

Example: Gary

When Mrs. Ibsen first began working with Gary, she was delighted with the quick progress she made in developing good rapport with him and with the speed with which Gary mastered initial communication skills to replace the aggression and self-injury that he had shown for so long in response to demands. Mrs. Ibsen was so confident after Gary's early successes that she decided to expand his skills immediately in the shopping mall, a situation that was difficult for Gary to manage. This proved to be a big mistake. Gary had not practiced his new communication skills long enough to use them automatically in the face of frustration. When Gary and his mother entered the mall, his mother asked him to take off his coat. Unfortunately, the zipper jammed. Although Gary had learned to ask for help in this situation, he had not practiced seeking assistance very much at this point. Rather than focusing on the need to ask his mother for help, Gary instead was focusing on the many interesting goods and activities present in the mall. He was particularly eager to explore the record store where one of his favorite rock videotapes was being played at the moment. When his zipper jammed and his mother tried to prompt him to ask for help, Gary became very frustrated at not being able to watch the videotape immediately and he tore his coat. Mrs. Ibsen tried to pull his coat off to prevent further damage, but by this time Gary was very agitated. He pushed by his mother and shoved one of the patrons in the store so that he could get a better look at the videotape monitor. When the patron responded angrily, Gary bit himself, much to the surprise of the patron who called over the store manager. By this time, Mrs. Ibsen was thoroughly embarrassed, and a large group of customers had gathered around in shocked silence. Mrs. Ibsen explained the situation to the manager who, although supportive, suggested that Mrs. Ibsen had better remove Gary from the store to avoid any further outbursts.

At first, Mrs. Ibsen was quite disappointed with the day's events but she soon recovered her optimism once she realized that the real problem had been a lack of sufficient preparation to enable Gary to generalize his new skills to such complicated and confusing situations as the shopping mall. Mrs. Ibsen decided that she would strengthen Gary's functional communication skills in the more controlled setting of their home before she ventured out again to try generalization in the shopping mall. Accordingly, she had Gary practice asking for help in a variety of home situations. Gary learned to request assistance in tasks related to dressing, food preparation, housecleaning, and grooming. These tasks were all naturalistic because Gary encountered them almost daily in his home life. Mrs. Ibsen found that the relaxed atmosphere at home contrasted sharply with the hustle and bustle of the shopping mall with its many distractions and interfering stimuli, and it was easier to control the initial generalization process in the home setting. It did not take long for Gary to generalize assistance-seeking skills across a wide variety of tasks at home. After Gary had learned to cope with frustration in the presence of 8–10 tasks, he began to show unprogrammed generalization to many additional tasks that had not been involved in the communication training.

When Gary had successfully generalized his communication skills across tasks, Mrs. Ibsen began to program generalization across people. She had other people carry out all the communication-

based interventions that she had been implementing—functional
equivalence training, enhancing receptive language, building tolerance for reinforcement delays, embedding, and providing opportunities for choice-making. Mrs. Ibsen involved her husband, her
other children, extended family, Gary's teachers, school bus driv-
ers, and neighbors in the process. Many new tasks were introduced
and Gary was learning that using his skills paid off with many different people. He was soon displaying these skills even to people
who had not been involved in the initial training, which means that
unprogrammed generalization across people began to occur. Gary
became increasingly competent at displaying functional communication instead of problem behavior in situations that were less and
less controlled and involved many people as well as a multitude of
distracting stimuli. Mrs. Ibsen felt that Gary was at last ready to
tackle more complicated but enriching settings in the broader community. To some extent, the process of programming generalization
across settings had already begun since Gary was now used to dealing with frustration arising from demands associated with the classroom and school bus as well as at home. However, Mrs. Ibsen
wanted to extend Gary's competence to additional naturalistic settings. She enlisted the help of family members as well as school
staff in encouraging Gary to use his communicative repertoire on
community outings to the supermarket, neighborhood park, fast
food restaurants, the swimming pool, on field trips, and even to the
infamous shopping mall. By this time Gary's skills were so well
established in both the controlled setting at home as well as the
less controlled classroom and school bus settings that he was able
to cope with the new demands presented by the various community
settings. Programming generalization in all of these additional settings became a matter of routinely reapplying all the procedures
that Gary was familiar with from previous experiences. Not only
did the programmed generalization go smoothly, but soon Gary was
displaying his functional communication skills in other settings
such as the doctor's office and a video arcade that were not included in the programming. Unprogrammed generalization across
settings began to occur. At this advanced stage of intervention, Gary
was showing both programmed and unprogrammed generalization
across tasks, people, and settings. His communication skills had
almost entirely replaced the aggressive and self-injurious behaviors
that he had shown for so long and in so many situations.

Comment: Naturalistic Settings

Controlled Situations Mrs. Ibsen's initial experience with
programmed generalization illustrates why it is a good idea to begin
working in a controlled situation before moving to a less controlled

one. The shopping mall had a large number of signals for problem behavior and many distracting stimuli. Trying to program generalization in this type of situation is difficult unless the person has a well established repertoire of communication skills and is used to dealing with many people and many potentially frustrating circumstances all at the same time. Gary initially lacked this repertoire, and consequently, when he experienced frustration at the mall, he immediately regressed to his usual way of dealing with frustration, namely, self-injury and aggression. When things got out of hand at the mall, Mrs. Ibsen did not have many options left to her because she was being pressured by others to end the crisis situation. If she had been at home, she might have been able to wait for Gary to calm down and then have prompted him to request assistance. She could have used the crisis as an opportunity for teaching Gary to expand and practice his newly acquired communication skills. At the mall, her only option was to leave. Having realized that the difficulties arose because of the uncontrolled aspects of the shopping mall, Mrs. Ibsen was right to change her programming to the more controlled situation represented by the home. She could gradually extend Gary's skills across a variety of tasks and people without having to worry about being pressured to stop working with Gary when a crisis arose.

It is important to stress that regardless of whether Mrs. Ibsen was working in the more controlled home situation or the less controlled shopping mall situation, she always chose naturalistic situations in which to teach Gary. The tasks, people, and settings involved were always related to situations that Gary could be expected to encounter in his daily life. This strategy made sense to Mrs. Ibsen because her ultimate goal was to help Gary to be as fully integrated into normal community living as possible. In the past, teachers of persons with disabilities would sometimes choose arbitrary tasks to work on such as putting pegs in a board or stringing beads. These teachers felt that the type of task did not matter very much as long as the person with disabilities got a lot of practice dealing with frustration in an educational context. Although the teachers were well intentioned, these types of tasks were not useful because they seldom, if ever, were an important part of daily living in the community. Therefore, even when the person with disabilities learned to ask for assistance in the context of performing such tasks, this communication skill typically did not generalize to the broader community environment because the types of tasks in real life were dramatically different from the limited ones taught in the classroom. By carefully choosing tasks, people, and settings so that they were representative of community living situations, Mrs. Ibsen avoided those generalization difficulties.

Multiple Situations   A critical part of generalization programming for Gary involved the use of *multiple* naturalistic situations. Mrs. Ibsen ensured that many different people taught Gary a
number of tasks in a wide variety of community settings. Much
research has shown that if you do not program generalization in
enough situations, the person with disabilities is relatively unlikely
to transfer his or her newly acquired skills to all the situations that
are desirable. Nevertheless, as Mrs. Ibsen's experience with Gary
showed, when you program generalization in a number of situations, you begin to see skills transfer to new situations that were
not involved in training. For example, after Gary was taught to use
his communication skills in several different settings, he generalized these same skills to new settings without the need for additional programming.

The principles of generalization programming that we have
been discussing are also applicable to problem behavior that is attention-seeking or tangible-seeking. Gary, for the most part, displayed problem behavior in order to escape from situations that he
found undesirable. Val and Juan, however, used problem behavior
primarily for attention and tangibles, respectively. For Val, Joan began intervention in a fairly controlled situation, with Val and Joan
working together in a corner of the classroom, and moved gradually
to less controlled situations such as the gymnasium, where many
different activities were taking place and large numbers of students
and staff were constantly coming and going. Joan, like Mrs. Ibsen,
took steps to ensure that Val was taught by many different people
on many different tasks across many different settings. The naturalistic situations that were chosen for generalization programming involved other students and staff in work and leisure activities. In
each situation, the focus was on Val's asking for attention rather
than aggressing and tantrumming to get attention. For Juan, Bill began with the controlled situation of Juan and Bill alone in the
kitchen and moved to less controlled situations such as Juan riding
on a minivan with the other residents from his home. Bill also
made sure that Juan practiced asking for a variety of items (instead
of aggressing) with many other people while engaged in a variety
of tasks in many different naturalistic settings. Both Val and Juan
showed unprogrammed generalization after programmed generalization had been carried out in a number of different situations.

It is important to emphasize that just as we use multiple intervention approaches to deal with multiple instances of problem behavior earlier in intervention, for example, teaching a person to ask
for assistance in one situation but to request tangibles in a different
situation, it is necessary when programming for generalization to
ensure that different skills are taught in different situations be-

cause, across situations, problem behavior is very likely to be controlled by more than one factor. Therefore, for example, it might be necessary to program generalization for Val in the supermarket by teaching her to ask for assistance in locating an item, but in the park, it might be necessary to program attention-seeking, and in the fast food restaurant, programming requests for tangibles might be needed. Typically, as parents, teachers, and group home staff program generalization in more and more situations, the procedures become routine and not very time-consuming. Most important of all is the gratification that comes from seeing the person with disabilities functioning successfully in the community by influencing others through communication skills rather than problem behavior.

We cannot emphasize enough that the focus on generalization provides a major way of achieving the ultimate goal of intervention, namely, lifestyle change. Joan, Mrs. Ibsen, and Bill were not satisfied that Val, Gary, and Juan eventually showed very little problem behavior. They wanted to promote community integration as well. They ensured that Val, Gary, and Juan generalized their skills to a wide variety of situations including the supermarket, neighborhood parks, fast food restaurants, swimming pools, and shopping malls. Val, Gary, and Juan had been living a life in which they were excluded from most community activities. Now, their lives changed for the better. In these many community settings, Val, Gary, and Juan encountered many people who did not have disabilities. Cashiers and other staff at supermarkets and shopping malls began to recognize Val, Gary, and Juan and greeted them and engaged them in conversation. Val, Gary, and Juan participated in a wider variety of activities than ever before as they learned to shop, swim, and order food, all with appropriate support from Joan, Mrs. Ibsen, and Bill. Val, Gary, and Juan became a part of their neighborhood community.

✔ CHECKLIST OF THINGS TO DO

1. Begin programming generalization in controlled situations and then gradually move to less controlled situations. A controlled situation is one that contains relatively few signals for problem behavior and few distracting stimuli. A controlled situation is also one in which it is possible to manage a crisis (should one develop) without having to leave because of social pressure, danger, or embarrassment.

(continued)

2. Always program generalization in naturalistic situations, which are situations that the person with disabilities encounters or is likely to encounter in his or her daily life in the community.
3. Use many different naturalistic situations when programming generalization. Programming should occur across a variety of tasks, people, and settings.
4. Remember that for most individuals with disabilities, problem behavior serves more than one purpose. Therefore, generalization programming should take into account that different situations probably require the teaching of different skills.
5. Monitor for success. Success means that the individual is displaying a wide variety of communication-based skills across many tasks, people, and settings in the community without displaying any significant problem behavior in these situations. As a result, the individual experiences a broader, more normalized lifestyle. Success also means that the desired generalization is occurring in new situations that were not involved in the original programming, which means that unprogrammed generalization is also taking place.

GENERALIZATION FAILURES

Generalization sometimes fails to occur despite your best efforts. We have found three common reasons for generalization failure: 1) inadequate rapport, 2) lack of an adequate functional assessment, and 3) the presence of strong signals for problem behavior that overpower the effects of intervention efforts. Each of these difficulties can be overcome, as the following examples make clear.

Example: Inadequate Rapport. Val

Early in the course of programming generalization, Joan noticed repeated failures when new people came to work with Val. Substitute teachers, volunteers, and new staff were frequently unable to get Val to use her communication skills. Instead, Val became quite aggressive and often seemed to be using problem behavior to get attention from her classmates and, even more so, from other staff whom she knew in the school. Joan made a point of discretely observing Val interacting with new people without Val seeing her. It became apparent to Joan that the difficulty was due to a lack of rapport between Val and the new people. Many of the communication skills that Val had been taught were intended to help Val get attention from other people. The assumption was that attention from those people was a reinforcer. This assumption turned out not to be operating in the case of new people. When Joan watched Val, she noticed that Val appeared indifferent to the new people and did not make eye contact with them or try to stay close to them. When they approached her, Val frequently walked away and tried to talk to the other students or people she knew who happened to be passing in the hallway. She rarely smiled or laughed in the presence of these new people and would sometimes ask when Joan was coming back. Val seemed not to care about these people and was therefore not motivated to communicate with them because she did not value their attention. In contrast, disrupting the class by aggressing against the other students was successful in getting attention from them (a longstanding reinforcer for Val), and occasionally major disruption resulted in other school staff (whom Val knew) coming into the classroom to help out. This type of attention was also a reinforcer for Val. Joan concluded that it was necessary for the new staff to establish rapport with Val so that she would be motivated to seek out their attention using her established communication skills. Joan helped the new staff implement a program in which they made themselves into signals for reinforcement, approach, and simple communication all within the context of shared interests. When this program had been in place for several days, Val began to show all the behaviors associated with successful rapport-building such as trying to stay close to the new people, making eye contact with them, and initiating interactions with them. Val now appeared to value their attention. Now, when these people prompted functional communication, Val used her communication skills to get attention and soon used those skills spontaneously. Her problem behaviors became rare in the presence of new people. Generalization failure gave way to generalization success.

Comment: Rapport-Building Is an Ongoing Part of Intervention

Communication skills are most likely to be used when they allow access to valued reinforcers. As the example with Val illustrates, attention from new people is not necessarily a reinforcer. This is not surprising because for most of us gaining the attention of people whom we scarcely know is typically not a reinforcer. People with disabilities react just as we would. When Val's communication skills did not help her to get the attention of someone she liked, she reverted to getting attention from other students and school staff by being aggressive. When her communication skills were no longer useful, she instead used her aggressive behavior to get attention as she had successfully done in the past. Generalization of the intervention effects of high levels of communication accompanied by low levels of problem behavior failed to occur in the presence of new people. Only when those people built rapport with Val did generalization occur. Rapport-building resulted in making attention from new people valuable to her. Therefore, it became easy for new people to prompt Val to use her functional communicative repertoire. In a short time, Val needed no prompts and displayed this repertoire spontaneously.

Example: Lack of an Adequate Functional Assessment. Gary

Gary became quite good at handling frustration in task situations, and he asked for a break or help as appropriate. Therefore, Mrs. Ibsen assumed that programming generalization to the school setting would be easy. The gym period at school had always been especially difficult for Gary. After a discussion with Mrs. Ibsen, Gary's gym teacher, Paul, decided to teach him to ask for breaks during various exercise activities, but Gary resisted the gym teacher's efforts. When Gary was given a break, he frequently responded by becoming even more aggressive to his classmates as well as to Paul. Paul decided to watch Gary more closely over several days to determine why generalization programming was not working. Paul ruled out rapport as a factor because he and Gary had an excellent relationship. Over time, Paul noticed that whenever he gave Gary a break, Gary would try to remain close to him and attempt to initiate conversations. Gary would sometimes try to leave the gym but, before he did, he would wait until Paul chased after him. When Gary aggressed against a classmate, he almost always did so when Paul was watching him. When this happened, Paul would run over and try to move Gary away from the victim. By carefully monitoring Gary's behavior and the reactions it produced from other people (including himself), Paul concluded that Gary's aggressive behavior in the gymnasium served a different purpose than the same behavior at home. At home, it was clear that aggression was a form of escape, but in the gym it was clear that it was a form of attention-seeking. In other words, the functional assessment that had been carried out at home was not relevant to the situation in the gym. Only when the assessment was repeated in the gym was the attention-seeking function of the behavior there determined. When Paul had determined that Gary's aggression in the gym was maintained by attention, he taught Gary new phrases such as "Chase me," and "Play ball with me," that enabled him to effectively solicit attention in that setting. These phrases, chosen as a result of the new assessment, were effective in reducing Gary's aggressive behavior to negligible levels.

Comment: Functional Assessment Is an Ongoing Part of Intervention

You have now seen the reason why we have repeatedly said that functional assessment is not something that can be done once and then discontinued. The same problem can serve more than one purpose depending on the situation in which it occurs. Gary's aggression at home was frequently a form of escape in the face of demands, but the same behavior in the gym was a form of attention-seeking. Unless additional functional assessments are carried out, you, as a teacher, parent, or group home staff-person may not fully identify all the various purposes that a particular problem behavior serves. Since intervention selection and success depend on a functional assessment, inadequate or incomplete assessments often result in the failure of previously successful interventions to generalize, even if generalization is carefully programmed. Generalization failures should therefore be a cue for you to ask whether you are assuming that a problem behavior has a particular purpose when in fact it does not. If your assumption is wrong, then you need to do an additional functional assessment just as Gary's teacher did. If the assessment indicates that the problem behavior does indeed serve a different purpose than you had thought, you need to develop a new intervention strategy to ensure successful generalization. When Gary's teacher changed strategies, Gary's aggression was quickly eliminated in the gym.

Example: Presence of Strong Signals for Problem Behavior. Juan

Juan was asking for breaks during his exercise routine and generalization had been successfully programmed across many group home staff. Juan frequently communicated his request for a break after a reasonable number of exercises had been completed and he was rarely aggressive. One day, Dave, who had worked with Juan a long time ago in another group home, was transferred to Juan's home. Dave was trained to use the communication-based intervention with Juan. From the beginning, however, Juan responded to Dave with explosive outbursts of screaming, kicking, and hitting. The attempt to program generalization to Dave failed. At a staff meeting at which the problem was discussed, Dave revealed that he had been Juan's primary support staff person at Juan's former home. Since the communication-based approach was not in effect at that home, Dave had frequently been in the position of having to restrain Juan to protect other residents as well as to try to calm him down. Because Juan did not like to be restrained, even temporarily, he and Dave had often been involved in unpleasant physical struggles that took place in an atmosphere of screaming and agitated behavior on the part of other residents. Because of this history, Dave gradually became a powerful signal for problem behavior on the part of Juan. It was not uncommon for Juan to strike out at Dave the moment that Dave came to work or to avoid Dave by leaving the room whenever Dave entered. Juan's current group home staff realized that the problem was the result of poor rapport. Dave was not a neutral person to Juan the way that a stranger would be but he had acquired negative attributes that functioned as a signal for aggression. To remedy this difficulty, the staff developed a rapport-building program in which Dave was gradually associated with a variety of items Juan enjoyed. Because Dave and Juan both enjoyed neighborhood walks and many of the same snack foods, these two individuals spent a lot of time together participating in these mutually enjoyable activities and Juan helped Dave to pop corn, make hot chocolate, and heat up turnovers. Juan began to approach Dave when he entered the room, stayed close to Dave, and initiated simple requests. In other words, rapport was built and Dave ceased being a signal for problem behavior. When this goal had been achieved, Dave was able to program generalization quickly using the communication-based strategies that he had been taught earlier.

Comment: Additional Contributions of Rapport-Building

The relationship between two individuals can be described as negative, neutral, or positive, but successful communication depends on positive rapport. Therefore, building rapport must be undertaken when a neutral or negative relationship exists between people. In the example involving Val and her substitute teacher, difficulties arose because of a lack of rapport or a neutral relationship. The substitute teacher was not a signal for problem behavior for Val the way Dave was for Juan. However, because the substitute teacher was also not a signal for approach and communication, rapport-building was indicated. In the example of Juan, however, the difficulty involved a negative relationship. A negative relationship commonly results from a situation in which two people have a long history that is characterized by frequent, unpleasant social interaction. After a time, the person with disabilities learns to use problem behavior to terminate further contact with the individual with whom he or she has been having the unpleasant interactions. These people, like Dave, become powerful signals for problem behavior. Such negative rapport is a poor starting point for communication-based intervention, and the presence of such powerful signals for problem behavior typically overwhelms the effect that any of the more positive signals associated with appropriate behavior may have. For example, Dave found that even when he tried to prompt Juan to ask for a break, Juan would ignore the prompt and instead attack Dave physically. Dave and the group home staff were therefore correct in returning to the very beginning of intervention by having Dave gradually build a more positive relationship. Through rapport-building, Dave slowly became a signal for approach and simple communication rather than aggression and avoidance.

To summarize, we have often found that generalization of communication skills to situations with a history of problem behavior is more difficult to achieve than generalization to situations that have no such history. When you encounter such a situation, it is best not to attempt to program generalization immediately but rather to try to decrease the signals for problem behavior that already exist using rapport-building and related strategies.

Redesigning the Environment There is one additional issue worth considering. It is sometimes possible to prevent generalization failures by redesigning the environment so that signals for problem behavior are no longer present. For example, if Dave were the only person with whom Juan had a negative relationship that evoked aggression, then it might be possible to reassign Dave to a different group home and assign a new person in his place who was not a signal for aggression. This solution can be quick and efficient and there are circumstances in which it is warranted, for example, if Dave were not a critical staff person for Juan to work with and if reassigning Dave were an administratively simple matter. However, if a person cannot be reassigned, then it is necessary to carry out rapport-building. It can be argued that it is important in general to rebuild negative relationships because it is likely that a person with disabilities who has been exhibiting severe aggression and self-injury for a long time will have negative relationships with quite a few people. This being the case, it is better to address the difficulty directly through rapport-building than to attempt to avoid the issue through repeated staff changes. Rebuilding formerly negative relationships may be seen as part of the process of eliminating many signals for problem behavior, which further extends successful generalization programming.

✔ CHECKLIST OF THINGS TO DO

1. Evaluate whether generalization failure has occurred. Failure means that although carefully programmed intervention has been successful in the past, you do not currently see increases in functional communication and decreases in problem behavior with respect to new people, new tasks, or new settings.

2. If there has been generalization failure, determine if the new people who have been asked to carry out intervention have neutral rather than good rapport with the person who has disabilities. If so, have them carry out the rapport-building procedures before proceeding with communication-based intervention.

(continued)

3. If generalization failure is not due to neutral rapport, carry out a functional assessment in the new situation to determine if the purpose of problem behavior in this situation is the same as that in situations in which interventions have been successful. If the purpose is not the same, redesign intervention to reflect the new purpose and then proceed with communication-based intervention.

4. Determine if the generalization situation contains powerful signals for problem behavior that overwhelm the effects of intervention. If so, redesign the situation to exclude these signals. If this strategy is not feasible or desirable, then alter the signals so that they no longer evoke problem behavior. For example, if a person is a signal for problem behavior because of a long-standing negative relationship with the person who has disabilities, then initiate rapport-building procedures to change the negative relationship. When these steps have been taken, proceed with communication-based intervention.

5. Monitor for success. Success means that increases in communication and corresponding decreases in problem behavior are now routinely achieved in those situations in which generalization programming had previously failed.

Chapter 14

Maintenance

Maintenance refers to how well the intervention effects last over time ("intervention durability," in scientific terminology). Consider a young man with mental retardation whose self-injury and aggression were reduced through communication-based intervention. His problem behaviors decreased to negligible levels in a variety of different situations, indicating that generalization had occurred. If, however, his problem behaviors suddenly increase again and remain frequent, then we would say that the intervention effects did not maintain. Parents, teachers, and residential staff, among others, are seldom satisfied with interventions whose effects do not maintain well over time. Many of the procedures that we have described are included partly because the scientific literature suggests that they are important factors in producing maintenance. The procedures of greatest interest relate to teaching functional skills and using intermittent reinforcers to strengthen those skills.

MAINTENANCE AND FUNCTIONAL SKILL DEVELOPMENT

Much research demonstrates that teaching functional skills is a good idea because, among other reasons, these skills are likely to maintain over time. Functional skills are those that allow an individual to get what he or she wants reliably and efficiently in daily life. For example, if a young girl with autism is especially interested in drawing pictures, then teaching her to request crayons and paints constitutes functional skill training. In contrast, teaching her to name animals when she has shown no interest in doing so represents teaching a nonfunctional skill. Because the latter skill does not produce a reinforcing outcome for the girl, it would be surprising if she were to use that skill over time, and research does demonstrate poor maintenance following such training. However, since crayons and paints are powerful reinforcers for her, the girl could be expected to use her newly taught communication skills to request these items and to continue to do so for as long as such items

were of interest to her, and research demonstrates good maintenance following this type of skill training. To continue the example, imagine that at first the girl did not know how to request the
paints and crayons because she had not yet been taught how to
request them. She had learned, like too many people with disabilities, to obtain desired items by throwing herself on the floor,
screaming, and striking out at others. People treated her behavior
as if it was a primitive way of requesting drawing supplies and
responded to the problem behavior by providing the relevant items.
In other words, the problem behavior had become functional because others responded to it positively by providing what she
wanted. Sadly, problem behavior has excellent maintenance properties and left untreated, it often persists for years. The whole logic
of communication-based intervention is to provide an individual
with new communication skills that are functionally equivalent to
problem behavior and, in fact, more efficient than such behavior in
obtaining desired outcomes. By teaching the young girl in our example to make requests that serve the same function as problem
behavior, we make such problem behavior unnecessary, particularly if the requests are more efficient than the tantrums in getting
what she wants. We have made this point repeatedly, but what is
important is that functional communication skills not only replace
problem behavior in the short run but continue to do so in the long
run. Maintenance of communication skills occurs because those
skills reliably and efficiently permit the person with disabilities to
get what is important to him or her on a regular basis. To put it
another way, if an individual can get what he or she wants simply
by making a request, then why would that individual ever stop
making those requests? If making requests is highly successful, then
why would the individual ever revert to the potentially less reliable
and inefficient mode of requesting through self-injury, aggression,
and tantrums? The answer to these two questions is that individuals frequently show long-term use of requests and long-term suppression or even elimination of problem behavior following functional skills training. Apparently, maintenance and functional skill
development go hand in hand.

MAINTENANCE AND INTERMITTENT REINFORCEMENT

There is another issue implicit in the procedures that we have described in this book that is also relevant to producing maintenance.
This concerns the use of intermittent reinforcement to strengthen
functional skills. As you may recall, when communication skills
are first taught, the individual using them may make requests very
frequently. We recommended that in the early stages of interven-

tion, parents and teachers, for example, should honor each request by providing the requested reinforcer. Thus, if a boy with mental retardation has learned to request his favorite music instead of engaging in self-injury to get others to provide the music, then parents and teachers should respond to each request by allowing the boy access to the music. Technically, providing a reinforcer for each request is referred to as "continuous reinforcement." We suggested that arranging for continuous reinforcement for requests was a good idea at the beginning of training because it would help strengthen valuable functional skills that compete with problem behavior. We noted that, eventually, however, parents and teachers get tired of honoring every request, and they do not like to be nagged. That is why we suggested the use of several procedures to teach the individual to tolerate delays of reinforcement. As you recall, individuals learn that not every request pays off. When the procedure is properly applied, requests pay off only intermittently, hence, the technical term "intermittent reinforcement." Thus, in our example, the boy's mother may eventually allow her son access to music only after he has completed a number of chores around the house. Should he request music several times during the course of completing his chores (a likely possibility), his mother would assure him that the music will be available just as soon as he completes his chores. The boy would have made several requests for music, only one of which is honored. If the procedure is repeated over many days, the boy is experiencing intermittent reinforcement of his requests. We suggested that the delay procedures were welcomed by most parents and teachers because these procedures have the effect of gradually reducing nagging when the individual has learned that multiple requests no longer are honored every time. In addition, the delay procedures are important for another reason besides reducing nagging. There are many demonstrations in the scientific literature showing that skills that have been strengthened using intermittent reinforcement maintain much better than those that have been strengthened using continuous reinforcement. There are technical explanations for this finding but, in terms of everyday experience, you can appreciate that you are much more likely to persist in doing something that has paid off only intermittently in the past (putting money in a slot machine and winning occasionally) than to persist in doing something that has continuously paid off in the past (putting money in a vending machine) but suddenly no longer does so (the machine breaks and you lose your money). Generally, the world is structured in such a way that intermittent reinforcement is a more common occurrence for most of us (especially with respect to requests) than continuous reinforcement. Therefore, skill training that emphasizes the use of intermittent reinforcement provides better preparation for living in the real world than training that emphasizes continuous reinforcement. Most important, good maintenance of functional communication skills helps to ensure good maintenance of problem behavior reduction, an outcome valued by everyone who is involved.

As noted, functionality and intermittent reinforcement are two issues related to maintenance that are covered implicitly in earlier sections of this book. There are, however, some additional issues that arise in the context of trying to achieve intervention durability and we examine several of these next.

MAINTENANCE PROBLEMS ARE SOMETIMES REALLY GENERALIZATION PROBLEMS

Even if you adhere closely to all the intervention recommendations made in this book, you will find, sooner or later, that problem behaviors are likely to occur again even after they have been eliminated for some time. At first, this situation may make you think that the interventions are no longer effective and need to be replaced with new ones. This may occasionally be true and you may need to develop new procedures, but generally it is not true. The procedures that you have been using are indeed adequate to do the job. If you look at the situation closely, you will often find that the problem is one of generalization, not maintenance.

In the section on generalization failure, we noted that if rapport is inadequate, generalization may not occur. Consider the example of Val. When Val encountered a substitute teacher with whom she had no rapport, problem behavior often reoccurred. It is easy to imagine a situation in which Val was successful in using her communication skills for a year or more without showing problem behavior and, then, due to administrative changes, new staff are brought in who have not yet established rapport with Val. If Val then reverts to tantrums and aggression, does that mean that the communication-based intervention is poor at producing maintenance and therefore needs to be replaced with new procedures? Of course not—what is required is that the new staff carry out the rapport-building procedures and then continue with the other interventions. The problem involves generalization failure, or the failure of intervention effects to transfer to new people, rather than maintenance failure, or failure of the intervention itself to produce a lasting effect.

MAINTENANCE PROBLEMS SOMETIMES RESULT FROM A DOUBLE STANDARD

From time to time, most of us become frustrated and angry, particularly when we encounter various obstacles in our daily lives. If our car stalls on a freezing winter morning, we may in exasperation kick one of the tires. If a vending machine jams and we lose our dollar bill, we may pound the side of the machine. If the Internal Revenue Service sends us a letter informing us that we will be audited, we may curse. If we have a splitting headache and one of our children refuses to go to bed at the regular time, preferring instead to race around the house pretending to be a spaceship, we may scream. Do these situations mean that we have problem behavior and therefore need an intervention? Most people would answer that unless we show such severe behavior frequently, no intervention is required. However, when people with disabilities show problem behavior in equally frustrating circumstances, there is a tendency to claim that some intervention must be implemented. This is using a double standard. Of course, it is true that we have concentrated on frequent and severe problem behavior. Thus, if a person with disabilities responds to a jammed vending machine by increasing incidents of head-banging that draw blood and require hospitalization, then some type of intervention is needed to avoid repeated occurrences of such behavior in the future. However, consider a situation in which a 4-year-old child with disabilities who once had a severe behavior problem was successfully taught to use communication skills (using the procedures we have been describing) instead of problem behavior. Following a period of 3 months in which there were no problem behaviors, the child's favorite toy breaks. The child responds with 5 minutes of screaming accompanied by intermittent light face-slapping. Does this situation constitute a failure of maintenance? Do we now say that a communication-based approach produces poor intervention durability? If the child did not have disabilities, we might express concern over how upset the child was and we might even go out and purchase a replacement for the broken toy. However, we would not be likely to institute a program of intervention. Unfortunately, we apply a different standard for the child with disabilities. Because that child once engaged in frequent and severe problem behavior, we regard any new outburst, however justifiable, as a dangerous situation that requires intervention. We begin to question whether the intervention that had been used successfully in the past was in fact successful at all, given the relapse. We may conclude that the intervention should not be recommended because it is associated with maintenance problems.

To be honest, we ought to apply the same standards to people with disabilities as we do to people without disabilities. Unless an individual shows severe and frequent bouts of problem behavior, we ought to assume that occasional instances of mild to moderate aggression, tantrums, or even self-injury may simply represent a response to frustration that may be seen in any person. Judgment is involved in this process, and concerned people such as teachers, parents, residential staff, and significant others in the community need to arrive at consensus as to what level of problem behavior is acceptable by community standards. Problem behavior that falls outside of those standards may require new or additional interventions and the possibility that the intervention was indeed a failure may need to be considered. However, it may be that the community is intolerant and has excessively strict standards, and some thought can be given to relaxing those standards through a process of public education and marshalling the support of community leaders. The adoption of more tolerant standards by the community may eliminate the need for changing the nature of intervention, thereby eliminating the issue of maintenance failure in many cases. To summarize, it is seldom reasonable to set as the goal of intervention the total elimination of all problem behavior for an indefinite time period. By tolerating occasional episodes of problem behavior under justifiable circumstances, we may find that genuine maintenance failures are in fact infrequent and that the intervention procedures generally do not need to be replaced with others.

MAINTENANCE FAILURE DUE TO BOREDOM

Although you have been conscientiously carrying out all relevant intervention procedures, you may sometimes find that the person with whom you are working gradually shows increasing levels of problem behavior even when such behavior had been eliminated for weeks or even months. The example that follows illustrates this situation.

Example: Val

Val no longer displayed tantrums and aggression while sorting clothes, washing them, and then putting them away because Joan had changed her relationship with Val through communication training and redesigning the social environment. Although communication-based intervention had successfully replaced all problem behavior for 6 months, and although the intervention was still in effect, Joan began to notice that week by week Val's behavior was steadily deteriorating. At first, Val worked more slowly at the laundry task, often failing to complete her chores, for example, walking away after she had folded only half the clothes. Then, she began to scream when Joan asked her to finish the job. Joan found in a few weeks that she had to prompt Val physically in order to get her to continue working. These prompts soon led to Val's throwing clothes across the room, spitting at Joan, and occasionally grabbing Joan's hair. Because Joan had been careful to keep in place all the elements of intervention that had so far been successful, she could not understand Val's worsening behavior. After watching Val closely for a few weeks and discussing the issue with other staff who were present during the laundry chore, Joan decided that the real issue was boredom on Val's part. She and Val had done the same laundry task together for months on end. Joan found that, without being aware of it, she had fallen into the trap of making the chore dull and repetitive. She found herself using the same jokes to motivate Val week after week. She engaged in the same topics of conversation, talking about Val's art work, her weekend activities, her cosmetics. She even sang the same songs with Val time and again. Joan reflected that if she had to live her own life in such a dull, repetitive way, then she too might be tempted to scream and avoid certain chores. In a word, Joan decided that Val was bored. The solution now seemed obvious to Joan: introduce flexibility and variety into the daily routine. Joan found some new things to joke with Val about while doing the laundry and she made sure to vary the nature of her joking every few days at a minimum. Joan also tried her best to keep her conversations with Val fresh and interesting. Joan asked Val's mother what important things for Val were happening at home. She asked other school staff who worked with Val the same question. In her own daily interactions with Val, Joan was constantly on the lookout for events that could lead to interesting conversations. Joan kept in mind all the information that she had gathered and used it to pick conversational topics that Val would enjoy while doing the laundry chore. Joan learned new songs to sing with Val and brought a variety of tapes and sometimes a radio to the laundry room in order to keep things lively. Finally, Joan arranged for other staff to substitute for her occasionally so that Val would have new partners to converse with while doing the laundry. When all these changes had been made, Val seemed enthusiastic again about completing her chores. The intervention procedures suddenly seemed to work again and problem behaviors disappeared. Val did her chores efficiently and quickly and was again happily engaged in social interactions with her laundry partners.

Comment: Reinforcer Satiation

Most of us find repetitive tasks such as laundry boring and aversive. We should therefore not be surprised to discover that people with disabilities react the same way to such tasks. It is easy to get into a rut in such situations. Parents, teachers, and others frequently find

that it is easier to go on "automatic" in boring situations and carry
out tasks in a rigid, repetitive fashion. This strategy does not work
when you are trying to prevent problem behaviors from recurring
in people with disabilities. For example, Val enjoyed the jokes, conversation, and singing that she received as a consequence of using
her functional communication skills. These forms of attention
helped to reduce the aversiveness of demand situations for her,
greatly limiting problem behaviors that served an escape function.
It follows that if these forms of attention are no longer interesting
to Val (lose their "reinforcing properties," in technical terms), then
an individual may revert to problem behaviors that in the past have
generated a variety of reinforcers or forms of attention. In technical
terms, the loss of reinforcer effectiveness may be due to a process
of "reinforcer satiation." This means that basically too much of a
good thing is not necessarily good. To illustrate, if you are hungry
and you like cake, the first one or two pieces may be powerful reinforcers for a variety of behaviors related to eating. However, if you
are given a third, fourth, and fifth piece, you at first become satiated
and then nauseated. Cake will no longer function as a reinforcer
and, more likely than not, you will exhibit behaviors associated
with leaving the dining situation rather than remaining in it. A similar process takes place with respect to attention. At first, Val appeared to enjoy the jokes and conversational topics, but after a
while she was satiated with these same jokes and conversations.
What at first had been something she desired soon became an aversive event. In the beginning, Val was eager to participate in the
laundry chore and its associated reinforcing social interactions. In
the end, Val was eager to avoid the chore and the associated social
interactions that were no longer reinforcing. Problem behavior previously was Val's most successful means for terminating unpleasant
situations. Therefore, following satiation of specific forms of attention, Val reverted to screaming and aggression, which had successfully extricated her in the past from aversive situations as well as
generated attention from those around her. It is important to emphasize that most of us would probably behave as Val did in this
same situation. Having to listen to the same jokes and same conversation topics for many months would provide a powerful motive
for escape behavior and avoidance of any chores associated with
such dull and repetitive social interactions. In such circumstances,
most of us would attempt to inject new life into the task scenario
and that was the strategy that Joan followed. By varying jokes, conversation topics, songs, and personnel, Joan prevented reinforcer
satiation, thereby reducing escape behavior as well as attention-
seeking problem behavior. Maintenance failure due to boredom
was reversed.

MAINTENANCE FAILURE DUE TO
INADEQUATE SOCIAL SUPPORT SYSTEMS

The social relationships that constitute the core of communication-based intervention do not occur in a vacuum. When parents, teachers, and group home staff are called upon to respond to the communicative efforts of the person with disabilities, many factors determine how well they respond or whether they will respond at all. If the person conducting intervention does a poor job of continuing intervention or stops the intervention altogether, then it is reasonable to expect maintenance failure. Maintaining intervention effects is not possible unless the people conducting the intervention themselves maintain intervention efforts. Breakdowns are likely to occur when the social systems in which parents, teachers, and residential staff live and work are inadequate to support intervention efforts. For example, parents who experience marital discord, chronic depression, or health problems are frequently so distracted by these difficulties that they are unlikely to maintain intervention efforts for long. Thus, if a mother goes into a protracted period of depression, her ability to carry out intervention consistently and for long periods of time is reduced and, more often than not, the consequences are a return of problem behavior in the person with disabilities. Clearly, in this situation as well as in the others mentioned, maintenance failure needs to be addressed by first providing social support systems that can address the depression or marital or health problems. Likewise, if teachers and group home staff find themselves with disorganized or, perhaps, hostile administrative supervisors, then these interpersonal problems are likely to undermine the consistency and longevity of intervention efforts. Again, maintenance failures are likely. Clearly, maintenance failure in this situation needs to be addressed first through administrative reorganization, personnel changes, or problem-solving discussion groups. An example helps to illustrate some of the points just made.

Example: Gary

Mrs. Ibsen had learned a long time ago that raising a child with disabilities can be an exhausting and demanding task. Like most parents in her situation, however, Mrs. Ibsen was able to have a satisfying family life and marriage. She enjoyed Gary and her other children. Nevertheless, from time to time Mrs. Ibsen felt a sense of social isolation. The many additional demands posed by Gary sometimes made it difficult for her to get together socially with other women or, for that matter, with her husband. Mrs. Ibsen began to feel depressed when this situation occurred frequently. When she was depressed, she found it difficult to be responsive to

Gary. Unfortunately, Gary would then react by engaging in problem behavior. Mrs. Ibsen realized after a while that these relapses (maintenance failures) on Gary's part were really the result of her undesirable social situation more than anything else. Therefore, she decided to join a social support group involving other mothers who had children with disabilities. When she heard other mothers talking about problems similar to hers, she felt less isolated. She also got some ideas from the other mothers about how to cope better. One idea concerned respite care. Several mothers had discovered that they could hire local college students to come to their homes a few hours a week to be with their children. Some mothers were able to persuade their local relatives to provide respite care. In either case, this time gave the mothers an opportunity to schedule visits, shopping expeditions with their friends, and other activities. Respite also allowed them an opportunity to go out with their husbands several Saturday nights per month. When Mrs. Ibsen arranged for respite care, she found that although her break was only a few hours a week, she looked forward to that time and it helped rejuvenate her. She enjoyed having regular and reliable contact with her friends. She and her husband also appreciated being able to focus on each other instead of only on their children and problems related to their children. Her periods of depression became very rare. As a consequence of her improved social opportunities, she felt more energetic and better able to focus on Gary. Gary's relapses became infrequent and his communicative exchanges with his mother were positive and engaging.

Comment: Support for People Who Support People with Disabilities

Most parents become tired, get depressed, or feel lonely from time to time. In these circumstances, it is too much to expect them to conscientiously carry out a lengthy and time-consuming series of interventions for problem behavior. Just as people with disabilities need to be supported, so also do the parents, teachers, direct support staff, and others responsible for helping and teaching them. As we have said so often, parents and others are not vending machines dispensing reinforcers whenever needed. Parents have personal and social needs and when these are not met, maintenance failure becomes more likely. Just as we construct social systems that support appropriate behavior in people with disabilities, so we also must construct social systems that support parents, teachers, and others who carry out the interventions. Intervention is not simply something that we do to a person with disabilities. Intervention is an altered social relationship between people with disabilities and people without disabilities. Part of that altered relationship involves providing for the needs of parents and others so that they will be better able to respond to the needs of people with disabilities. It may sometimes be necessary to change the social support system so that it more favorably affects parents, teachers, and residential staff. For example, the support system was altered to provide more opportunities for Mrs. Ibsen to socialize with her friends and her husband. This change reduced the frequency of her episodes of depression, enabling her to be more responsive to Gary. The result was that Gary showed fewer relapses of problem behavior. The example makes clear that successful maintenance involves building support systems for parents and others in addition to building support systems for the people for whom they care.

✔ CHECKLIST OF THINGS TO DO

1. Evaluate whether maintenance difficulties are occurring, that is, whether problem behaviors are increasing after a period of time in which they disappeared or were infrequent.
2. If there are maintenance difficulties, then evaluate if you have been continuing to teach functional skills and strengthening them using intermittent reinforcement. If not, reinstate functional skill training and the use of intermittent reinforcement.
3. If functionality and intermittent reinforcement are not an issue, then evaluate whether the maintenance difficulty may be due to generalization problems such as inadequate rapport. Reread the section concerning generalization problems for information on how to correct them. If generalization is the issue, then use the appropriate procedures to correct the problem.
4. If generalization is not an issue, then evaluate whether your standards for adequate intervention durability are too strict and whether an unfair double standard is being applied just because the person with disabilities once had a serious behavior problem. If the issue centers on inappropriate standards, change those standards by educating all people involved in the intervention process about what an appropriate and reasonable standard should be.
5. If standards are not the issue, then evaluate whether maintenance failure is due to boredom (reinforcer satiation) on the part of the person with disabilities. If so, introduce more variety into the living situation thereby preventing overexposure (satiation) to the relevant reinforcers.
6. If reinforcer satiation is not an issue, evaluate whether maintenance failure is due to inadequate social support systems for parents,

(continued)

teachers, residential staff, and others. If so, change the structure of these systems so that these are more conducive to supporting the intervention efforts of these people.

7. Consider the possibility that circumstances may arise in which several or perhaps all of the issues just described are relevant to particular individuals. For example, maintenance difficulties may arise because of *simultaneous* problems with standards, reinforcer satiation, and social support systems. If this situation occurs, you will need to address all of these issues together.

8. Monitor for success. Success means that the intervention relapse will be reversed, and once again the person with disabilities shows few if any problem behaviors over time and exhibits his or her functional communication skills consistently and appropriately.

Epilogue

It is unfortunate that for too many people with disabilities exhibiting severe problem behavior is an important way, sometimes the only way, of influencing others. Throughout this book, we have recognized explicitly that problem behaviors may serve important purposes for the individuals displaying them. Therefore, it is critical not to focus efforts simply on eliminating problem behaviors but rather to focus on replacing them with new, socially acceptable behaviors that serve the same purposes as the problem behaviors but do so more efficiently. Education, not behavior reduction, is the real priority. Through education, people with disabilities are better able to achieve their goals without resorting to self-injury and aggression. Through education, people with disabilities are better able to gain more influence over their lives thereby becoming more similar to people without disabilities. Last, and most important, through education, people with disabilities can enter into social relationships with parents, teachers, direct support staff, and other members of the community, relationships that are characterized not by control but by reciprocity, not by passivity but by participation, and not by being a category but by being a friend.

Resource Materials

The ideas and procedures described in this book are drawn from many sources in the professional and scientific literature. We provide some of these sources, referenced by chapter, so that parents, teachers, residential staff, and other professional support staff can follow up on a number of issues in more detail. We also provide sources of information about other educational approaches related to the ones described in this book.

CHAPTER 2. CRISIS MANAGEMENT

Brown, F. (1991). Creative daily scheduling: A nonintrusive approach to challenging behaviors in community residences. *Journal of The Association for Persons with Severe Handicaps, 16*, 75–84.

Dorsey, M.F., Iwata, B.A., Reid, D.H., & Davis, P.A. (1982). Protective equipment: Continuous and contingent application in the treatment of self-injurious behavior. *Journal of Applied Behavior Analysis, 15*, 217–230.

Milan, M.A., Mitchell, Z.P., Berger, M.I., & Pierson, D.F. (1981). Positive routines: A rapid alternative to extinction for elimination of bedtime tantrum behavior. *Child Behavior Therapy, 3*, 13–25.

Silverman, K., Watanabe, K., Marshall, A.M., & Baer, D.M. (1984). Reducing self-injury and corresponding self-restraint through the strategic use of protective clothing. *Journal of Applied Behavior Analysis, 17*, 545–552.

Touchette, P.E., MacDonald, R.F., & Langer, S.N. (1985). A scatter plot for identifying stimulus control of problem behavior. *Journal of Applied Behavior Analysis, 18*, 343–351.

Wacker, D.P., Northup, J., & Kelly, L. (in press). Proactive treatment of self-injurious behavior based on functional analysis. In E. Cipani & N. Singh (Eds.), *Treatment of severe behavior problems: A handbook for practitioners.* New York: Springer-Verlag.

CHAPTER 3. THE PURPOSEFUL NATURE OF PROBLEM BEHAVIOR: CONCEPTUAL AND EMPIRICAL BACKGROUND

Bird, F., Dores, P.A., Moniz, D., & Robinson, J. (1989). Reducing severe aggressive and self-injurious behaviors with functional communication training. *American Journal on Mental Retardation, 94*, 37–48.

Carr, E.G., & Durand, V.M. (1985a). Reducing behavior problems through functional communication training. *Journal of Applied Behavior Analysis, 18*, 111–126.

Carr, E.G., & Durand, V.M. (1985b). The social-communicative basis of severe behavior problems in children. In S. Reiss & R. Bootzin (Eds.), *Theoretical issues in behavior therapy* (pp. 219–254). New York: Academic Press.

Carr, E.G., Robinson, S., Taylor, J.C., & Carlson, J.I. (1990). Positive approaches to the treatment of severe behavior problems in persons with developmental disabilities: A review and analysis of reinforcement and stimulus-based procedures. *Monographs of The Association for Persons with Severe Handicaps, 4.*

Cipani, E. (1990). The communicative function hypothesis: An operant behavior perspective. *Journal of Behavior Therapy and Experimental Psychiatry, 21*, 239–247.

Day, R.M., Rea, J.A., Schussler, N.G., Larsen, S.E., & Johnson, W.L. (1988). A functionally based approach to the treatment of self-injurious behavior. *Behavior Modification, 12*, 565–589.

Doss, S., & Reichle, J. (1989). Establishing communicative alternatives to the emission of socially motivated excess behavior: A review. *Journal of The Association for Persons with Severe Handicaps, 14*, 101–112.

Duker, P.C., Jol, K., & Palmen, A. (1991). The collateral decrease of self-injurious behavior with teaching communicative gestures to individuals who are mentally retarded. *Behavioral Residential Treatment, 6*, 183–196.

Durand, V.M., & Carr, E.G. (1987). Social influences on "self-stimulatory" behavior: Analysis and treatment application. *Journal of Applied Behavior Analysis, 20*, 119–132.

Durand, V.M., & Carr, E.G. (1991). Functional communication training to reduce challenging behavior: Maintenance and application in new settings. *Journal of Applied Behavior Analysis, 24*, 251–256.

Durand, V.M., & Kishi, G. (1987). Reducing severe behavior problems among persons with dual sensory impairments: An evaluation of a technical assistance model. *Journal of The Association for Persons with Severe Handicaps, 12*, 2–10.

Dyer, K. (1993, January). Functional communication training: Review and future directions. *Behavior Therapist*, 18–21.

Goldiamond, I. (1974). Toward a constructional approach to social problems. *Behaviorism, 2*, 1–84.

Horner, R.H., & Budd, C.M. (1985). Acquisition of manual sign use: Collateral reduction of maladaptive behavior, and factors limiting generalization. *Education and Training of the Mentally Retarded, 20*, 39–47.

Horner, R.H., & Day, H.M. (1991). The effects of response efficiency on functionally equivalent competing behaviors. *Journal of Applied Behavior Analysis, 24*, 719–732.

Horner, R.H., Sprague, J.R., O'Brien, M., & Heathfield, L.T. (1990). The role of response efficiency in the reduction of problem behaviors through functional equivalence training: A case study. *Journal of The Association for Persons with Severe Handicaps, 15*, 91–97.

Reichle, J., & Wacker, D. (Eds.). (1993). *Communicative alternatives to challenging behavior: Integrating functional assessment and intervention strategies.* Baltimore: Paul H. Brookes Publishing Co.

Smith, M.D. (1985). Managing the aggressive and self-injurious behavior of adults disabled by autism. *Journal of The Association for Persons with Severe Handicaps, 10*, 228–232.

Wacker, D.P., Steege, M.W., Northup, J., Sasso, G., Berg, W., Reimers, T., Cooper, L., Cigrand, K., & Donn, L. (1990). A component analysis of functional communication training across three topographies of severe behavior problems. *Journal of Applied Behavior Analysis, 23,* 417–429.

CHAPTER 4. FUNCTIONAL ASSESMENT: DESCRIBE
CHAPTER 5. FUNCTIONAL ASSESMENT: CATEGORIZE

Alessi, G. (1988). Direct observation methods for emotional/behavior problems. In E.S. Shapiro & T.R. Kratochwill (Eds.), *Behavioral assessment in schools* (pp. 14–75). New York: The Guilford Press.

Axelrod, S. (1987). Functional and structural analyses of behavior: Approaches leading to reduced use of punishment procedures? *Research in Developmental Disabilities, 8,* 165–178.

Bailey, J.S., & Pyles, D.A.M. (1989). Behavioral diagnostics. In E. Cipani (Ed.), *The treatment of severe behavior disorders* (pp. 85–107). *Monographs of the American Association on Mental Retardation, 12.*

Carr, E.G. (1977). The motivation of self-injurious behavior: A review of some hypotheses. *Psychological Bulletin, 84,* 800–816.

Carr, E.G., & Carlson, J.I. (1993). Reduction of severe behavior problems in the community using a multicomponent treatment approach. *Journal of Applied Behavior Analysis, 26,* 157–172.

Carr, E.G., & McDowell, J.J. (1980). Social control of self-injurious behavior of organic etiology. *Behavior Therapy, 11,* 402–409.

Carr, E.G., & Newsom, C.D. (1985). Demand-related tantrums: Conceptualization and treatment. *Behavior Modification, 9,* 403–426.

Carr, E.G., Newsom, C.D., & Binkoff, J.A. (1976). Stimulus control of self-destructive behavior in a psychotic child. *Journal of Abnormal Child Psychology, 4,* 139–153.

Carr, E.G., Newsom, C.D., & Binkoff, J.A. (1980). Escape as a factor in the aggressive behavior of two retarded children. *Journal of Applied Behavior Analysis, 13,* 101–117.

Cooper, L.J., Wacker, D.P., Sasso, G.M., Reimers, T.M., & Donn, L.K. (1990). Using parents as therapists to evaluate appropriate behavior of their children: Application to a tertiary diagnostic clinic. *Journal of Applied Behavior Analysis, 23,* 285–296.

Dunlap, G., Dunlap, L.K., Clarke, S., & Robbins, F.R. (1991). Functional assessment, curricular revision, and severe behavior problems. *Journal of Applied Behavior Analysis, 24,* 387–397.

Durand, V.M., & Crimmins, D.B. (1988). Identifying the variables maintaining self-injurious behavior. *Journal of Autism and Developmental Disorders, 18,* 99–117.

Edelson, S.M., Taubman, M.T., & Lovaas, O.I. (1983). Some social contexts of self-destructive behavior. *Journal of Abnormal Child Psychology, 11,* 299–312.

Groden, G. (1989). A guide for conducting a comprehensive behavioral analysis of a target behavior. *Journal of Behavior Therapy and Experimental Psychiatry, 20,* 163–169.

Hawkins, R.P. (1986). Selection of target behaviors. In R.O. Nelson & S.C. Hayes, *Conceptual foundations of behavioral assessment* (pp. 311–385). New York: Guilford Press.

Holdgrafer, G.E., & Dunst, C.J. (1990). Use of low structured observation for assessing communicative intents in young children. *First Language, 10,* 243–253.

Iwata, B.A., Dorsey, M.F., Slifer, K.J., Bauman, K.E., & Richman, G.S. (1982). Toward a functional analysis of self-injury. *Analysis and Intervention in Developmental Disabilities, 2,* 3–20.

Iwata, B.A., Pace, G.M., Kalsher, M.J., Cowdery, G.E., & Cataldo, M.F. (1990). Experimental analysis and extinction of self-injurious escape behavior. *Journal of Applied Behavior Analysis, 23,* 11–27.

Lennox, D.B., & Miltenberger, R.G. (1989). Conducting a functional assessment of problem behavior in applied settings. *Journal of The Association for Persons with Severe Handicaps, 14,* 304–311.

Luiselli, J.K. (1991). Assessment-derived treatment of children's disruptive behavior disorders. *Behavior Modification, 15,* 294–309.

Mace, F.C., Lalli, J.S., & Lalli, E.P. (1991). Functional analysis and treatment of aberrant behavior. *Research in Developmental Disabilities, 12,* 155–180.

Maisto, C.R., Baumeister, A.A., & Maisto, A.A. (1978). An analysis of variables related to self-injurious behaviour among institutionalized retarded persons. *Journal of Mental Deficiency Research, 22,* 27–36.

Miltenberger, R.G., & Fuqua, R.W. (1985). Evaluation of a training manual for the acquisition of behavioral assessment interviewing skills. *Journal of Applied Behavior Analysis, 18,* 323–328.

Northup, J., Wacker, D., Sasso, G., Steege, M., Cigrand, K., Cook, J., & DeRaad, A. (1991). A brief functional analysis of aggressive and alternative behavior in an outclinic setting. *Journal of Applied Behavior Analysis, 24,* 509–522.

Oliver, C. (1988). Self-injurious behaviour in people with a mental handicap. *Current Opinion in Psychiatry, 1,* 567–571.

O'Neill, R.E., Horner, R.H., Albin, R.W., Storey, K., & Sprague, J.R. (1990). *Functional analysis of problem behavior: A practical assessment guide.* Sycamore, IL: Sycamore Press.

O'Neill, R.E., Horner, R.H., O'Brien, M., & Huckstep, S. (1991). Generalized reduction of difficult behaviors: Analysis and intervention in a competing behaviors framework. *Journal of Developmental and Physical Disabilities, 3,* 5–21.

Repp, A.C., Felce, D., & Barton, L.E. (1988). Basing the treatment of stereotypic and self-injurious behaviors on hypotheses of their causes. *Journal of Applied Behavior Analysis, 21,* 281–289.

Repp, A.C., Singh, N.N., Olinger, E., & Olson, D.R. (1990). The use of functional analyses to test causes of self-injurious behaviour: Rationale, current status and future directions. *Journal of Mental Deficiency Research, 34,* 95–105.

Romanczyk, R.G. (1986). Self-injurious behavior: Conceptualization, assessment, and treatment. *Advances in Learning and Behavioral Disabilities, 5,* 29–56.

Sasso, G.M., & Reimers, T.M. (1988). Assessing the functional properties of behavior: Implications and applications for the classroom. *Focus on Autistic Behavior, 3,* 1–15.

Sasso, G.M., Reimers, T.M., Cooper, L.J., Wacker, D., Berg, W., Steege, M., Kelly, L., & Allaire, A. (1992). Use of descriptive and experimental analyses to identify the functional properties of aberrant behavior in school settings. *Journal of Applied Behavior Analysis, 25,* 809–821.

Schroeder, S.R., Rojahn, J., Mulick, J.A., & Schroeder, C.S. (1981). Self-injurious behavior. In J.L. Matson & J.R. McCartney (Eds.), *Handbook of behavior modification with the mentally retarded* (2nd ed., pp. 141–180). New York: Plenum Press.

Sprague, J.R., & Horner, R.H. (1992). Covariation within functional response classes: Implications for treatment of severe problem behavior. *Journal of Applied Behavior Analysis, 25,* 735–745.

Steege, M.W., Wacker, D.P., Berg, W.K., Cigrand, K.K., & Cooper, L.J. (1989). The use of behavioral assessment to prescribe and evaluate treatments for severely handicapped children. *Journal of Applied Behavior Analysis, 22,* 23–33.

Vyse, S.A., & Mulick, J.A. (1988). Ecobehavioral assessment of a special education classroom: Teacher-student behavioral covariation. *Journal of the Multihandicapped Person, 1,* 201–216.

Wiesler, N.A., Hanson, R.H., Chamberlain, T.P., & Thompson, T. (1985). Functional taxonomy of stereotypic and self-injurious behavior. *Mental Retardation, 23,* 230–234.

CHAPTER 6. FUNCTIONAL ASSESSMENT: VERIFY

Bailey, J.S., & Pyles, D.A.M. (1989). Behavioral diagnostics. In E. Cipani (Ed.), *The treatment of severe behavior disorders* (pp. 85–107). *Monographs of the American Association on Mental Retardation, 12.*

Baumeister, A.A., & MacLean, W.E. (1984). Deceleration of self-injurious and stereotypic responding by exercise. *Applied Research in Mental Retardation, 5,* 385–393.

Bijou, S.W., & Baer, D.M. (1961). *Child development I: A systematic and empirical theory.* Englewood Cliffs, NJ: Prentice Hall.

Bijou, S.W., & Baer, D.M. (1978). *Behavior analysis of child development.* Englewood Cliffs, NJ: Prentice Hall.

Boe, R.B. (1977). Economical procedures for the reduction of aggression in a residential setting. *Mental Retardation, 15,* 25–28.

Brown, F. (1991). Creative daily scheduling: A nonintrusive approach to challenging behaviors in community residences. *Journal of The Association for Persons with Severe Handicaps, 16,* 75–84.

Carr, E.G., Reeve, C.E., & Magito-McLaughlin, D. (in press). Contextual influences on problem behavior in people with developmental disabilities. In D.M. Baer, E. Pinkston, & E. Reese (Eds.), *Stimulus control: Current knowledge, enduring issues.*

Carr, E.G., Robinson, S., & Palumbo, L.W. (1990). The wrong issue: Aversive versus nonaversive treatment. The right issue: Functional versus nonfunctional treatment. In A. Repp & N. Singh (Eds.), *Perspectives on the use of nonaversive and aversive interventions for persons with developmental disabilities* (pp. 361–379). Sycamore, IL: Sycamore Publishing Co.

Dorsey, M.F., Iwata, B.A., Reid, D.H., & Davis, P.A. (1982). Protective equipment: Continuous and contingent application in the treatment of self-injurious behavior. *Journal of Applied Behavior Analysis, 15,* 217–230.

Dumas, J.E., & Wahler, R.G. (1985). Indiscriminate mothering as a contextual factor in aggressive-oppositional child behavior: "Damned if you do and damned if you don't." *Journal of Abnormal Child Psychology, 13,* 1–17.

Dunlap, G. (1984). The influence of task variation and maintenance tasks on the learning and affect of autistic children. *Journal of Experimental Child Psychology, 37,* 41–64.

Dunlap, G., & Koegel, R.L. (1980). Motivating autistic children through stimulus variation. *Journal of Applied Behavior Analysis, 13*, 619–627.

Gardner, W.I., Cole, C.L., Davidson, D.P., & Karan, O.C. (1986). Reducing aggression in individuals with developmental disabilities: An expanded stimulus control, assessment, and intervention model. *Education and Training of the Mentally Retarded, 21*, 3–12.

Gardner, W.I., Karan, O.C., & Cole, C.L. (1984). Assessment of setting events influencing functional capacities of mentally retarded adults with behavior difficulties. In A.S. Halpern & M.J. Fuhrer (Eds.), *Functional assessment in rehabilitation* (pp. 171–185). Baltimore: Paul H. Brookes Publishing Co.

Horner, R.H., Day, H.M., Sprague, J.R., O'Brien, M., & Heathfield, L.T. (1991). Interspersed requests: A nonaversive procedure for decreasing aggression and self-injury during instruction. *Journal of Applied Behavior Analysis, 24*, 265–278.

Kantor, J.R. (1959). *Interbehavioral psychology*. Granville, OH: Principia Press.

Kern, L., Koegel, R.L., Dyer, K., Blew, P.A., & Fenton, L.R. (1982). The effects of physical exercise on self-stimulation and appropriate responding in autistic children. *Journal of Autism and Developmental Disorders, 12*, 399–419.

Krantz, P.J., & Risley, T.R. (1977). Behavioral ecology in the classroom. In K.D. O'Leary & S.G. O'Leary (Eds.), *Classroom management* (2nd. ed., pp. 349–366). New York: Pergamon Press.

Lancioni, G.E., Smeets, P.M., Ceccarani, P.S., Capodaglio, L., & Campanari, G. (1984). Effects of gross motor activities on the severe self-injurious tantrums of multihandicapped individuals. *Applied Research in Mental Retardation, 5*, 471–482.

Mace, F.C., Hock, M.L., Lalli, J.S., West, B.J., Belfiore, P., Pinter, E., & Brown, D.K. (1988). Behavioral momentum in the treatment of noncompliance. *Journal of Applied Behavior Analysis, 21*, 123–141.

McAfee, J.K. (1987). Classroom density and the aggressive behavior of handicapped children. *Education and Treatment of Children, 10*, 134–145.

McGimsey, J.F., & Favell, J.E. (1988). The effects of increased physical exercise on disruptive behavior in retarded persons. *Journal of Autism and Developmental Disorders, 18*, 167–179.

Michael, J. (1982). Distinguishing between discriminative and motivational functions of stimuli. *Journal of the Experimental Analysis of Behavior, 37*, 149–155.

Podboy, J.W., & Mallory, W.A. (1977). Caffeine reduction and behavior change in the severely retarded. *Mental Retardation, 15*(6), 40.

Silverman, K., Watanabe, K., Marshall, A.M., & Baer, D.M. (1984). Reducing self-injury and corresponding self-restraint through the strategic use of protective clothing. *Journal of Applied Behavior Analysis, 17*, 545–552.

Singer, G.H.S., Singer, J., & Horner, R.H. (1987). Using pretask requests to increase the probability of compliance for students with severe disabilities. *Journal of The Association for Persons with Severe Handicaps, 12*, 287–291.

Touchette, P.E., MacDonald, R.F., & Langer, S.N. (1985). A scatter plot for identifying stimulus control of problem behavior. *Journal of Applied Behavior Analysis, 18*, 343–351.

Wahler, R.G. (1980). The insular mother: Her problems in parent–child treatment. *Journal of Applied Behavior Analysis, 13,* 207–219.

Wahler, R.G., & Fox, J.J. (1981). Setting events in applied behavior analysis: Toward a conceptual and methodological expansion. *Journal of Applied Behavior Analysis, 14,* 327–338.

Wahler, R.G., & Graves, M.G. (1983). Setting events in social networks: Ally or enemy in child behavior therapy? *Behavior Therapy, 14,* 19–36.

Winterling, V., Dunlap, G., & O'Neill, R.E. (1987). The influence of task variation on the aberrant behaviors of autistic students. *Education and Treatment of Children, 10,* 105–119.

CHAPTER 7. BUILDING RAPPORT

Aronson, E. (1984). *The social animal* (Chap. 7. Attraction: Why people like each other). New York: W. H. Freeman & Co.

Egan, G. (1975). *The skilled helper: A model for systematic helping and interpersonal relating.* Monterey, CA: Brooks/Cole.

Flannery, K.B., Horner, R.H., Albin, R.W., Shukla, S., & Heathfield, L.T. (1993). *A descriptive analysis of rapport development and its effects on problem behaviors.* Unpublished manuscript, University of Oregon, Eugene.

McClannahan, L.E., McGee, G.G., MacDuff, G.S., & Krantz, P.J. (1990). Assessing and improving childcare: A personal appearance index for children with autism. *Journal of Applied Behavior Analysis, 23,* 469–482.

Patzer, G.L., & Burke, D.M. (1988). Physical attractiveness and child development. In B.B. Lahey & A.E. Kazdin (Eds.), *Advances in clinical child psychology* (Vol. II, pp. 325–368). New York: Plenum.

CHAPTER 8. CHOOSING COMMUNICATION FORMS

Carr, E.G. (1982). *How to teach sign language to developmentally disabled children.* Austin, TX: PRO-ED.

Carr, E.G. (1988). Functional equivalence as a mechanism of response generalization. In R. Horner, G. Dunlap, & R.L. Koegel (Eds.), *Generalization and maintenance: Life-style changes in applied settings* (pp. 221–241). Baltimore: Paul H. Brookes Publishing Co.

Carr, E.G., & Durand, V.M. (1987, November). See me, help me. *Psychology Today,* 62–64.

Carr, E.G., Robinson, S., & Palumbo, L.W. (1990). The wrong issue: Aversive versus nonaversive treatment. The right issue: Functional versus nonfunctional treatment. In A. Repp & N. Singh (Eds.), *Perspectives on the use of nonaversive and aversive interventions for persons with developmental disabilities* (pp. 361–374). Sycamore, IL: Sycamore Press.

Durand, V.M. (1990). *Severe behavior problems: A functional communication training approach.* New York: Guilford Press.

Hunt, P., Alwell, M., & Goetz, L. (1988). Acquisition of conversation skills and the reduction of inappropriate social interaction behaviors. *Journal of The Association for Persons with Severe Handicaps, 13,* 20–27.

Hunt, P., Alwell, M., & Goetz, L. (1991). *Teaching conversation skills to individuals with severe disabilities with a communication book adaptation: Instructional handbook.* Unpublished manuscript, Department of Special Education, San Francisco State University, San Francisco.

Hunt, P., Alwell, M., Goetz, L., & Sailor, W. (1990). Generalized effects of conversation skill training. *Journal of The Association for Persons with Severe Handicaps, 15,* 250–260.

Mirenda, P., & Iacono, T. (1990). Communication options for persons with severe and profound disabilities: State of the art and future directions. *Journal of The Association for Persons with Severe Handicaps, 15,* 3–21.

Neel, R.S., & Billingsley, F.F. (1989). *Impact: A functional curriculum handbook for students with moderate to severe disabilities.* Baltimore: Paul H. Brookes Publishing Co.

Prizant, B.M., & Wetherby, A.M. (1987). Communicative intent: A framework for understanding social-communicative behavior in autism. *Journal of the American Academy of Child and Adolescent Psychiatry, 26,* 472–479.

Reichle, J.E., & Yoder, D.E. (1979). Assessment and early stimulation of communication in the severely and profoundly mentally retarded. In R.L. York & E. Edgar (Eds.), *Teaching the severely handicapped* (Vol. 4, pp. 180–218). Seattle: American Association for the Education of the Severely/Profoundly Handicapped.

Reichle, J., York, J., & Sigafoos, J. (1991). *Implementing augmentative and alternative communication: Strategies for learners with severe disabilities.* Baltimore: Paul H. Brookes Publishing Co.

Siegel-Causey, E., & Guess, D. (1989). *Enhancing nonsymbolic communication interactions among learners with severe disabilities.* Baltimore: Paul H. Brookes Publishing Co.

Steege, M.W., Wacker, D.P., Cigrand, K.C., Berg, W.K., Novak, C.G., Reimers, T.M., Sasso, G.M., & DeRaad, A. (1990). Use of negative reinforcement in the treatment of self-injurious behavior. *Journal of Applied Behavior Analysis, 23,* 459–467.

Wacker, D.P., Steege, M.W., Northup, J., Sasso, G., Berg, W., Reimers, T., Cooper, L., Cigrand, K., & Donn, L. (1990). A component analysis of functional communication training across three topographies of severe behavior problems. *Journal of Applied Behavior Analysis, 23,* 417–429.

CHAPTER 9. CREATING AN APPROPRIATE CONTEXT FOR COMMUNICATION

Brown, L., Nietupski, J., & Hamre-Nietupski, S. (1976). Criterion of ultimate functioning. In M.A. Thomas (Ed.), *Hey, don't forget about me!* (pp. 2–15). Reston, VA: Council for Exceptional Children.

Ford, A., Schnorr, R., Meyer, L., Davern, L., Black, J., & Dempsey, P. (Eds.). (1989). *The Syracuse community-referenced curriculum guide for students with moderate and severe disabilities.* Baltimore: Paul H. Brookes Publishing Co.

Janicki, M.P., Krauss, M.W., & Seltzer, M.M. (Eds.). (1988). *Community residences for persons with developmental disabilities: Here to stay.* Baltimore: Paul H. Brookes Publishing Co.

Matson, J.L., & Mulick, J.A. (Eds.). (1983). *Handbook of mental retardation.* New York: Pergamon Press.

Meyer, L.H., Peck, C.A., & Brown, L. (Eds.). (1991). *Critical issues in the lives of people with severe disabilities.* Baltimore: Paul H. Brookes Publishing Co.

Rusch, F.R. (1990). *Supported employment models, methods, and issues.* Sycamore, IL: Sycamore Publishing Co.

Smith, M.D. (1990). *Autism and life in the community: Successful interventions for behavioral challenges.* Baltimore: Paul H. Brookes Publishing Co.

Wehman, P., & Schleien, S. (1981). *Leisure programs for handicapped persons: Adaptations, techniques, and curriculum.* Baltimore: University Park Press.

Creating Communication Opportunities

Halle, J.W. (1984). Arranging the natural environment to occasion language: Giving severely language-delayed children reasons to communicate. *Seminars in Speech and Language, 5,* 185–197.

Haring, T.G., Neetz, J.A., Lovinger, L., Peck, C., & Semmel, M.I. (1987). Effects of four modified incidental teaching procedures to create opportunities for communication. *Journal of The Association for Persons with Severe Handicaps, 12,* 218–226.

Hart, B. (1980). Pragmatics and language development. In B.B. Lahey & A. E. Kazdin (Eds.), *Advances in clinical child psychology* (Vol. 3, pp. 383–427). New York: Plenum Press.

Hart, B.M., & Risley, T.R. (1982). *How to use incidental teaching for elaborating language.* Austin, TX: PRO-ED.

Hunt, P., Goetz, L., Alwell, M., & Sailor, W. (1986). Using an interrupted behavior chain strategy to teach generalized communication responses. *Journal of The Association for Persons with Severe Handicaps, 11,* 196–204.

Koegel, R.L. Koegel, L.K., & Surratt, A. (1992). Language intervention and disruptive behavior in preschool children with autism. *Journal of Autism and Developmental Disorders, 22,* 141–153.

Koegel, R.L., O'Dell, M.C., & Koegel, L.K. (1987). A natural language teaching paradigm for nonverbal autistic children. *Journal of Autism and Developmental Disorders, 17,* 187–200.

Laski, K.E., Charlop, M.H., & Schreibman, L. (1988). Training parents to use the natural language paradigm to increase their autistic children's speech. *Journal of Applied Behavior Analysis, 21,* 391–400.

McGee, G.G., Krantz, P.J., Mason, D., & McClannahan, L.E. (1983). A modified incidental teaching procedure for autistic youth: Acquisition and generalization of receptive object labels. *Journal of Applied Behavior Analysis, 16,* 329–338.

Rogers-Warren, A., & Warren, S.F. (1980). Mands for verbalization: Facilitating the display of newly trained language in children. *Behavior Modification, 4,* 361–382.

Warren, S.F., & Rogers-Warren, A.K. (Eds.). (1985). *Teaching functional language: Generalization and maintenance of language skills.* Austin, TX: PRO-ED.

CHAPTER 10. BUILDING TOLERANCE FOR DELAY OF REINFORCEMENT

Fowler, S.A., & Baer, D.M. (1981). "Do I have to be good all day?" The timing of delayed reinforcement as a factor in generalization. *Journal of Applied Behavior Analysis, 14,* 13–24.

Koegel, R.L., & Rincover, A. (1977). Research on the difference between generalization and maintenance in extra therapy responding. *Journal of Applied Behavior Analysis, 10,* 1–12.

Sulzer-Azaroff, B., & Mayer, G.R. (1977). *Applying behavior-analysis procedures with children and youth* (pp. 339–340; 402–404). New York: Holt, Rinehart & Winston.

CHAPTER 11. EMBEDDING

Charlop, M.H., Kurtz, P.F., & Milstein, J.P. (1992). Too much reinforcement, too little behavior: Assessing task interspersal procedures in conjunction with different reinforcement schedules with autistic children. *Journal of Applied Behavior Analysis, 25,* 795–808.

Dunlap, G., & Morelli-Robbins, M. (1991). *A guide for reducing situation-specific behavior problems with task interspersal.* Unpublished manuscript, Florida Mental Health Institute, University of South Florida, Tampa.

Horner, R.H., Day, H.M., Sprague, J.R., O'Brien, M., & Heathfield, L.T. (1991). Interspersed requests: A nonaversive procedure for decreasing aggression and self-injury during instruction. *Journal of Applied Behavior Analysis, 24,* 265–278.

Mace, F.C., Hock, M.L., Lalli, J.S., West, B.J., Belfiore, P., Pinter, E., & Brown, D.K. (1988). Behavioral momentum in the treatment of noncompliance. *Journal of Applied Behavior Analysis, 21,* 123–141.

Singer, G.H.S., Singer, J., & Horner, R.H. (1987). Using pretask requests to increase the probability of compliance for students with severe disabilities. *Journal of The Association for Persons with Severe Handicaps, 12,* 287–291.

Winterling, V., Dunlap, G., & O'Neill, R.E. (1987). The influence of task variation on the aberrant behaviors of autistic students. *Education and Treatment of Children, 10,* 105–119.

CHAPTER 12. PROVIDING CHOICES

Bannerman, D.J., Sheldon, J.B., Sherman, J.A., & Harchik, A.E. (1990). Balancing the right to habilitation with the right to personal liberties: The rights of people with developmental disabilities to eat too many doughnuts and take a nap. *Journal of Applied Behavior Analysis, 23,* 79–89.

Dyer, K., Dunlap, G., & Winterling, V. (1990). Effects of choice making on the serious problem behaviors of students with severe handicaps. *Journal of Applied Behavior Analysis, 23,* 515–524.

Guess, D., Benson, H.A., & Siegel-Causey, E. (1985). Concepts and issues related to choice-making and autonomy among persons with severe disabilities. *Journal of The Association for Persons with Severe Handicaps, 10,* 79–86.

Houghton, J., Bronicki, G.J.B., & Guess, D. (1987). Opportunities to express preferences and make choices among students with severe disabilities in classroom settings. *Journal of The Association for Persons with Severe Handicaps, 12,* 18–27.

Koegel, R.L., Dyer, K., & Bell, L.K. (1987). The influence of child-preferred activities on autistic children's social behavior. *Journal of Applied Behavior Analysis, 20,* 243–252.

Shevin, M., & Klein, N.K. (1984). The importance of choice-making skills for students with severe disabilities. *Journal of The Association for Persons with Severe Handicaps, 9,* 159–166.

CHAPTER 13. GENERALIZATION
CHAPTER 14. MAINTENANCE

Baer, D.M. (1981). *How to plan for generalization*. Austin, TX: PRO-ED.

Clark, D.B., & Baker, B.L. (1983). Predicting outcomes in parent training. *Journal of Consulting and Clinical Psychology, 51,* 309–311.

Foxx, R.M., & Livesay, J. (1984). Maintenance of response suppression following overcorrection: A 10-year retrospective examination of eight cases. *Analysis and Intervention in Developmental Disabilities, 4,* 65–79.

Griest, D.L., & Forehand, R. (1982). How can I get any parent training done with all these other problems going on? The role of family variables in child behavior therapy. *Child and Family Behavior Therapy, 4,* 73–80.

Griest, D.L., & Wells, K.C. (1983). Behavioral family therapy with conduct disorders in children. *Behavior Therapy, 14,* 37–53.

Horner, R.H., Albin, R.W., & Mank, D.M. (1989). Effects of undesirable, competing behaviors on the generalization of adaptive skills: A case study. *Behavior Modification, 13,* 74–90.

Horner, R., Dunlap, G., & Koegel, R.L. (Eds.). (1988). *Generalization and maintenance: Life-style changes in applied settings*. Baltimore: Paul H. Brookes Publishing Co.

Kazdin, A., & Esveldt-Dawson, K. (1981). *How to maintain behavior*. Austin, TX: PRO-ED.

Stokes, T.F., & Baer, D.M. (1977). An implicit technology of generalization. *Journal of Applied Behavior Analysis, 10,* 349–367.

Sulzer-Azaroff, B., & Mayer, G.R. (1977). *Applying behavior analysis procedures with children and youth* (pp. 324–368). New York: Holt, Rinehart & Winston.

SOURCES FOR RELATED EDUCATIONAL APPROACHES

Dunlap, G., Kern-Dunlap, L., Clarke, S., & Robbins, F.R. (1991). Functional assessment and curricular revision, and severe behavior problems. *Journal of Applied Behavior Analysis, 24,* 387–397.

Evans, I.M., & Meyer, L.H. (1985). *An educative approach to behavior problems: A practical decision model for interventions with severely handicapped learners*. Baltimore: Paul H. Brookes Publishing Co.

Foxx, R.M. (1982). *Increasing behaviors of severely retarded and autistic persons*. Champaign, IL: Research Press.

Gardner, W.I., & Cole, C.L. (1989). Self-management approaches. In E. Cipani (Ed.), *The treatment of severe behavior disorders* (pp. 19–35). Washington, DC: American Association on Mental Deficiency.

Horner, R.H., Sprague, J.R., & Flannery, K.B. (1993). Building functional curricula for students with severe intellectual disabilities and severe problem behaviors. In R. Van Houten & S. Axelrod (Eds.), *Effective behavioral treatment: Issues and implementation* (pp. 47–71). New York: Plenum Press.

Kamps, D.M., Leonard, B.R., Dugan, E.P., Boland, B., & Greenwood, C.R. (1991). The use of ecobehavioral assessment to identify naturally occurring effective procedures in classrooms serving students with autism and other developmental disabilities. *Journal of Behavioral Education, 1,* 367–397.

Koegel, L.K., Koegel, R.L., Hurley, C., & Frea, W.D. (1992). Improving social skills and disruptive behavior in children with autism through self-management. *Journal of Applied Behavior Analysis, 25,* 341–353.

Koegel, R.L., Koegel, L.K., & Parks, D.R. (1988). *How to teach self-management skills to people with severe disabilities: A training manual.* Unpublished manuscript, University of California at Santa Barbara, Santa Barbara.

Koegel, R.L., Schreibman, L., Good, A., Cerniglia, L., Murphy, C., & Koegel, L.K. (1989). *How to teach pivotal behaviors to children with autism: A training manual.* Unpublished manuscript, University of California at Santa Barbara, Santa Barbara.

LaVigna, G.W., Willis, T.J., & Donnellan, A.M. (1989). The role of positive programming in behavioral treatment. In E. Cipani (Ed.), *The treatment of severe behavior disorders* (pp. 59–83). Washington DC: American Association on Mental Retardation.

Meyer, L.H., & Evans, I.M. (1989). *Nonaversive intervention for behavior problems- A manual for home and community.* Baltimore: Paul H. Brookes Publishing Co.

Sanders, M.R., & Glynn, T. (1981). Training parents in behavioral self-management: An analysis of generalization and maintenance. *Journal of Applied Behavior Analysis, 14,* 223–237.

Schreibman, L. (1988). *Autism.* Newberry Park, CA: Sage Publications.

Turnbull, A.P., Patterson, J.M., Behr, S.K., Murphy, D.L., Marquis, J.G., & Blue-Banning, M.J. (Eds.). (1993). *Cognitive coping, families, and disability.* Baltimore: Paul H. Brookes Publishing Co.

Appendix

Results of Field Tests

We carried out field tests on the assessment and intervention procedures that are described in this book. These field tests followed a 1-year period in which the procedures had been taught to various individuals associated with two different agencies serving people with developmental disabilities. The results of these field tests are described below. Four administrative supervisors from the two agencies rated the performance of several hundred interventionists, who included group home staff, teachers, and parents. We wanted to know whether these intervention agents used the assessment and intervention procedures. The various assessment and intervention procedures were grouped into skill clusters, which are described at length below. The supervisors then rated each intervention agent's performance on each skill cluster on a 7-point scale that ranged from 1 (the intervention agent never used the procedure) to 7 (the intervention agent often used the procedure). Then, the ratings were averaged across all the intervention agents and rounded off to one decimal place. As the reader can see from the detailed results below, the intervention agents frequently implemented almost all of the skill clusters. The only exception was the embedding cluster, which was implemented somewhat less frequently.

The fact that the procedures were typically used often was an important first step. However, we also wanted to know whether the procedures had desirable effects on people with developmental disabilities. To answer this question, we asked the supervisors to rate almost 200 people with developmental disabilities with respect to the various outcomes and behavior changes described at length below. Again, ratings were made using the 7-point scale noted earlier. As you can see from the results, various desirable outcomes and behavior changes occurred frequently, with most measures rated as occurring often. The different aspects of functional assessment were rated as often producing useful information on the nature of the problem behavior and its controlling variables. Crisis management procedures were generally effective. Our approach was also seen as helpful in enhancing rapport, building initial communication skills, and decreasing problem behavior as a result of the rapport-building and communication training. Embedding was generally successful in producing good mood, and choice-making increased when opportunities were provided for the individual to make choices. Functional communication continued to improve over time and across situations as the interventions were progressively applied. Problem behavior decreased to low levels over long periods of time and across many different situations. Finally, and most important, there were lifestyle changes and the individual with disabilities was spending more time in the community, taking advantage of the many kinds of activities available.

In summary, a variety of intervention agents were able to carry out the assessment and intervention procedures described in this book and generally chose to use them often. Furthermore, the assessment and intervention procedures, when implemented, produced a variety of desirable and educationally sound changes in people with developmental disabilities including a broadening of their lifestyle.

Field Test: Communication-Based Intervention for Problem Behavior I. Crisis Management and Functional Assessment/Analysis

Raters: Administrative supervisors (*N* = 4)
Intervention agents rated: Group home staff/teachers/parents
(*N* = 450)
Individuals with disabilities rated: Group home residents/
school-age children (*N* = 182)

Scale used:

Never   Sometimes   Often

Were the procedures used?

1. <u>Crisis management cluster</u> Crisis management strategies are used appropriately either to nip problems in the bud before they escalate or to deal with problem behavior that has reached a dangerous level.

Average rating: 7

2. <u>Functional assessment: Description cluster</u> Interviews and direct observations are made to determine the nature of the problem behavior, the interpersonal context (antecedents), and the social reaction (motivation/purpose). Additional interviews and direct observations are made when: 1) there are discrepancies between various sources of information regarding problem behavior, 2) there are new problem behaviors associated with important changes in the person's life situation, 3) there is residual problem behavior after intervention, 4) problem behaviors that were once under control begin to recur. Interviews and direct observations are made periodically even after intervention has begun in order to identify newly emerging problem behaviors.

Average rating: 6.3

3. <u>Functional assessment: Categorization cluster</u>   Based on the descriptive information, hypotheses concerning the purpose of the problem behaviors are made. Situations in which various problem behaviors appear to serve the same specific purposes are grouped together as an aid to intervention planning.

Average rating: 6.9

4. <u>Functional analysis: Verification cluster</u>   For a sample of situations, the reinforcer for a problem behavior and its alternative is systematically manipulated to verify the purpose of the problem behaviors. Where appropriate, setting events are manipulated to determine whether they influence the presence or absence of problem behavior.

Average rating: 6.3

What effects did the procedures have?

1. <u>Changes in problem behavior following crisis management</u>   Following the use of one or more of the crisis intervention strategies, problem behavior stops quickly and for a long enough period of time for you to begin implementing long-term educationally based strategies.

Average rating: 5.7

2. <u>Assessment outcome: Description</u>   When you use the methods of description that you were taught, you are able to identify the problem behavior, its interpersonal context, and the social reaction to it.

Average rating: 6.7

3. <u>Assessment outcome: Categorization</u>   The assessors are able to agree with one another, more than 90% of the time, on what the purpose of the problem behavior is. For the vast majority of severe problem behavior, the purposes fall into one of the socially-mediated categories (attention, escape, tangibles). Within each category, it is possible to group situations so that they fall into a relatively small number of themes.

Average rating: 6.9

4. <u>Assessment outcome: Verification</u>   For a given interpersonal context, problem behavior is observed to fluctuate systematically when its consequences (social reaction) are manipulated. When setting events are manipulated, problem behavior is observed to fluctuate systematically as a function of the presence/absence of the setting events.

Average rating: 6.2

Field Test: Communication-Based Intervention for Problem Behavior II. The Core Intervention

Raters: Administrative supervisors ($N = 4$)
Intervention agents rated: Group home personnel/teachers/ parents ($N = 355$)
Individuals with disabilities rated: Group home residents/school-age children ($N = 176$)

Scale used:

| 1 | 4 | 7 |
| Never | Sometimes | Often |

Were the procedures used?

1. Rapport cluster   Is there an attempt to engage the individual in games, conversation, and other rewarding activities? Is there an attempt to reward approach and simple conversation? Is there a concern to help the individual to look his or her best (physical appearance)? Is there an attempt to identify shared interests and then to engage the individual in these shared interests?

Average rating: 7

2. Communication cluster   Is there an attempt to make sure that the new communication form serves the same function as the old problem behavior form and does so more efficiently? Is a communication system chosen that can be acquired quickly and can be readily understood by others? Is there a focus (initially) on choosing communication forms that can be widely used by the individual? Is there an attempt made to enhance receptive language so that the individual is able to participate in longer communicative interactions? Are opportunities provided to practice skills in problem situations?

Average rating: 6.4

3. Appropriate context cluster   Are an adequate number of people available to attend to communication? Do people share an intervention philosophy in which communication (more specifically) and functional education (more generally) are central to activity planning? Is there a community orientation, that is, an effort to involve the individual in neighborhood activities, employment, and community recreation? Is independent living a primary goal in intervention planning?

Average rating: 6.4

What effects did the procedures have?

1. Changes in rapport   Does the individual show more proximity-seeking with respect to other people? Attend more to other people? Initiate more social interaction with others? Make more frequent requests of others? Accept social initiations more from others? Engage more often in activities of shared interest with others?

Average rating: 5.9

2. Changes in initial communication skills   Are the new communication forms displayed in situations that formerly evoked problem behavior? Do the communication forms generally produce a quick response from others? Is there a tendency toward longer communicative exchanges as receptive language increases?

Average rating: 5.6

3. Changes in problem behavior   Did problem behavior decrease in situations that used to evoke it? Is the level and/or intensity of problem behavior now acceptable to others?

Average rating: 5.9

Field Test: Communication-Based Intervention for Problem Behavior III. Additional Procedures and Programming for Generalization and Maintenance

Raters: Administrative supervisors (*N* = 4)
Intervention agents rated: Group home personnel/teachers/ parents (*N* = 355)
Individuals with disabilities rated: Group home residents/school-age children (*N* = 176)

Scale used:

| 1 | 4 | 7 |
| Never | Sometimes | Often |

Were the procedures used?

1. Delay of reinforcement cluster. After communication skills have been established, is there an attempt to teach the individual to tolerate a delay of reinforcement following a request by requiring that some activity first be completed and/or engaged in until such time as other people are ready/willing to respond to the communicative request?

Average rating: 5.0

2. Embedding cluster If the individual repeatedly shows problem behavior in response to specific demands from others, is there an attempt to induce good mood prior to presenting the demands again (i.e., embedding the demands in a positive context)?

Average rating: 3.8

3. Choice cluster Is the individual given an array of options from which to choose with respect to the tasks in which he/she needs to

work, the people with whom he/she may interact, tangible reinforcers and social activities that he/she may access?

Average rating: 6.4

4. Generalization cluster   Is there an attempt to program generalization across a wide variety of *naturalistic* tasks, people, and settings? If generalization does not occur, is there an attempt to solve the problem by building rapport (where appropriate), conducting additional functional assessments, and/or redesigning the daily environment to exclude or minimize signals for problem behavior?

Average rating: 6.0

5. Maintenance cluster   When maintenance failures occur, is there an attempt to address the issue by considering whether unreasonable outcome criteria have been set; introducing more variety in the living situation in an attempt to avoid dull, repetitive routines; and/or improving social support systems for parents, teachers, group home staff, and other caregivers so that the intervention efforts of these people will be strengthened?

Average rating: 6.0

What effects did the procedures have?

1. Changes in developed communication skills   Does the individual continue to make requests in spite of the fact that such requests are sometimes not honored immediately? Does the individual display a wide variety of communication-based skills across many tasks, people, and settings? Does the individual continue to show his or her functional communication skills consistently and appropriately over long periods of time?

Average rating: 6.0

2. Changes that result from embedding   Does the individual display behaviors indicative of a good mood following an attempt to create a positive context for demands?

Average rating: 5.5

3. Changes that result from offering choices   When the person with disabilities is provided with options does he or she respond by choosing one of the options?

Average rating: 5.6

4. Changes in problem behavior   Is the individual able to tolerate reasonable delay of reinforcement without displaying problem behavior? Following good mood induction with respect to frustrating demands, is the individual now able to carry out the demands without displaying problem behavior? When choices are honored within the context of situations that typically evoke problem behavior, does the behavior become less frequent or disappear? Does problem behavior decrease to an acceptable level across a wide variety of tasks, people, and settings? Does problem behavior remain at a low, acceptable level across long periods of time?

Average rating: 6.0

5. Changes in lifestyle   After you used the various intervention procedures described in the book, did you find that the individual with disabilities was able to spend more time in the community and take better advantage of social, vocational, and leisure activities available in the community?

Average rating: 6.1

Index

Page numbers followed by t or f indicate tables or figures, respectively.

243